1,001 Things You Always Wanted to Know About Angels, Demons, and the Afterlife

J. STEPHEN LANG

THOMAS NELSON PUBLISHERS
Nashville

Published in Nashville, Tennessee, by Thomas Nelson, Inc.

Unless otherwise noted Scripture quotations are from the NEW KING
JAMES VERSION of the Bible. Copyright © 1979, 1980, 1982,
Thomas Nelson, Inc., Publishers.

Scripture quotations noted KJV are from the KING JAMES VERSION
of the Bible.

Scripture quotations noted NIV are from the HOLY BIBLE: NEW
INTERNATIONAL VERSION®. Copyright 1973, 1978, 1984 by
International Bible Society. Used by permission of Zondervan
Publishing House. All rights reserved.

Library of Congress Cataloging-in-Publication Data

Lang, J. Stephen.
    1,001 things you always wanted to know about angels, demons
and the afterlife but never thought to ask / J. Stephen Lang.
        p.cm.
    ISBN 0-7852-6861-8
    1. Angels—Miscellanea. 2. Demonology—Miscellanea. 3. Future
life—Miscellanea. I. Title.

BT966.2 .L24 2000
235—dc21   00-037234
                                              CIP

Printed in the United States of America
1 2 3 4 5 6 7 - 05 04 03 02 01 00

Contents

1

Questions & Controversies

1. "literal" hell and heaven?

Is hell a hot furnace? Is heaven a cloudy place with harps and golden streets? The Bible says little about the physical attributes of either place. The book of Revelation pictures heaven as a praise-filled city with streets of gold and pearly gates. Revelation uses these images to communicate the ideas of beauty and fellowship with God. Revelation also refers to the devil and evil people being destroyed in a lake of fire. Jesus Himself spoke of the fire of hell—the idea being that the person apart from God is in agony. Is it a "literal" fire? That question misses the point. The point is that the person who chooses to separate himself from God is in the worst possible circumstance.

2. animals in heaven?

People who love their pets often ask the poignant question, "Are there animals in heaven?" The Bible doesn't shed much light on this matter, although Psalm 36:6 says of God, "Your judgments are a great deep; O LORD, You preserve man and beast." Does this mean animals are "saved" as humans are? Hard to say. Author C. S. Lewis, a respected lay theologian (and a cat lover, by the way), believed that domestic animals could somehow be saved "in" their masters.

Some people point to the famous incident of Elijah, taken from earth to heaven in a chariot drawn by "horses of fire" (2 Kings 2:11). Were these real horses? Again, hard to say.

The book of Revelation's images of heaven do not include animals—but that doesn't necessarily mean that animals are not part of the eternal plan.

3. do angels have wings?

Not always, according to the Bible, which tells us that some people have "entertained angels unawares" (Heb. 13:2 KJV). We can assume people would be *aware* if they were entertaining a winged creature. The Bible presents several stories of angels appearing extremely human—which leaves artists with the challenge of how to communicate that this particular person really is a divine messenger. One way to do this is with wings—suggesting swiftness, flight, abilities beyond the human range. They are shown soft and feathery like birds' wings—an attractive image, unlike the scaly wings of insects or the clawed wings of bats.

In the Bible, some angels do have wings. The prophet Isaiah had a vision in the temple, seeing seraphs (a type of angel), each with six wings (Isa. 6). The prophet Ezekiel saw four "living creatures" (usually interpreted as angels), each with four wings, and four faces to boot (Ezek. 1; 10). But, most important of all were the two cherubim (again, a type of angel), shown in gold images on the lid of the famous ark of the covenant.

See 84 (cherubim).

4. reincarnation?

The Bible does not teach reincarnation, though some thinkers (such as Edgar Cayce, who considered himself a Christian) believe that it does. They interpret Jesus' words to Nicodemus—"You must be born again"(John 3:3)—in the sense of being reborn into another body and life. Also, they point to the healing of the man born blind in John 9. Jesus' disciples asked Him, "Rabbi, who sinned, this man or his parents, that he was born blind?" (v.2).Their question suggests (to people who already believe in reincarnation) that the man had lived a past life, and his blindness was punishment for sins in that life. But the Bible is consistent in the belief stated very directly in Hebrews 9:27: "It is appointed for men to die once, but after this the judgment."

5. gender of angels?

Artworks show angels of both sexes—though sometimes the male angels are so feminine as to be "unisex." The Bible indicates that angels are sexless (Matt. 22:30), since they have no need to reproduce. Whenever an angel is mentioned in the Bible, it is always a "he," which doesn't mean "male," but only means that the person who saw him took him to be male in appearance—the invisible taking on a recognizable shape for the benefit of human eyes.

6. can angels eat?

We can assume that spirits do not need food and drink as humans do, but twice in the Bible angels are described as eating and drinking with human hosts. Three angels visited Abraham, who provided them with food and drink (Gen. 18:1–8). The two angels who visited Lot in order to save him from the wicked city of Sodom also dined as Lot's guests (Gen. 19).

7. "giants on the earth"?

In many translations, Genesis 6:4 reads, "There were giants on the earth in those days." The Hebrew word translated "giants" is *nephilim*, and it is used in Numbers 13 to describe the hulking inhabitants of Canaan, who so intimidated the Israelite reconnaissance men. *Nephilim* may not mean giants of supernatural origin, but simply a tribe of large-framed, powerful men. When military strength was a man's most important asset, such men were, of course, feared and respected. Genesis 6 says these giants were the offspring of the "sons of God" (see 47) and mortal women.

8. pleasure in watching hell?

Do the people in heaven see the people in hell? Jesus' parable of Lazarus and the rich man (see 298) suggests that they do. In the parable, the beggar Lazarus is in heaven while the coldhearted rich man who snubbed him is in hell, where Lazarus can see and hear him. Some prominent theologians, such as Augustine and Thomas Aquinas, claimed that one of the pleasures of heaven is seeing the torments of those in hell. This strikes us as rather cruel, but consider what they meant: Sin is receiving its just punishment, so those in heaven should rejoice because justice is done and because they themselves have escaped such horror.

9. are we angels after death?

The Smothers Brothers had a sitcom in which brother Tommy played a deceased man who had become an angel (no wings), reporting to an unseen celestial supervisor named Ralph and intervening in the life of brother

Dick. The series reflected a popular belief that when people pass on, they become angels (or, at least, *good* people do). What is the basis of this belief, other than wishful thinking?

Does the Bible anywhere suggest that a person really becomes an angel after death? The answer is "No, but . . ." Consider Acts 12, in which the apostle Peter has been freed from prison by an angel. Once free, Peter went to the house of some fellow believers. Rhoda, the young woman who went to answer Peter's knock at the door, was overjoyed to hear his voice and ran to tell the others. Believing he could not possibly have escaped prison, they insisted that she was wrong, but when she persisted, they said to her, "It is his angel" (Acts 12:15). How do we interpret this? Some commentators claim that there was a popular belief that a man's guardian angel could take on the appearance of the man himself. So the passage does not necessarily suggest that Peter's friends thought he had died and become an angel.

10. what about suicides?

The Bible has practically nothing to say about suicide. Judas Iscariot, the disciple who betrayed Jesus, hanged himself. Samson, the strongman of ancient Israel, toppled a Philistine temple with his own hands, killing not only the Philistines but himself as well. Saul, Israel's first king, killed himself rather than fall into the hands of the triumphant Philistines. But these incidents and the few other suicides in the Bible pass without comment about the rightness or wrongness of the deed, and what fate awaits the person after suicide.

But Christian tradition has always been against it. While Japanese warriors and Roman aristocrats approved suicide as a noble death, Christians have not. Many Christians have been martyred for their faith, willing to face torture and execution, but not willing to end their own lives to avoid such agony. In reply to the philosophical question "Whose life is it, anyway?" the church has always replied, "God's, who gave it to you." And since it is God's to give, it is God's—and only His—to take. This was the view of such influential authors as Augustine (see 596), who saw suicide as cowardly and as self-murder, as horrible as murdering someone else. Thomas Aquinas (see 606) wrote that no person had the right to reject God's gift of life. Official church approval of such beliefs led to the prohibition (until very recently) of burying a suicide in a church cemetery. Whatever individuals may have thought about the final fate of suicides, the churches as a whole leaned toward the view that the person went to hell. In Dante's *Divine Comedy*, a special section of hell is reserved for suicides. In our own time, C. S. Lewis echoed the older beliefs and stated that suicide was like "deserting one's post."

Attitudes toward suicide have changed dramatically. Few people nowadays would make the sweeping statement that everyone who commits suicide goes to hell. As stated before, the Bible itself, our final authority on spiritual matters, gives us no clear guidance on the subject.

11. what about infants?

Some people imagined there was an eternal resting place for children who died before they could be baptized. Obviously no one wanted to believe that innocent babes would be sent to hell, but, being unbaptized, they could not be in heaven, either. In the Middle Ages, Catholic theologians thought that there was Limbo (see 935), a region that was neither heaven nor hell nor purgatory, for such persons as the feebleminded or unbaptized children to spend eternity. It was called the *Limbus Puerorum*, Limbo of Children. There they would live eternally in peace, though not experiencing the fuller joys of heaven.

12. creation of angels?

The Bible says nothing about when or how the angels were created. Master theologian Augustine (see 596) had a suggestion: They were created at the very beginning, when God gave the first command in creation: "Let there be light" (Genesis 1:14). Angels are beings of light, partakers of God's eternal light. So though Genesis 1 doesn't mention them by name, they very well could have been made right at the beginning of it all.

13. how could God make a Satan?

According to Christian tradition, He did not. Satan was originally Lucifer, a good angel (see 131 [Lucifer]). Through his own pride and envy, Lucifer rebelled against God and was cast out of heaven. The rebel angels who joined with Lucifer fell by their own evil will.

14. how big is heaven?

According to Revelation 21:16, it is a perfect cube, 12,000 stadia (about 1,400 miles) on each side. While that is huge, could it contain all the saints who have died through the ages? Some critics have said that heaven will be too crowded, with the saints pressed together like sardines. Most Christians believe the measurements in Revelation are to be taken symbolically, a reminder to us that heaven is huge (and certainly huge enough for everyone who goes there).

15. sorrow in heaven?

One important truth about heaven is that there will be no sadness there (Rev. 21:4). Yet might people in heaven not sorrow for their loved ones on earth or for the sufferings of saints undergoing persecution? Part of being human is sympathizing and empathizing—we might say that there is a kind of joy in sharing the pain of others. While the inhabitants might (though we can't say for sure) feel sadness for those left behind, the Bible is clear that nothing can take away from the overall joy of being in God's presence.

16. laughter in heaven?

Heaven, the Bible assures us, is a place of joy. What about laughter? On earth the two often go together, yet the Bible says nothing about laughter in heaven. However, Jesus did promise that those who now weep will laugh (Luke 6:21), and perhaps He meant "in heaven." Of course, our earthly laughter is most often "comic relief" from the difficulties of earthly life, and that kind of relief is unnecessary in heaven. But laughter just for the fun of it? Why not?

17. the age of the blessed?

People sometimes wonder, *What age are we in heaven?* The great theologian Thomas Aquinas (see 606) believed that thirty-three was the ideal age (since Jesus had been resurrected at that age). But a place where everyone had a thirty-three-year-old "look" would be quite boring, and we have no reason to think that heaven will be full of clones. We simply don't know what age we will appear to be, or that it will matter.

18. boredom forevermore?

Critics of the Christian view of heaven point out that it will be incredibly boring. Who would enjoy (they ask) eternally walking on golden streets, playing a harp, and worshiping God? We can only reply that the Bible presents us with glimpses (but not the complete picture) of heaven. Several times in the New Testament the authors admit that they are trying to describe the indescribable. Jesus' image of a jolly wedding banquet sounds pleasant enough, particularly when everyone would be kind to one another, with no cattiness or feuding as at earthly gatherings. We can only assume that in a place of joy and love we would not be bored, and might not even be conscious of the passage of time at all.

19. "spirits in prison"?

This phrase has puzzled the Bible commentators for centuries. Christ, says 1 Peter, was put to death but made alive by the Spirit, "by whom also He went and preached to the spirits in prison, who formerly were disobedient, when once the longsuffering of God waited in the days of Noah" (3:19-20). Meaning what? The commentators have come up with a thousand interpretations, none of them satisfying to everybody. One possibility that has fascinated artists: Between His death and resurrection, Christ preached the message of salvation to people who had died before His coming. Some commentators explain that this is how the saints of the Old Testament—Abraham, Moses, and David, for example—came to be "Christians" and thus fit to be in heaven.

CONTROVERSIES

20. Christianity and liberalism

In the 1920s, a war of words and ideas was being fought between liberal and conservative Christians. One of the feistiest warriors on the conservative side was J. Gresham Machen (1881–1937), whose masterwork was *Christianity and Liberalism*. In Machen's view, liberalism wasn't just one form of Christianity but was an entirely different religion. He observed that liberalism really had no use for heaven, for "this world is really all in all." This present world is the center of liberal thought, and thus religion "has become a mere function of the community or of the state." The hope for heaven is replaced with the hope for earthly utopia (see 927).

21. soul sleep

Does the soul go directly to heaven or hell when the person dies, or is there a "wait"? "Soul sleep" refers to the soul sleeping, or waiting, between death and the resurrection. While some Bible passages suggest such a "sleep," others suggest that we go directly to our final end. (Jesus' promise to the thief on the cross that the two would be together in paradise certainly supports the latter view [Luke 23:43].) In the past, denominations have fought and split over this issue, but most Christians today would agree that it is of fairly minor importance. (See 22 [intermediate state].)

22. intermediate state

Fact 1, based on our experience: Individuals die. Fact 2, based on the Bible: Christ will return to earth to judge the living and the dead, rewarding the saved and punishing the unsaved. With these two facts in mind, we still aren't absolutely sure what happens to individuals who die. Are they already in heaven or hell, or are they conscious and reflecting on their lives, or are they "asleep," unconscious until the Lord returns? The Bible gives support to all three positions. (The third is sometimes called "soul sleep" [see 21].) While the issue has been hotly debated over the centuries, Christians should bear in mind the essential belief: The righteous will live with Christ forever.

23. election

As a Christian term, this refers to God's choice of people to be saved. In essence, it means that God does not save certain people because of their own efforts, but simply because He chooses to do so. Some people are horrified at this belief, aghast that heaven would be populated only by God's "chosen." But the Old and New Testaments do mention election. Paul did, believing that God's chosen are able to share the glory of Christ and bear His moral image. For Paul, the believer's knowledge of being chosen made him glory more in God, since he saw that his own efforts were not what saved him. And believing that one is chosen does not (as some say) lead to loose living—quite the contrary, for believing one is chosen to live eternally leads to a gratitude-centered life, living morally out of gratitude to God. (For key Bible passages on election, see Rom. 8:29–30; 9:23–24; 11:33–36; 1 Cor. 1:30; 2 Cor. 3:18; Eph. 1:3–14; 5:5–6; Col. 3:12–17; 1 Thess. 1:3–10.)

24. devil in the radio

Christians have made wide use of radio in ministry, but in the early days of radio many believers were suspicious of it. Ephesians 2:2 refers to Satan as the "prince of the power of the air," and some believers have applied this to radio, since it is an "air" form of communication. Since radio then and now was seen as mostly a form of entertainment—*worldly* entertainment to boot—many believers felt that Christians should shun it altogether. The same criticism was later applied to TV. Clearly, most Christians today are happy to use both radio and TV to spread the faith.

25. Satan and tongues

More than a few Christian scholars have stated that speaking in tongues is the work of the devil. Possible? Perhaps, for Paul warned the early Christians that Satan "masquerades as an angel of light" (2 Cor. 11:14 NIV). Thus Satan could, in theory, cause "counterfeit" spiritual gifts, including tongues. But the fact is that Paul and the other New Testament writers did not suggest that tongues was the work of the devil. True, tongues could be faked—but what would Satan have to gain from it? Paul, Peter, and other apostles warned against false *teaching*, but never mentioned what evil (if any) might result from speaking in tongues.

26. *Demons and Tongues*

Published in 1912, this book by Alma White summarized the reaction of many Holiness Christians to the growing Pentecostal movement. The book put forward the view that speaking in tongues was caused by demons, not by the Spirit. It is a sad curiosity in history that Christians so readily pounce on one another whenever a difference of opinion arises. Christians have proved willing and eager to attribute their opponents' beliefs and activities to the work of devils. However, times have changed, and many people in the Holiness Movement today also consider themselves Pentecostals, accepting and even encouraging speaking in tongues.

27. the Salem witch trials

"Thou shalt not suffer a witch to live" (Ex. 22:18 KJV) sounds cruel, but it is part of the Old Testament's key message of worshiping only God and avoiding the barbarity and immorality of pagan religion (which often involved human sacrifice and ritual prostitution). People who dabbled in the demonic were, as Israel's history shows, a threat to a faith centered on the true God. In contrast, the

New Testament shows Christianity spreading in the Roman Empire, where all sorts of religions and magical arts had to coexist. Nothing in the New Testament would condone killing a witch. But the Christians who settled Massachusetts in the 1600s were bent on preserving a pure religion, and they were willing to exile—and, in a few cases, execute—people who would not conform. The execution of twenty people for witchcraft in Salem, Massachusetts, in 1692, is a blot on Christian history.

THE UNIVERSALIST DEBATE

28. annihilationism

Is hell really forever, or does God simply snuff out the wicked? Charles F. Parham, one of the "founding fathers" of the Pentecostal revival in the twentieth century, claimed that annihilationism was "the most important doctrine in the world today." Later, Pentecostals took pains to emphasize that, yes, hell really was permanent. Parham's statement indicates that in the early days of Pentecostalism, not everyone saw speaking in tongues as the key feature of the movement. Annihilationism is also called *conditional immortality*.

29. Origen (c. 185–c. 254)

He was probably one of the most brilliant Christians of his time, or any time. Origen's father had been a Christian martyr, and he halfway martyred himself. (He castrated himself, making himself, as he saw it, a "eunuch for the kingdom of God.") Later, he died from injuries suffered under Roman persecution. Origen wrote hundreds of works of theology and Bible commentary. Most of these writings were perfectly in line with the Bible—but not all. Origen speculated that reincarnation might be a reality. He toyed with universalism, suggesting that all human beings—and even the devil and all his demons—might eventually find salvation. Being an extremely influential teacher (whose morals were never questioned, even if his beliefs were), Origen's writings were widely circulated. Christian authorities feared that these might undermine Christian belief, so in the year 543 a church council declared some of his beliefs to be heretical.

30. the Synod of Constantinople, 543

In the year 543, a council of bishops from across the empire gathered at the capital city of Constantinople (which is now Istanbul, Turkey). Among other subjects, the council discussed the idea, popular in some circles, that hell might not be eternal. Some people were teaching that hell might only be a temporary punishment—or that there might not be a hell at all, and that people who did not enter heaven might simply be annihilated, ceasing to exist but not tormented in hell. The Christian scholar Origen (see 29), who had been dead for centuries, had taught such ideas. The council condemned these ideas and all people who taught them: "If anyone shall say or think that there is a time limit to the torment of demons and ungodly persons, or that there will ever be an end to it, or that they will ever be pardoned or made whole again, then let him be excommunicated."

31. *apokatastasis*

This cumbersome-looking Greek word refers to the idea of universal redemption—that is, eventually all human beings (and perhaps even demons) will find salvation. While the New Testament makes it clear that not all people will turn to God, and that the followers of Satan will eventually meet their doom along with Satan himself, many Christians in the past believed (or hoped) that in time everyone would freely choose salvation. The Christian scholar Origen (see 29) flirted with this idea, and even toyed with the idea that souls might move closer to God through a long string of reincarnations. If God is infinitely loving, Origen said, then eventually (and it might take thousands of years), everyone will return to Him and find happiness, and even Satan's evils will melt away in the refining fire of God's love. An appealing idea? It is, and it has a lot going for it except that it so blatantly contradicts the Bible, including the clear teaching of Jesus Himself. (See 32 [universalists].)

32. universalists

Universalism is the belief that all people will eventually find salvation—that is, heaven for everyone, hell for no one. It is definitely *not* taught in the New Testament, and the church at large has never accepted it. But many wishful-thinking people (including many Christians) are uncomfortable with the idea that anyone would suffer eternal torment, so there have been and probably always will be universalists.

As an organized religion, Universalism began in America in the 1700s, with the first congregation organized in 1779. The Winchester Platform of 1803 stated that man is perfectible and all men will eventually be saved. Since their beliefs did not square with the Bible, Universalists gained a reputation for being unorthodox. They became increasingly less comfortable under the designation of "Christian" (even though they had started out that way), and in 1942 they affirmed that they welcomed all "humane" people, whether or not they called themselves Christian. In 1961 they merged with another notably liberal group, the Unitarians, forming the Unitarian-Universalist Association. Burdened with this cumbersome name, the members now refer to themselves simply as Unitarians. (See 33 [Hosea Ballou].)

The Universalists—the "no hell" people, as their opponents called them—played down human sinfulness and played up man's potential. But orthodox Christians saw them as taking a too-rosy view of humankind, ignoring the reality that mankind desperately needs a Savior and is in danger of hell without one. The Universalists of the 1800s did number a few celebrities among their members, including showman P. T. Barnum and education pioneer Horace Mann.

33. Hosea Ballou (1771–1852)

You might call him the "Apostle of Universalism." Ballou, son of a Baptist minister, was a conventional Christian in his early life, but he later began to doubt certain basic Christian beliefs, notably that there is a hell. He was ordained in the Universalist Church (see 32) in 1794 and became one of its most noted leaders. While the early Universalists were orthodox Christians (excepting their belief that all men will finally be saved), Ballou pushed the church in a more liberal direction. He reasoned (and it makes sense) that if there is no hell to be saved from, what is the need for all the other important Christian doctrines? So he cast doubt on belief in the Trinity, the divinity of Christ, and (of course) the authority of the Bible. He would have been pleased that, more than a century after his death, the Universalists merged with the extremely liberal Unitarians.

THE PROTESTANT-CATHOLIC DIVIDE

34. purgatory

Heaven and hell are, according to the New Testament, the two final destinations for human beings. Catholics teach that there is another state after death, purgatory, where people whose eventual destination is heaven must spend time "purging away" sins they have accumulated in their earthly lives. Catholics base this teaching on a section in the Apocrypha, 2 Maccabees 12:39–45, which speaks of offering sacrifices for dead persons "that they might be delivered from their sin." Theologians such as Augustine taught that sins that had gone unrepented at the time of the Christian's death would be purged by fire in purgatory—not the punishing fire of hell, but a purifying fire, readying the person for heaven. Part of Catholic teaching regarding purgatory is that people still alive can do deeds to benefit people in purgatory. Since the Reformation, most Protestants have rejected the belief in purgatory (partly because the Catholic church had abused the doctrine, partly because Protestants did not regard 2 Maccabees as divinely inspired Scripture). (See 489 [upper Gehenna].)

35. Apocrypha

Apocrypha means "hidden things." The books were mainly written in the period between the Old and New Testaments. The books are: 1 and 2 Maccabees, Tobit, Judith, The Wisdom of Solomon, Ecclesiasticus (not the same as Ecclesiastes), Baruch, and additions to Esther and Daniel. Of these books, most readers find the most profit in Wisdom and Ecclesiasticus, which are similar to Proverbs in their wise advice. Valuable information about the period between the Testaments is found in 1 Maccabees. Centuries ago, Bible translators struggled with a question: Do we include the Apocrypha? Around A.D. 400, the scholar Jerome was working on his great translation into Latin. Living in the Holy Land, Jerome learned that the Jewish scholars had chosen not to include certain books in their Bibles (what Christians call the Old Testament). He and other Christian scholars agreed that if the Jews did not consider these books sacred, neither should Christians. But these "questionable" books had been around a long time, and Jerome was pressured to include them in his Latin Bible, the Vulgate.

With the Reformation in the 1500s came a renewed interest in translating the Bible from the original Hebrew and Greek. The Reformers went back to Jerome's question: Should we include these books that the Jews do not consider sacred? Some said yes, some said no. Martin Luther included them in his German translation. He said they were not equal to the other books but were "profitable and good to read."

The Catholic position was fixed at the Council of Trent (1546), which said that, yes, the Apocrypha was definitely sacred Scripture, inspired by God. The council also pronounced damnation on anyone who took a different view.

One reason Catholics were adamant about the divine inspiration of the Apocrypha is that the doctrine of purgatory, which had become extremely important in the Catholic system, is taught nowhere in the Old or New Testament but is taught (or hinted at) in the Apocrypha. Thus Catholics were eager to retain the Apocrypha, and Protestants were just as eager to put it aside.

36. Mary and purgatory

"Pray for us sinners now and at the hour of our death."
This is a Catholic prayer to the Virgin Mary, probably one
of the most repeated prayers in the history of the world.
In the Middle Ages, as belief in purgatory became more
and more widespread, Mary took on a new and enhanced
role. She, more so than Christ Himself, was the one who
could soften a soul's punishment and time in purgatory.
While Christ was thought of as the just Judge of human
sins, Mary played the role of comforter, who could lessen
the punishments of those who prayed to her. As belief in
purgatory became more important in the church's life, so
did devotion to the Virgin Mary. When the Protestant
Reformation came along in the 1500s, the Reformers
attacked both the belief in purgatory and also the exces-
sive devotion to Mary.

37. Our Lady of the Angels

The Roman Catholic Church holds a much higher view of
the Virgin Mary than do Protestants, and some Catholics
refer to her as Queen of Heaven or Our Lady Queen of
the Angels. She is sometimes pictured in Catholic art as a
crowned figure surrounded by adoring choirs of angels.
As Queen of the Angels, Mary is sometimes prayed to,
with people asking her aid in sending the angels to ward
off some evil.

38. *ego te absolvo*

These Latin words mean "I absolve you." In the Middle Ages, when most people accepted hell as a reality and feared it, these words were of extreme importance. One confessed one's sins to a priest. If he was convinced that repentance was sincere then he released the person from his guilt with the words "I absolve you." People who expected to die soon naturally wanted a priest near at hand, for how horrid it would be to go to hell just because one's final sins had gone unconfessed. With the coming of the Protestant Reformation in the 1500s, the Reformers complained that people had developed a cynical attitude toward God and their own sins—after all, one could live a scandalous life and still hope that, at the end, everything would be made right with the words *ego te absolvo.*

39. the three monastic vows

Monks and nuns of the Catholic and Orthodox churches are bound by three strict vows: poverty, chastity, and obedience. These three, dating from centuries ago, stemmed from the monks' belief that their lives should be as much like that of angels as possible. Thus poverty is the rule (since angels own nothing and need nothing), as is chastity (for the Bible says angels do not mate, marry, or reproduce), and so is obedience (the angels obey God strictly, and the monks must likewise obey the head of the monastery).

40. virginity

The Old Testament is distinctly pro-family and pro-chil-dren—the more children, the better. The New Testament takes a different view: Marriage and children are all right for Christians, but Jesus and Paul both stated that celibacy was good—not for everyone, but for a select few. Such influential authors as Jerome and Augustine constantly praised celibacy as the best path to heaven. Augustine had had a promiscuous youth, and as a Christian he turned to the other extreme, describing celibacy as the *vita angelica*, "the way of the angels," freeing oneself from earthly lusts and allowing more time for God. In Augustine's day (the early 400s), the Catholic church had no fixed position on whether or not ministers should marry. As the pro-virgin-ity writings of men like Augustine were widely read, the church shifted to the position that all ministers should be celibate, a position the Roman Catholic Church still holds.

41. heaven versus earth

Augustine (see 596), one of the most influential theolo-gians, taught that the church on earth has only a limited vision of God, while the church in heaven beholds Him more completely. Our goal on earth, Augustine said, is to become as much like the church in heaven as possible. This is why *contemplation of God* became such an impor-tant feature of Catholicism in the Middle Ages. Just as the angels and people in heaven spent their time in joyful contemplation of God, so Christians on earth could do the same. Augustine and others encouraged monasticism, withdrawing from the world and devoting as much time as possible to prayer, worship, and contemplation of the divine—that is, becoming as much like angels as possible. Many men in monasteries defined their calling as "the angelic life." Protestants have generally rejected this version of the Christian life.

2

Angels in the Bible

42. The archangel Michael

There are several Michaels in the Bible, but the truly important one is Michael the archangel (meaning a sort of "ruling angel," head over other angels). The prophet Daniel referred to him as a "prince," a sort of heavenly protector of Israel (Dan. 10:13, 21; 12:1). The book of Revelation pictures a conflict at the end of time, with Michael and his angels fighting against the dragon, Satan (12:7). The image of the winged and armored Michael standing triumphant over the dragon is a popular subject in art.

Michael is one of only two angels with names in the Bible, the other being Gabriel.

While the Bible mentions his name only five times, Jewish and Christian folklore had much to say about him. Jewish tradition says that he was the mysterious "man" who wrestled with Jacob, that he passed on the Law to Moses on Sinai, that he played a role in the heavenly ascensions of

Enoch and Elijah, that he was the seraph who touched Isaiah's lips with a live coal, and that he replaced the rebellious Lucifer (Satan) as leader of the heavenly choirs.

As a biblical angel and a major figure in angel folklore, Michael is mentioned many times elsewhere in this book.

43. the angel Gabriel

Gabriel plays a role in the story of Jesus' birth and the birth of His kinsman John the Baptist. Luke 1 tells of the priest Zechariah, who saw the angel in the temple. Gabriel announced that Zechariah's wife, Elizabeth, would bear a son who would "make ready a people prepared for the Lord" (v. 17). Zechariah, who was old, had doubts, and Gabriel, who said he stood "in the presence of God," punished Zechariah with muteness till the birth occurred.

Gabriel went to Mary in Nazareth and told her she was to bear a child, "the son of the Highest" (Luke 1:32). Mary said she was a virgin, but Gabriel told her, "The Holy Spirit will come upon you, and the power of the Highest will overshadow you; therefore, also, that Holy One who is to be born will be called the Son of God" (Luke 1:35).

Gabriel appears in the book of Daniel as an interpreter of Daniel's mysterious visions (8:16; 9:21), and as one who granted Daniel wisdom and understanding.

Between the Old and New Testaments, many legends about Gabriel took shape. Some of these are mentioned in this book's chapter on folklore and legends.

As a biblical angel, Gabriel is a common figure in literature and art. In Milton's *Paradise Lost*, he is a mighty warrior in battle against the devils.

An old Christian tradition has it that Gabriel will blow the trumpet to signal the end of the world, but the Bible does not mention his name in this connection. Also, while Christian tradition says that Gabriel is an archangel, he is never called that in the Bible.

THE OLD TESTAMENT

44. "let us make man"

According to Genesis 1, the high point of God's creation of all things was the creation of man. On the sixth day, after creating all the animals, God said, "Let us make man in our image, in our likeness" (1:26 NIV). Generations of Bible readers have asked the obvious question: Who is this "us," since God is the only God? This has kept the commentators busy. In the first place, the common Hebrew name for God is *elohim*, which is plural. Christians believe that the plural pronoun reflects the Trinity—that is, the one God, but also the Trinity of Father, Son, and Holy Spirit. But before Christianity the Jews saw another meaning in "us" and "our": God was speaking to the angels, His heavenly court. Is this interpretation correct? Hard to say. Certainly the Bible puts forth the idea that the angels were present when God created man (Ps. 8:5). The meaning "our image" seems to be this: God has just created animals, but man is special, made to be like God and like the angels in many ways.

45. when were angels created?

Christian belief has always been that only God is eternal—so all else (including the angels) was created at some point in time. Angels are not mentioned in the creation sequence in Genesis 1, but Psalm 148 refers to their creation (though not to the time), and so does Colossians 1:16. But it is clear from the book of Job that they had already been created when God began creating the earth, for God asked Job, "where were you when I laid the foundations of the earth? . . . When the morning stars sang together, and all the sons of God shouted for joy?" (Job 38:4, 7). It is generally agreed that the "morning stars" and the "sons of God" were angels.

Outside the Bible, the Jewish writings known as the Book of Jubilees, written between the Old and New Testaments, give information about the time the angels were created: It was the first day of Creation.

46. the Bible's first angels

People always connect the Garden of Eden with the tempter, Satan. But there were angels connected with Eden as well, though not in any pleasant sense. After the serpent tempted Adam and Eve, they ate the forbidden fruit, and because they disobeyed God, they were banished from Eden. The entryway of Eden was guarded by cherubim (angels) and a flaming sword, a vivid symbol that once man had sinned he could never go back to Eden (Gen. 3:24).

47. the sons of God

Bible scholars run into some problems that just cannot be solved. One is found in Genesis 6:1–4: "When men began to multiply on the face of the earth, and daughters were born to them, . . . the sons of God saw the daughters of men, that they were beautiful . . . The sons of God came in to the daughters of men and they bore children to them. Those were the mighty men who were of old, men of renown." Just who were these "sons of God"? Angels? Fallen angels? Demons? No one knows for sure. But the widely read book of Enoch, written between the Old and New Testaments, states that the "sons of God" of Genesis 6 were fallen angels, whose union with human women produced all kinds of evils on the earth. (See 7 ["giants in the earth?"].)

48. Ishmael's guardian

Ishmael was the son of Abraham and his concubine, Hagar. After he was born, Abraham's wife, Sarai, drove mother and child away, but an angel saved them from perishing (Gen. 16). The nation of Israel was descended from Abraham's son Isaac, but Genesis records that a great nation was descended from Ishmael also. Arabs trace their ancestry to Ishmael, called *Ismail* in the Koran, the Muslims' holy book. The Koran, in contrast with the Bible, says that Ismail, not Isaac, was the favorite son of Abraham.

49. Old Testament Trinity—or angels?

Genesis 18 relates that the Lord appeared to Abraham as he was sitting in his tent doorway. But "the Lord" appeared as three men. Abraham entertained them hospitably, and "He" (the Lord—but which of the three men was speaking?) predicted that when He came again later, Abraham's wife, Sarah, would have a child. Sarah, listening nearby, laughed, since she and Abraham were both old. But the prophecy came true, for she gave birth to Isaac.

This passage fascinates Bible readers, since it refers to "the Lord" and "He" but also insists that three men, not one, visited Abraham. Was one of the three men God in the flesh, while the other two were angels? Some readers have suggested that this was the Trinity—what the New Testament refers to as God the Father, the Son, and the Holy Spirit. So perhaps Abraham's visitors were a kind of "Old Testament Trinity."

50. Lot, his wife, and Sodom

Lot, the nephew of Abraham, was the only resident (along with his family) of the sinful city of Sodom that God chose to save. Genesis 19 tells the pathetic tale of two divine visitors who were almost raped by the men of Sodom. The visitors urged Lot to flee the doomed city. They fled, and God rained down fire on Sodom. The angels had told the family not to look back, but Lot's wife did, and she became a pillar of salt. (Jesus said, "Remember Lot's wife!" a warning not to look back on one's past.)

51. the sacrifice of Isaac

This is one of the most touching stories in the Bible. Abraham finally had a son, Isaac (as God had promised), in his old age (a hundred years old, in fact). But, surprisingly, God later commanded Abraham to "take now your son, your only son Isaac, whom you love, and go to the land of Moriah, and offer him there as a burnt offering" (Gen. 22:2). Abraham, the role model of trust in God, obeyed. The story relates that the boy Isaac asked his father why there were fire and wood but no lamb for a sacrifice. Abraham answered, "God will provide" (v. 8). Abraham bound the boy and raised his knife to kill him, but was stopped by an angel, who said, "Do not lay your hand on the lad, or do anything to him; for now I know that you fear God" (v. 12). The angel said that because of Abraham's faith God would surely bless him.

Many ancient nations near Israel practiced child sacrifice. Israel always condemned it.

The near-sacrifice of Isaac has been a favorite subject for artists.

52. Jacob's ladder

The patriarch Jacob led an exciting life. Fleeing his brother, Esau (whom he had cheated out of his inheritance), Jacob spent a night in the wilds, using a stone for a pillow. He had a dream of a stairway to heaven, with angels going up and down it. (Older translations use "ladder" instead of "stairway.") Above the stairway God Himself spoke and renewed His covenant with Jacob's grandfather Abraham, promising blessing on Jacob's descendants. Jacob awoke and concluded, "Surely the LORD is in this place . . . This is none other than the house of God, and this is the gate of heaven!" (Gen. 28:16–17). Jacob named the spot Bethel ("house of God").

"Jacob's Ladder" is a popular campfire song, and it is also the name of the rope ladders used on ships.

53. wrestling God (or an angel)

Jacob, grandson of Abraham, had a colorful life, and Genesis 32 tells of how he literally wrestled God, or God's angel. On the lam from his angry brother, Esau, Jacob met a man who wrestled with him till daybreak. The man ripped Jacob's hip out of its socket, then demanded to go, but Jacob replied, "I will not let You go unless You bless me!" (v. 26). The man (or angel) told Jacob that from then on his name would be Israel, meaning "struggles with God," because Jacob had "struggled with God and with men, and [had] prevailed" (v. 28). The man (or angel) would not tell Jacob his own name, and Jacob—now renamed Israel—concluded that he had seen God face to face.

54. the burning bush

Exodus 3 tells the famous story of Moses encountering the burning bush in the wilderness: "And the Angel of the LORD appeared to him in a flame of fire from the midst of a bush. So he looked, and behold, the bush burned with fire, but the bush was not consumed" (v. 2). But later on in the story there is no mention of the angel of the Lord, just the Lord Himself. So who was there—the Lord or the angel? This is one of several places in the Bible where the answer seems to be "both." Clearly the angel of the Lord was one that the author took to be God Himself.

55. the angel at the Red Sea

As the movie *The Ten Commandments* depicts so vividly, the Israelite slaves' exit from oppressive Egypt was dramatic. Their exodus seems so unlikely that it can be explained only as divine intervention. Just before the famous parting of the Red Sea, Exodus records that "the Angel of God, who went before the camp of Israel, moved and went behind them; and the pillar of cloud went from before them and stood behind them. So it came between the camp of the Egyptians and the camp of Israel. Thus it was a cloud and darkness to the one, and it gave light by night to the other, so that the one did not come near the other all that night" (14:19–20). Thus God's angel served as a kind of buffer until God parted the Red Sea for the Israelites to pass through safely.

56. the angel on Sinai

The book of Exodus tells us that God Himself gave the Law directly to Moses on Mount Sinai. In the book of Acts, the martyr Stephen had it somewhat differently, referring to the angel who spoke to Moses on Sinai (7:38). A contradiction? Not necessarily. Key events in the Bible are often reported in different ways: A man meets with God Himself in one version of a story, with the Lord's angel in another. Either way, the main idea is that God's power came through in the meeting.

57. the Israelites' angel

Exodus 23 contains some promises—and threats—to Israel, God's people. God promised that He would send an angel "to keep you in the way and to bring you into the place which I have prepared. Beware of Him and obey His voice; do not provoke Him, for He will not pardon your transgressions; for My name is in Him" (vv. 20–21). In these verses God is not speaking about an angel that anyone can see or hear, but rather an invisible guide.

Some Christians later applied these words to Christ, saying that He will guide God's people to the place prepared for them—not to Canaan, but to heaven.

58. Christ in the Old Testament

The early Christians, since most of them were Jews, read and loved the Old Testament. Because they believed that Jesus Christ was the Messiah who the prophets had predicted, they searched the Old Testament for anything that might appear to be a prophecy of the Christ. Some went so far as to say that the "angel of the Lord" mentioned many times in the Old Testament was Christ Himself, making an appearance before He was actually born as a human baby in Bethlehem.

59. Passover

Still celebrated by Jews, Passover commemorates God's "passing over" the Hebrews' homes as He caused the death of the firstborn of the Egyptians. Moses told the people to mark their homes with blood, and the angel of death "passed over" them (Ex. 12:23). This last of the ten plagues on the Egyptians had the desired effect: Pharaoh released the Hebrew slaves. The popular movie *The Ten Commandments* depicted the death angel as a sort of sinister, lethal fog moving over the landscape.

60. Balaam's donkey

Can a donkey speak? The prophet Balaam had such an animal, at least on one occasion. As the Israelites journeyed from Egypt to their home in Canaan, they passed through the hostile land of Moab. The Moabite king sent his prophet Balaam to curse Israel. As Balaam rode toward the Israelites his donkey saw an angel with a drawn sword in the road. The donkey veered off, and Balaam beat her, not seeing the angel himself. The poor beast finally lay down, and Balaam beat her again. This time she spoke: "What have I done to you, that you have struck me these three times?" (Num. 22:28). God opened Balaam's eyes, and he saw the angel and fell facedown. He changed his plans (naturally), and instead of cursing the Israelites, he prophesied that they would be a great nation, blessed by God (Num. 22–24).

61. "Joshua Fit de Battle of Jericho"

The old spiritual is based on Joshua 5:13–6:27. Joshua, leader of the Israelites after Moses died, was told by an angel (the "commander of the LORD's army") how to capture the strongly fortified city of Jericho. Instead of attacking, the Israelites were to march around the city for six days, carrying the ark of the covenant. On the seventh day, priests were to blow trumpets and the people were to shout. When they did this, the city walls fell (as the song says, "and de walls come tumblin' down"), and the Israelites captured the city.

The "Commander of the LORD's army" had to tell Joshua to take off his shoes, for he was standing on holy ground. This is almost exactly what the Lord commanded Moses to do when speaking from the burning bush, so we have reason to think that the "Commander" was the Lord Himself.

62. the angel at Bochim

The Hebrew word *Bochim* means "weeping," and it was at Bochim that the people of Israel had good cause to weep. Judges 2 speaks of the angel of the Lord meeting with the people there, reminding them that they had been unfaithful to the Lord. As a result, the heathen tribes around them "shall be thorns in your side, and their gods shall be a snare to you" (v. 3). Hearing of this, the people broke into weeping. As the book of Judges makes clear, the angel's prophecy came true.

63. Gideon's angel

Judges 6 begins the story of the military leader Gideon. While threshing wheat, Gideon was greeted by an angel with the words "The LORD is with you, you mighty man of valor!" (v. 12) Gideon was skeptical and stated that the Lord was not with him, nor his nation, for the Lord had let the Midianites oppress them. (The Midianites—the rapacious "camel jockeys" of the Old Testament—were a constant thorn in Israel's side.) But the angel insisted that Gideon would be the one to deliver Israel from the Midianites. As often happens in the Old Testament, this mysterious visitor is identified as "the angel of the Lord" but then is called "the Lord" a few verses later. Were the authors confused? No. The main point was that the messenger was speaking the word of God. At any rate, Gideon wanted a sign that the visitor was truly divine. He set some uncooked meat and bread on a rock, and the angel set them on fire with the end of his staff. Then the angel disappeared. Gideon was awestruck: "Alas, O Lord GOD! For I have seen the Angel of the LORD face to face" (Judg. 6:11–22).

64. Samson's birth

The Hebrew strongman is one of the more interesting Bible characters, maybe because his story involves violence, lust, betrayal, and revenge. His story is told in Judges 13–16. Samson was one of Israel's "judges"—not a judge in the modern sense, but more like a deliverer or military leader. Israel was plagued constantly by the pagan Philistines. Samson was born to a woman who had long been barren, and an angel told his parents to dedicate the child to God.

65. the post-census plague

King David commanded a census of Israel, something that angered the Lord greatly. The prophet Gad told

David that divine punishment was on its way, and it came in the form of a plague that killed seventy thousand people. The plague was apparently the work of the Lord's angel. Seeing all the destruction, the Lord halted the angel. "Then David spoke to the LORD when he saw the angel who was striking the people" (2 Sam. 24:10–17). As so often happens in the Bible, we have no idea what the angel looked like or how David could determine that he was an angel. At any rate, David repented of his folly and built an altar to the Lord, and the plague was ended.

66. the heavenly host

The King James Version of the Bible uses *host* in an old sense, meaning "army" or "multitude." In the KJV, *host* usually refers to a literal human army, but several times it specifically refers to "the host of heaven" or "heavenly host," which are clearly celestial beings. These could be angels, but "host of heaven" can also represent the stars and planets. The prophet Micaiah claimed that he "saw the LORD sitting on His throne, and all the host of heaven standing by, on His right hand and on His left" (1 Kings 22:19). The phrase "the LORD of hosts" occurs many times in the Bible, referring to God's power and majesty.

Probably the most famous mention of the heavenly host occurs in the story of the angels and the shepherds of Bethlehem: "And suddenly there was with the angel a multitude of the heavenly host praising God and saying: 'Glory to God in the highest, and on earth peace, good-will toward men!'" (Luke 2:13–14).

67. Elijah's angel

Israel's prophets constantly preached against their people's idol worship. The Canaanite fertility god Baal was one of many false gods the Israelites worshiped. The great prophet Elijah challenged 450 prophets of Baal to a showdown on Mount Carmel (1 Kings 18). There the frenzied Baal prophets had no success in calling down Baal to devour the animals they sacrificed, but Elijah's God sent down fire (possibly lightning) to consume the sacrifice. When the people saw that God was the true God, "they fell on their faces; and they said, 'The LORD, He is God!'" (v. 39).

The incident made Queen Jezebel, a notorious Baal-worshiper, determined to kill Elijah. So, fresh from his triumph over Baal's prophets, he fled to the desert, where God comforted him. "As he lay and slept under a broom tree, suddenly an angel touched him, and said to him, 'Arise and eat.' Then he looked, and there by his head was a cake baked on coals, and a jar of water" (1 Kings 19:5–6).

68. Elijah and Beelzebub

Angels made more than one appearance in the colorful life of the prophet Elijah. In 2 Kings 1 is the story of how

Israel's king Ahaziah, injured from a fall, sent messengers to the Philistine god Beelzebub (see 174). In other words, a man fearing death asked the servants of a false god whether he would live or die. "But the angel of the LORD said to Elijah the Tishbite, 'Arise, go up to meet the messengers of the king'" (v. 3). The angel instructed Elijah to chide the king for ignoring Israel's own God and inquiring of a pagan idol. (This was the equivalent of dabbling in the occult.) The message got even worse: The king would die from his injuries. It came to pass as predicted.

69. the destruction of Sennacherib

The righteous King Hezekiah's reign is described in 2 Kings 18–20. He rebelled against the empire of Assyria, which led to Jerusalem's being threatened by the mighty King Sennacherib. The prophet Isaiah told Hezekiah that God would deliver them from the brutal Assyrians. The angel of the Lord struck down 185,000 Assyrian soldiers and Sennacherib returned home—to be murdered by his own sons. A famous poem, "The Destruction of Sennacherib," was written by the loose-living English poet Byron.

70. the assembled sons of God

The book of Job opens with a description of the righteous man Job, followed by a sort of "court scene": "Now there was a day when the sons of God came to present themselves before the LORD, and Satan also came among them" (1:6). Though they are not referred to as angels, we can only assume that that is what these "sons of God" are.

71. charging the angels with error

Can angels make mistakes? In the book of Job, Job's three friends try to explain to him why so many calamities have befallen him. Eliphaz, one of the three friends, asked Job if he really thought himself so righteous: "If He [God] puts no trust in His servants, if He charges His angels with error, how much more those who dwell in houses of clay" (4:18–19). Put another way, if God's own heavenly attendants can err (and Eliphaz implies that they can), then surely no mere human is above making a mistake now and then.

72. "the morning stars sang"

In the ancient world, the faraway stars and planets seemed mysterious—even divine. Thus, most ancient peoples fell into the error of worshiping the heavenly bodies. Israel's prophets constantly railed against this (and the worship of anything except the true God). The Hebrews would not accept the heavenly bodies as gods, yet the Bible hints that they believed the stars were angels. Consider Job 38, where the Lord Himself confronts Job and questions him:

"Where were you when I laid the foundations of the earth? . . . When the morning stars sang together, and all the sons of God shouted for joy?" (38:4, 7). Clearly the "morning stars" and the "sons of God" refer to angels.

73. "a little lower than the angels"

Psalm 8 is a song of praise to God, admiring the glories of creation. Compared with all this vastness, where does man fit in? "When I consider Your heavens, the work of Your fingers, the moon and the stars, which You have ordained, what is man that You are mindful of him, and the son of man that You visit him? For You have made him a little lower than the angels, and You have crowned him with glory and honor" (vv. 3–5). We have the term "angels" in our English translation, but the actual Hebrew word is *elohim*, which can be translated as "gods" or "heavenly beings." But "angels" is a fair translation, since the psalm is obviously referring to God's "heavenly court."

74. God's transportation

According to Psalm 18, God can use an angel as a mode of transportation: "He rode upon a cherub, and flew; He flew upon the wings of the wind" (v. 10). This type of cherub is not the cute, pudgy baby angel most people think of, but an awe-inspiring, winged creature, such as the two on the top of the ark of the covenant (see 84 [cherubim]).

75. angel security

Psalm 34 is a lovely statement of trust in divine protection. Consider verse 7: "The angel of the LORD encamps all around those who fear Him, and delivers them." The word *encamps* suggests not just one angel, but a whole army of angels, circling to protect the person. The people of Israel had witnessed again and again the saving actions of God and His angels, so it is appropriate that this song of trust refers to the angels and their protective work.

76. angels in pursuit

Psalm 35 is the cry of a persecuted man praying for deliverance and vengeance on his persecutors. "Let those be put to shame and brought to dishonor who seek after my life . . . Let them be like chaff before the wind, and let the angel of the LORD chase them. Let their way be dark and slippery, and let the angel of the LORD pursue them" (vv. 4–6). While this strikes some readers as vengeful (even unchristian) we have to read it for what it is: the heartfelt cry of one being persecuted. The man is not seeking his own vengeance, but is asking God and His angels to bring it about.

77. chariots of God

A proper title for Psalm 68 might be "God Rules!" It is a song of triumph, as though God were a celestial conqueror marching in glory to Jerusalem. "The chariots of God are twenty thousand, even thousands of angels" (68:17 KJV). Does this mean that God literally rides angels as a man would ride in a chariot? Of course not. It is simply a poetic way of saying that God, the Ruler of the universe, is accompanied by many thousands of angels, a fact mentioned more than once in the Bible.

78. evil angels in Egypt

The very long Psalm 78 is a kind of quick review of Israel's history, the good and the bad. Several verses refer to the plagues sent upon Egypt. Note verse 49: "He cast on them the fierceness of His anger, wrath, indignation, and trouble, by sending angels of destruction among them." (Instead of "angels of destruction," some translations have "evil angels.") This verse calls to mind the sinister fog in the movie *The Ten Commandments*. Instead of an actual angel with wings, the angel of death (which kills all the firstborn of the Egyptians) is depicted as a black fog creeping across the land.

79. "they shall bear you up"

One of the most comforting of the "protection" psalms is Psalm 91, with its promises of divine aid. Consider this section: "He shall give His angels charge over you, to keep you in all your ways. In their hands, they shall bear you up, lest you dash your foot against a stone" (vv. 11–12). Sound familiar? These words were quoted by Satan when he tempted Jesus to throw Himself off the pinnacle of the temple (Matt. 4:6). No doubt Jesus knew this beautiful psalm well, but He could see that Satan was twisting the words for his own purposes. Jesus countered with His own quotation from Scripture: "You shall not tempt the LORD your God" (Deut. 6:16).

80. angelic sing-along

Praise is a key theme of many of the psalms, and definitely Psalm 103 is one of the most heartfelt outpourings of praise anywhere in the Bible. David, its author, begins by praising God with his inmost being, but at the end he enlists the aid of other voices: "Bless the LORD, you His angels, who excel in strength, who do His word, heeding the voice of His word. Bless the LORD, all you His hosts, you ministers of His, who do His pleasure" (vv. 20–21).

81. Genesis set to music

One Bible commentary gives this name to Psalm 104, a hearty song of praise for God's creation. Naturally, angels figure into the song: "He lays the beams of His upper chambers in the waters, who makes the clouds His chariot, who walks on the wings of the wind, who makes His angels spirits, His ministers a flame of fire" (vv. 3–4).

"Flame of fire" here may simply mean lightning. It is as if God is riding upon storm clouds, surrounded by angels in the form of winds and lightning. This psalm was rewritten in rhyming form in 1561 by William Kethe, and it became the hymn we know as "O Worship the King," which sings of how "His chariots of wrath the deep thunderclouds form, / And dark is His path on the wings of the storm."

82. Isaiah's vision

In Isaiah 6, the prophet recorded his "commissioning" by God, which occurred in a vision in which seraphs (angels) were singing praise to God. Isaiah was so awestruck that he cried out, "Woe is me!" lamenting that he was an impure man living among impure people. One of the seraphs took a live coal from the altar, touched Isaiah's mouth, and declared him purified. Then God asked, "Whom shall I send?" The prophet replied, "Here am I! Send me."

83. seraphim

Like the cherubim (see 84) the seraphim were a sort of angel. (*Seraphim* is plural—one seraph, two seraphim.) Their name means, so far as we know, "burning ones." They are mentioned in Isaiah's vision in the temple, and they made quite an impression: "Each one had six wings: with two he covered his face, with two he covered his feet, and with two he flew" (Isa. 6:2). This is the only mention of seraphim in the Bible.

Jewish folklore holds that the seraphim were the highest order among the angels. They were not messengers, like most other angels, but were attendants to God, ever praising His power and holiness. The influential work called *The Celestial Hierarchy* (page 598) by the so-called Pseudo-Dionysius also stated that they were the highest of the angels.

In art, seraphim are usually shown in red (since they are the "burning ones"), often carrying the *flabellum*, a flaming sword inscribed with "Holy, holy, holy," the words they spoke in Isaiah's vision.

84. cherubim

The term "cherubs" usually refers to the cute, pudgy angels found on Christmas cards. But in the Bible they are awesome, almost frightening creatures. The prophet Ezekiel had a strange vision of the cherubim (that's plural—one cherub, two cherubim): "Their whole body, with their back, their hands, their wings, and the wheels that the four had, were full of eyes all around . . . Each one had four faces: the first face was the face of a cherub, the second face the face of a man, the third the face of a lion, and the fourth the face of an eagle" (Ezek. 10:12, 14). Much earlier, cherubim had served as sentries, brandishing flaming swords to keep Adam and Eve out once they were banished from Eden (Gen. 3:24).

The most commonly seen cherubim—or, at least, figures of them—were the two on the lid of the ark of the covenant. The ark is described in detail in Exodus 25, including the two winged figures who face each other, their wings touching (and portrayed accurately, by the way, in the movie *Raiders of the Lost Ark*). Israel was prohibited from making images of God Himself, but apparently they thought of the space between the cherubim as the place where God was present: The phrase "LORD Almighty, enthroned between the cherubim" occurs many times in the Bible.

85. "the Angel of His presence"

Isaiah 63 reads like a psalm, with its fond remembrances of God's aid in the past to the Israelites: "In all their affliction He was afflicted, and the Angel of His presence saved them" (v. 9). We don't know if this angel was a particular angel, or if this is just a poetic way of saying, "His presence saved them."

86. Ezekiel's living creatures

The book of the prophet Ezekiel opens with a bang, the prophet's bizarre vision of four unearthly beings. In the midst of an ominous whirlwind were "four living creatures." They were human in shape, but each one had four wings, and their feet were like calves' feet. They sparkled like burnished bronze. Each had four faces: a lion, a man, an ox, and an eagle. They moved, and they gave the impression of fire and lightning. More impressive than the creatures was the glory of the Lord Himself above them. This stunning vision caused Ezekiel to fall on his face, whereupon the Lord commissioned him as a prophet to the people of Israel.

We learn in Ezekiel 10 that these "living creatures" are cherubim (see 84), the guardians of the Lord's throne. Since this vision took place in Babylon, where Ezekiel was in exile, one message seems to be that the Lord's throne is anywhere He wishes it to be, not necessarily tied to a location in Israel.

87. angel eyes

Ezekiel 10 records the prophet's dramatic encounter with the cherubim (a type of angel). Unlike most other angels in the Bible, these cherubim were totally unearthly in appearance: "Their whole body, and their backs, and their hands, and their wings, and the wheels, were full of eyes round about" (v. 12 KJV). This description is why some artists have portrayed angels with eyes on their wings. (The eyes indicate that the angels see everything, of course.) Some angels have even been portrayed with wings that look like peacock feathers, probably because the circlets at the ends of peacock feathers look much like eyes.

88. a friend in the furnace

There is something exotic and musical about the names of the prophet Daniel's three friends: Shadrach, Meshach, and Abed-Nego. Daniel 3 tells the story of how wicked King Nebuchadnezzar of Babylon had the three friends thrown into a fiery furnace. Afterward, the king learned that not only were the three men surviving the furnace, but there were "four men loose, walking in the midst of the fire; and they [were] not hurt, and the form of the fourth [was] like the Son of God" (v. 25). Nebuchadnezzar was so impressed that he said, "Blessed be the God of Shadrach, Meshach, and Abed-Nego, who sent His Angel and delivered His servants" (v. 28).

89. angel in the lion's den

Daniel the Hebrew prophet faced the challenge of living under foreign rulers who worshiped other gods. Daniel 6 tells the familiar story of how the Persian king Darius had Daniel thrown into a den of lions for praying to his own God. The next morning, much to everyone's surprise, Daniel was alive and well. He told the king, "My God sent His angel and shut the lions' mouths" (6:22).

90. watchers and holy ones

Angels play a prominent role in the book of Daniel. In Daniel 4, the prophet relates, "I saw in the visions of my head while on my bed, and there was a watcher, a holy one, coming down from heaven" (v. 13). We can probably assume that this watcher and holy one was an angel.

Jewish legend relates that angels never slept. Jewish legend also has it that the watchers were the "sons of God" mentioned in Genesis 6, who cohabited with human women and gave birth to a race of giants.

91. Daniel's heavenly interpreter

The book of Daniel, like the book of Revelation in the New Testament, contains visions that are hard to interpret. Daniel had a vision of four strange beasts coming out of the ocean. The angel Gabriel was the heavenly interpreter who explained the visions to Daniel. The angel told Daniel, "Understand, son of man, that the vision refers to the time of the end . . . I am making known to you what shall happen in the latter time of the indignation" (Dan. 8:17, 19).

92. the man clothed in linen

Not all angels in the Bible are identified with the word *angel*. Both Ezekiel and Daniel mention "a man clothed in linen," and in the contexts it is clear that it was an angel being referred to. In Ezekiel 9 and 10, the man in linen has a writer's inkwell at his side, so clearly this angel is a kind of heavenly scribe. Jewish tradition says it was the angel Michael or Enoch the patriarch.

93. Zechariah's angels

Unique among all the books of the prophets in the Old Testament, Zechariah records several encounters with angels. Almost at the beginning of his book, he speaks of a "man" (it is soon clear that this is an angel) riding a red horse, with three other horses behind him. The prophet learns that the horses and riders have been going to and fro throughout the earth (1:7–11). Later in the book, an angel interprets various symbols to the prophet, including a lampstand, a flying scroll, and a woman in a basket. In chapter 6, the prophet sees horses and chariots of four different colors, and the angel explains that they are "four spirits of heaven, who go out from their station before the Lord of all the earth" (v. 5).

94. stork angels?

The book of the prophet Zechariah mentions angels several times, primarily in the role of interpreting visions. (An angel played the same role for the prophet Daniel.) But Zechariah also mentions something else that sounds faintly angelic: "Then I raised my eyes and looked, and there were two women, coming with the wind in their wings; for they had wings like the wings of a stork" (5:9).

95. *malakh*

The Hebrew word used for "angel" in the Old Testament is *malakh*, meaning "messenger," not necessarily a supernatural one. We have to determine from the context that the particular *malakh* is indeed an angel, not an ordinary human messenger. Incidentally, the prophet Malachi, whose book ends the Old Testament, bears a name that translates as "my messenger." Bible scholars aren't sure if he was named Malachi or if the book is sort of anonymous—as if it were titled "A Prophecy by God's Messenger."

THE LIFE OF JESUS

96. *logos* and angel of the Lord

John's gospel begins with "In the beginning was the Word, and the Word was with God, and the Word was God." As he proceeds further, it is obvious that he identifies this Word with Christ. The early Christians generally believed that Christ had in some way existed from the very beginning. He was the preexisting Word (which translates the Greek word *logos*). Some early Christians noted the number of times in the Old Testament that the phrase "angel of the Lord" appears and decided that the angel of the Lord might be the *Logos* making His appearance before He became the man Jesus. In other words, the *Logos* had been putting in appearances among human beings for several centuries.

97. John the Baptist

John was the kinsman and forerunner of Jesus Christ and one of the Bible's most interesting characters. John's birth was, like Jesus', announced by the angel Gabriel, and he was born to the elderly couple Zechariah and Elizabeth. Gabriel foretold that the child would act "in the spirit and power of Elijah . . . to make ready a people prepared for the Lord" (Luke 1:17).

98. Joseph, the angel, and dreams

The first mention of an angel in the four Gospels occurs in connection with the birth of Jesus. Mary, Joseph's fiancée, was pregnant through the work of the Holy Spirit. Faced with a difficult situation, Joseph was visited in a dream by an angel, who told him, "Joseph, son of David, do not be afraid to take to you Mary your wife, for that which is conceived in her is of the Holy Spirit. And she will bring forth a Son, and you shall call His name JESUS, for He will save His people from their sins" (Matt. 1:20–21). Joseph heeded the angel's words, married Mary, and named the child Jesus.

After the birth of Jesus and the visit of the wise men from the East, Joseph received another visit from the angel, and for good reason: Wicked King Herod had heard the rumor that a "king of the Jews" had been born, and he planned to take bloody action. The angel told Joseph, "Arise, take the young Child and His mother, flee to Egypt, and stay there until I bring you word; for Herod will seek the young Child to destroy Him" (Matt. 2:13). Herod (known to history as "Herod the Great," even though everyone agrees he was thoroughly vile) ordered all the male children in Bethlehem slaughtered, but by this time Jesus was safely in Egypt. The angel visited Joseph again and let him know it was safe to return home (vv. 13–23).

99. angels and the Temptation

After Jesus' baptism He went into the wilderness where He was tempted by Satan. Jesus triumphed in this ordeal, yet apparently it was quite strenuous. "The devil left Him, and behold, angels came and ministered to Him" (Matt. 4:11). Since He was the Son of God, why would He need the assistance of angels? Remember: Even though He was the Son of God, He was also fully human. It is possible that after a time in the wilderness He was hungry and thirsty and needed food and drink as any man would. It is possible also that the angels supplied some sort of spiritual support after this critical confrontation with Satan.

100. the ninety and nine

Jesus offended many of the religious people of His day by mingling with people they considered to be sinners. In response to criticism, He told the parable of the lost sheep: If a shepherd has a hundred sheep, and one is lost, he goes after it, rejoices when he finds it, and asks his neighbors to share in his rejoicing. "I say to you that likewise there will be more joy in heaven over one sinner who repents than over ninety-nine just persons who need no repentance" (Luke 15:7). Thus the salvation of a sinner is something that gives the angels delight.

101. Jesus the ladder

The early Christians thought of Jesus as the divine Mediator between sinful man and the holy God. In John's gospel, Jesus uttered these mysterious words: "You shall see heaven open, and the angels of God ascending and descending upon the Son of Man" (1:51). Clearly Jesus had in mind the dream of Jacob in Genesis 28, in which he saw a ladder (or stairway) to heaven, with angels going up and down upon it. The angels' coming and going represented God's communication with man, which Jesus indicates now takes place through Him.

102. the angel of the pool

John's gospel mentions a pool in Jerusalem, a pool with miraculous powers of healing. "An angel went down at a certain time into the pool and stirred up the water; then whoever stepped in first, after the stirring of the water, was made well of whatever disease he had" (5:4). The story continues with Jesus' healing a poor man who had tried in vain to get to the pool's healing waters but was never the first one in. An old Christian legend has it that it was the angel Raphael who stirred the waters (since the name Raphael means "God heals").

103. angel in the garden

The Gospels tell us that Jesus, being fully human, suffered agony before His arrest, knowing that He would be crucified. Luke's gospel records that in the garden on the Mount of Olives He prayed to God, "'Father if it is Your will, remove this cup from Me; nevertheless not My will, but Yours, be done.' Then an angel appeared to Him from heaven, strengthening Him" (Luke 22:42–43). Some readers wonder why the Son of God would need such aid, but we need to remember that Jesus was fully human and could benefit from angelic support just as any human would. In many paintings of Jesus' agony in the garden, an angel is shown.

104. twelve legions

Jesus' betrayal by Judas and His arrest in the Garden of Gethsemane caused one of His followers to lash out in violence. Jesus hurriedly told him, "Put your sword in its place, for all who take the sword will perish by the sword. Or do you think that I cannot now pray to My Father, and He will provide Me with more than twelve legions of angels?" (Matt. 26:52–53). It is clear that Jesus was conscious of the power of God to act on His behalf, but He knew that the way of suffering and dying on the cross was the only way.

105. the angel and the stone

To the question "How did Jesus get out of His tomb?" the Gospels provide an answer: "Behold, there was a great earthquake; for an angel of the Lord descended from heaven, and came and rolled back the stone from the door, and sat on it. His countenance was like lightning, and his clothing as white as snow. And the guards shook for fear of him, and became like dead men" (Matt. 28:2–4). To the devoted women who had come to the tomb, the angel said that Jesus was not there, for He had risen (28:5–6). It seems appropriate, since there were angels connected with Jesus' conception and birth, that an angel would be at the scene of the Resurrection.

106. the angels in the tomb

All the Gospels record angels in connection with Jesus' empty tomb. John's gospel relates that Mary Magdalene, the devoted follower of Jesus, came early on Easter morning to the tomb and found it empty. "And she saw two angels in white sitting, one at the head and the other at the feet, where the body of Jesus had lain" (20:12).

107. the ignorance of angels

When is the end of time? When will Jesus return to earth? People have been speculating about this for centuries, and no one has gotten it right yet. Not only are people ignorant of the time, but also, Jesus said, are the angels: "Of that day and hour no one knows, not even the angels of heaven, but My Father only" (Matt. 24:36).

ANGELS AND THE APOSTLES

108. the apostles' liberator

Acts 5 relates that the Jewish authorities slapped the apostles in prison. They weren't there long, for "at night an angel of the Lord opened the prison doors and brought them out, and said, 'Go, stand in the temple and speak to the people all the words of this life.' And when they heard that, they entered the temple early in the morning and taught." (vv. 19–20) The prison guards reported, "We found the prison shut securely, and the guards standing outside before the doors; but when we opened them, we found no one inside!" (v. 23).

109. Philip's angel

The book of Acts tells us much about Philip, one of the seven "deacons" who assisted the Christians in Jerusalem. He is usually called "Philip the evangelist" because Acts records his carrying the gospel to far-flung locales. He was prodded to do so by a heavenly messenger: An angel told him to go toward a desert road, where he met an official of the queen of the Ethiopians. Apparently this official was a "God-fearer," a non-Jew who was attracted to the Jewish religion. When Philip found him, he was in his chariot. Philip explained the gospel to him and immediately baptized him. Apparently the experience was wonderful, for the Ethiopian "went on his way rejoicing" (Acts 8:26–39). Thus, in a short time after Jesus' resurrection, the gospel had already moved as far as the kingdom of Ethiopia.

110. Cornelius and Peter

One of the most appealing characters in the New Testament is Cornelius, a Roman centurion. Acts 10 describes him as "one who feared God," which meant he practiced a Jewish spirituality, including prayer and aiding the poor. Acts 10 relates his being visited by an angel, who told him that his kindness and good works had not gone unnoticed by God. The angel linked him with the apostle Peter. After his meeting with Peter, he became a Christian, the first Roman convert to the faith.

111. angels, not evangelists

Angels in the Bible do many things to benefit human beings, including announcing the birth of the Savior

(Luke 2). But there is one distinctive activity that angels do *not* do: preach the gospel. One example: Acts 10 tells us of the righteous Roman soldier Cornelius (see 110), who was told by an angel to send for the apostle Peter, the man who would preach to him the gospel. Why didn't the angel himself present the gospel? This never happens in the Bible, nor anywhere in Christian history. The gospel is the good news of sinners being saved from their sin—something the angels cannot experience themselves. Only a saved sinner can preach the gospel to sinners.

112. Peter and the angel

As Jesus predicted, His apostles were persecuted, imprisoned, and even killed. Peter was thrown into prison by Herod and bound in chains with a soldier on each side. Peter was sleeping but awakened to a glowing angel, who made Peter's chains fall off. Peter followed him out and went to a home where some fellow Christians were praying for him. When Peter knocked, the servant girl was hysterical at seeing him set free. Peter's miraculous deliverance had an unfortunate consequence for his guards: Herod had them executed (Acts 12).

113. the death of Herod

Acts 12 records the persecution of Christians by the violent ruler Herod. He killed the apostle James and had

Peter imprisoned for a time. But a dire fate awaited Herod himself. Appearing in his royal robes and giving an eloquent speech before a crowd, Herod made such an impression that the people yelled, "The voice of a god and not of a man!" Perhaps Herod's ego had swelled too big: "Then immediately an angel of the Lord struck him, because he did not give glory to God. And he was eaten by worms and died" (Acts 12:23).

114. Paul's shipwreck

Paul the apostle had a life with many interesting scrapes and escapes, and Acts 27 tells of a dramatic storm and shipwreck. The storm raged for days, and almost everything was thrown overboard. The crew was about to despair, but Paul (on his way to trial in Rome) announced that an angel had assured him that he would reach Rome, and though the ship would be lost, no one would die. The ship ran aground on Malta, and the soldiers on board planned to kill the prisoners, fearing they would try to escape. But a Roman centurion who apparently liked Paul kept the soldiers from killing anyone.

115. a spectacle before the angels

Are angels really "watchin' over me," as the old camp song says? Indeed. Paul wrote that "we have been made a spectacle to the world, both to angels and to men" (1

Cor. 4:9). Within Paul's own lifetime, some of the spectacles took the form of persecution in the huge Roman arenas, where Christians were tortured and brutally killed for the amusement of the heartless audiences. The angels were watching. So while Christians who suffered in the Roman spectacles might hear laughter and sneers from their audiences, they were aware that God and His angels were a more important audience.

116. angels or Spirit?

For the most part, angels are invisible to man, as is the Holy Spirit. Some people confuse the two, believing that the Spirit is an angel. The Bible is clear that angels are "ministering spirits" (Heb. 1:14), but also clear that angels are not to be worshiped (Col. 2:18). Angels are creatures, not the Creator, and only the Creator is to be worshiped (Rom. 1:24–25). The Spirit is the triune God Himself, convicting men of sin and judgment (John 16:8), revealing and interpreting Christ to men, and never revealing Himself in human form, as angels sometimes do. The Spirit can be in more than one place at a time, but an angel cannot. The Spirit is all-present, all-knowing, and all-powerful. While angels' abilities far exceed our own, they do not possess the abilities of the Spirit.

117. judging the angels

Paul the apostle stated in 1 Corinthians, "Do you not know that the saints will judge the world? . . . Do you not know that we shall judge angels?" (6:2–3). This causes many readers to pause. How can mere mortals ever be put in the position of judging the heavenly angels? Several places in the New Testament indicate that some of the angels will be judged (Matt. 25:41; 2 Peter 2:4; Jude 6). There is certainly no reason why the resurrected believers, reigning with Christ, would not participate in the judging of angels who had gotten out of line.

118. armor of angels

The apostle Paul spoke in Romans 13:12 of the "armor of light" and in 2 Corinthians 6:7 of the "armor of right-eousness" that Christians should wear. Angels have often been portrayed in art as wearing armor also. This seems appropriate, since tradition has it that they are the "hosts" (armies) of the Lord. The archangel Michael, whom the Bible mentions as making war on Satan, is almost always pictured in armor of some sort.

119. company of angels

For the Jews, Mount Sinai was a special place, the place where God gave His holy Law to Moses. The letter to the

Hebrews claims that there is now a holier place than Sinai: "the city of the living God, the heavenly Jerusalem" with its "innumerable company of angels," the place of "the firstborn who are registered in heaven" and "the spirits of just men made perfect" (12:22–23).

120. curious angels

According to 1 Peter, the preaching of the Christian gospel of salvation is such a wonderful thing that even the angels desire to look into it (1:12).

121. the court scene

Jesus in heaven is (figuratively speaking) at the right hand of God (see 241). In 1 Peter 3:22, we learn that Christ "is at the right hand of God, angels and authorities and powers having been made subject to Him." Peter was picturing a heavenly court, with the angels, authorities, and powers (three different categories of angels) subject to their Ruler, Christ.

122. nothing will separate us

The apostle Paul was certain that once a sinner was redeemed by Christ, nothing whatsoever could separate him from God. "I am persuaded that neither death nor life, nor angels nor principalities nor powers, nor things present nor things to come, nor height nor depth, nor any other created thing, shall be able to separate us from the love of God which is in Christ Jesus our Lord" (Rom. 8:38–39). This is one of a few places in the Bible that refer to different categories of angels (the "principalities" and "powers" are types of angels). Paul was saying that, as powerful as angels are, even they cannot do us eternal harm.

123. Christ above the angels

Angels played a major role in Jewish folklore, which gave them a role in giving the Law to Moses. Many people—including some of the Jews who became Christians—may have been on the borderline of worshiping the angels. The letter to the Hebrews makes it clear that Christ is superior to the angels, for He is the unique Son of God, the one divine Mediator between God and mankind. Hebrews emphasizes that the angels themselves worship Christ, and so should all human beings (1:4–14).

124. angels unawares

"Be not forgetful to entertain strangers: for thereby some have entertained angels unawares" (Heb. 13:2 KJV). The author of Hebrews had in mind the story of Abraham entertaining three angels who, we gather, looked like normal human beings (Gen. 18:1–5) and who ate human food. This story raises the possibility that anyone we entertain might be an angel in disguise.

125. in flaming fire

Jesus' second coming is good news for those who have faith in Him, bad news for those who reject Him. Paul spoke of Jesus' returning to earth "from heaven with His mighty angels, in flaming fire taking vengeance on those who do not know God, and on those who do not obey the gospel of our Lord Jesus Christ. These shall be punished with everlasting destruction" (2 Thess. 1:7–9). The word *everlasting* here suggests that people who believe that hell is only temporary are wrong, as are those who believe in annihilationism (see 28).

126. the four living creatures

Revelation 4 pictures for us the throne room of heaven, in which are four "living creatures," each with six wings and "full of eyes around and within" (v. 8). One of the creatures was like a lion, the second like a calf, the third like a man, the fourth like an eagle. Day and night they chanted, "Holy, holy, holy, Lord God Almighty, Who was and is and is to come!" (v. 8). Were these angels? Obviously yes, though not the normal, human-appearing angels. They were similar to the seraphim in Isaiah's vision (Isa. 6), who also attended upon God and sang, "Holy, holy,

holy." Their animal-like appearance also suggests Ezekiel's "living creatures" (Ezek. 1; 10), which were also covered with eyes.

127. the book from an angel

Revelation is the only book of the Bible that actually claims to have been the result of a visit from an angel: "The Revelation of Jesus Christ, which God gave Him to show His servants—things which must shortly take place. And He sent and signified it by His angel to His servant John" (1:1). It is appropriate that Revelation mentions an angel in its first verse: the book contains more than seventy references to angels, more than any other book of the Bible.

3

Satan and Demons in the Bible

128. Satan

The evil being known as Satan (Hebrew for "adversary") or the devil appears very rarely in the Old Testament, but several times in the New. In spite of his being pictured with horns and a pitchfork, the Bible says nothing about his looks. (Since Satan is evil, artists naturally portray him as ugly.) Satan and the devils/demons who serve him are depicted as harmful to mankind, tempting us to do evil things and to reject God. The Bible's last book, Revelation, claims that Satan and his followers will be annihilated at the end of time. For the present, Satan and the devils can lead people astray—but not unless the people are willing. Comedian Flip Wilson's old line "The devil made me do it" doesn't square with the Bible. In the Bible, human beings are responsible for their own sins. The devil may tempt people, but people themselves choose to do wrong.

129. Satan as serpent

The first villain in the Bible is merely an animal, although a clever (and talking) one. This is the serpent, which, according to Genesis 3, tempted Eve to eat of the forbidden fruit. The serpent told the woman the first lie: He claimed that, contrary to what God said, the man and the woman had much to gain by eating the forbidden fruit. In fact, they would be like gods! Eve believed this, ate the fruit, then gave it to her husband to eat. Too late, they discovered that the serpent had lied, and no good came of their disobedience of God's command. The couple were punished, but so was the serpent. "So the LORD God said to the serpent: 'Because you have done this, you are cursed more than all cattle, and more than every beast of the field; on your belly you shall go, and you shall eat dust all the days of your life. And I will put enmity between you and the woman, and between your seed and her Seed; He shall bruise your head, and you shall bruise His heel" (Gen. 3:14–15).

Was the serpent Satan? Genesis does not say so. The Old Testament doesn't say anything on the subject, but Jewish tradition clearly developed the idea that the snake was more than just a mere reptile. By the time the New Testament was written, Satan was clearly "the tempter," so everyone identified him with the serpent of Genesis 3.

130. "as the serpent deceived Eve . . ."

The apostle Paul constantly admonished Christians to be on guard against false teaching—and against the devil. He wrote to the Corinthians, "I fear, lest somehow, as the serpent deceived Eve by his craftiness, so your minds may be corrupted from the simplicity that is in Christ" (2 Cor. 11:3). This is one of the few mentions in the Bible of the Garden of Eden story; but even though it is seldom referred to, it is clear that all Jews (and, later, all Christians) knew the story of the serpent and his malicious effects on the first humans.

131. the name Lucifer

The name actually means "light-bearer." It occurs only once in the Old Testament, Isaiah 14:12–15: "How art thou fallen from heaven, O Lucifer, son of the morning! how art thou cut down to the ground, which didst weaken the nations! For thou hast said in thine heart, I will ascend into heaven, I will exalt my throne above the stars of God . . . Yet thou shalt be brought down to hell" (KJV). Generations of Bible readers believed that Lucifer was Satan, a proud angel who rebelled against God and was expelled from heaven. (See 151 [angel of light].)

132. Satan in the book of Job

The book of Job is a profound consideration of the question "Why do good people suffer?" Job, who was wealthy but also righteous, was tested when God allowed Satan to afflict Job with all kinds of troubles. The book pictures God holding court when the "sons of God" assemble, and Satan enters the assembly (something the author of Job seems to accept as perfectly normal). Satan is more of a tester than a tempter. The Hebrew name Satan means simply "adversary," and Satan in this book is a kind of heavenly court prosecutor, working to show that the saintly Job is saintly only during the good times, not the bad. Satan does what he does only with God's approval and (in a sense) on God's behalf. Even so, Satan seems to take some delight in afflicting poor Job, and it is easy to see how the prosecutor-adversary evolved into the outright enemy of man.

Job's children and wealth were taken, his skin was afflicted with boils, and his wife urged him to "curse God and die!" Yet through all the afflictions Satan sent upon him, Job would not curse God. By "hanging in there," he proved Satan's accusation wrong.

133. sacrificing to demons

The idea that the gods of the pagans are demons was a common one among the Jews, an idea picked up by the Christians. (It forms the background for John Milton's

Paradise Lost, in which most of the demons have the names of pagan gods.) We see a reference to this belief in Psalm 106, which is a kind of review of Israel's past sins: "They served their idols, which became a snare to them. They even sacrificed their sons and their daughters to demons" (vv. 36–37). The Israelites were horrified at child sacrifice, but the heathen nations around them practiced it regularly. The god Moloch was depicted in idols that formed a sort of furnace, into which howling infants were thrown to their deaths, with cymbals and drums to drown out their cries. It is easy to see how the Israelites could believe that such horrid worship would be the worship of demons, not of a loving god.

134. Ezekiel and the king of Tyre

Ancient Tyre was a busy commercial seaport, famed for its wealth and luxurious living. The prophet Ezekiel directed the words of God against the king of Tyre, condemning his pride. While the book of Ezekiel makes it clear that it is this specific historical person who is being condemned, the prophet's words sound as if they might be describing someone else as well: "Your heart was lifted up because of your beauty; you corrupted your wisdom for the sake of your splendor; I cast you to the ground, I laid you before kings, that they might gaze at you" (28:17). Could this be referring to Satan, who was expelled from heaven because of his pride? Generations of Christians have interpreted Ezekiel 28 as referring not only to an earthly king but also to the proud angel who became too haughty and was thrown out of heaven.

135. Satan in Zechariah

The book of the prophet Zechariah was written comparatively late, which explains its position at the end (almost) of the Old Testament. Zechariah contains the last Old Testament reference to Satan: "Then he [God] showed me Joshua the high priest standing before the Angel of the LORD, and Satan standing at his right hand to oppose him. And the Lord said to Satan, 'The LORD rebuke you, Satan!'" (3:1–2). This is the only hint in the Old Testament that God and Satan are in direct opposition to each other. While in the book of Job, Satan is only a kind of tester of man's moral fiber, in Zechariah he seems to be a force directly opposed to God. We are not too far here from the willful and thoroughly evil Satan of the New Testament.

136. Satan or God?

In the historical books dealing with Israel's judges and kings, Satan is mentioned only once, in 1 Chronicles 21:1, which records that he incited King David to take a census of Israel. But, take note: That same incident is covered in 2 Samuel 24:1 (which is older than 1 Chronicles), which claims that God, angry with Israel, incited David to take the census. So who egged David on—God or Satan? We don't know. It's clear from the tone of 1 Samuel 24:1 that its author saw the census as a bad thing. God was angry when He told David to do it. Perhaps the author of 1 Chronicles saw it as such a bad thing that he attributed it to Satan, not God.

SATAN IN THE NEW TESTAMENT

137. the temptation of Jesus

The Gospels report that after Jesus' baptism by John the Baptist He went into the desert, where for forty days He was tempted by the devil. The three-part Temptation is told in Matthew 4 and Luke 4. Jesus was hungry, and the devil suggested, "If You are the Son of God, command that these stones become bread." Jesus replied with a verse from Deuteronomy, "Man shall not live by bread alone, but by every word that proceeds from the mouth of God." In this He was resisting the temptation to be a sort of wonder-worker. The devil then took Him (in a vision, perhaps) to the highest point of the temple and said, "If You are the Son of God, throw Yourself down." The devil then quoted the Bible to the effect that angels would protect Jesus. Jesus replied that God was not to be put to the test this way. Then, from a high mountain, the devil showed Jesus "all the kingdoms of the world and their glory." "All these things I will give You if You will fall down and worship me." Jesus replied, quoting Scripture, "You shall worship the LORD your God, and Him only you shall serve."

By resisting the temptation to be a wonder-worker or a worldly king, Jesus proved He was fit to be the world's Savior. In a sense He undid the temptation of Adam and Eve, who yielded to the temptation to be godlike and powerful.

138. the parable of the sower

Jesus' longest and most complex parable is a story of how people respond differently to the gospel. In the parable, a farmer sowed seed, some of it falling on good ground, on rocky soil, among thorns, and along the path. Jesus explained the parable in this way: The seed is the Word of God. The seed on the path is eaten by birds—that is, Satan takes away what is sown. The seed on rocky soil grows but withers away—people receive the Word, but it never takes root. The seed among thorns grows but is choked out—people receive the Word, but worldly worries keep it from growing. The seed on good soil grows and produces "some thirtyfold, some sixty, and some a hundred" (Mark 4:1–9).

139. your father, the devil

Among the Jews, "father" didn't imply just a biological relationship. It implied obedience and submission—in other words, if you disobey your father, you are not a true son. Likewise, a true child of God is one who obeys God.

The Jews were proud of their descent from Abraham, the great man of faith in Genesis. But in John 8, Jesus made it clear that biological descent meant nothing unless the people proved they were Abraham's *spiritual* descendants by imitating Abraham's faith. No, Jesus said, you are neither the children of Abraham nor the children of God, for "you are of your father the devil, and the desires of your father you want to do" (v. 44). This implies no biological connection with the devil, only that Satan's "children" are those who follow after him.

140. "deliver us from evil"

The familiar Lord's Prayer (found in Matt. 6:9–13) contains the phrase "lead us not into temptation, but deliver us from evil" (KJV). But the wording in the Greek may actually mean "deliver us from the evil one," as many modern translations have it. "The evil one" is, of course, Satan himself. While it doesn't make a major difference if we pray to be delivered from evil or the evil one, "evil one" does remind us that we face not just evil as an abstract idea, but a living, personal force: Satan.

141. Satan and sickness

Luke 13 records Jesus' healing of a woman "who had a spirit of infirmity eighteen years, and was bent over and could in no way raise herself up." Jesus healed her, and immediately she praised God. Jesus spoke of her as one "whom Satan has bound" for these eighteen years (13:11–16). It was common in Jesus' day to attribute any kind of illness—physical or mental—to the work of Satan or demons. In a way this makes sense: It is God's ultimate will that we be whole and healed, whereas it is Satan's will to do us harm in any way.

142. Satan on the inside

Can Satan himself possess a person? The Gospel authors said yes. According to Luke, "Satan entered Judas, surnamed Iscariot, who was numbered among the twelve. So he went his way and conferred with the chief priests and captains, how he might betray Him to them. And they were glad, and agreed to give him money" (Luke 22:3–5). Thus the horrible betrayal of Jesus by one of His own chosen disciples is not just the work of Judas himself, but also the work of the devil. While Satan had disappeared from the story after failing to tempt Jesus, he had returned to do his worst.

143. Satan and lightning

Luke's gospel speaks of a broader group of disciples known as the Seventy (see 183). After being sent out to do good works, they returned and reported that the demons are subject to them in Jesus' name. Jesus replied,

"I saw Satan fall like lightning from heaven" (Luke 10:18). It appears that Jesus was telling the Seventy that, yes, their mission was indeed having an effect on the kingdom of Satan and his demons. (Some commentators add a further interpretation: Since the Son of God existed from all eternity, He actually did witness the long-ago fall of Satan from heaven.)

Jesus may have intended an additional meaning: Just as Satan fell through pride, Christians can become too proud of their spiritual successes. In other words, as you triumph over Satan, don't commit the same sin Satan did.

The verse that follows is important: "Behold, I give you the authority to trample on serpents and scorpions, and over all the power of the enemy" (10:19). Is there any connection between Satan and serpents? Most assuredly.

144. the prince of this world

Three times in the gospel of John, Jesus referred to Satan as "the prince of this world." In John's gospel, "this world" is another way of saying "the world where evil and sin seem to have the upper hand." Jesus told Pilate that His kingdom is not of this world (John 18:36), for His kingdom is eternal, a kingdom of love and selflessness. Satan's kingdom is this world, or a large share of it, a kingdom of selfishness, but it will not last forever. Jesus told His disciples that the prince of this world will be cast out (12:31), that he has no power over Jesus Himself (14:30), and that he will be judged and condemned (16:11).

145. "get behind Me, Satan!"

One of the oddest passages in the Gospels concerns a quick and shocking turnaround in Jesus' attitude toward one of His disciples. As reported in Matthew 16:13–23, Jesus had just asked His disciples, "Who do men say that I, the Son of Man, am?" After several guesses by the disciples, Peter gave the correct answer: "You are the Christ, the Son of the living God." Jesus then pronounced a blessing on Peter, giving him the "keys of the kingdom of heaven." But soon after, when Jesus announced that as the Christ He must suffer and finally be killed, Peter took his Master aside and scolded Him: "Far be it from You, Lord; this shall not happen to You!" Jesus reacted with harshness: "Get behind Me, Satan! You are an offense to Me, for you are not mindful of the things of God, but the things of men." Did Jesus mean that His devoted disciple had become (or was possessed by) Satan? Hardly. Remember, the original meaning of the Hebrew word *Satan* was "adversary." Peter wasn't being evil, just contrary, opposing what Jesus had just described to him as the clear will of God.

146. *diabolos*

This Greek word is the source for our word *devil* (as well as the adjective form, *diabolic*). It means "slanderer" or "accuser" or "one who gives false information." It can even mean "one who opposes" (which is exactly the meaning of the Hebrew *Satan*). It is the most commonly used word for the devil in the New Testament.

147. the God of peace, crushing

Near the end of his letter to the Romans, Paul gave this promise: "The God of peace will crush Satan under your feet shortly" (16:20). The wording strikes some readers as almost humorous: The "God of peace" is going to "crush" someone? Yet it makes perfect sense, in a way. The world can never have perfect peace as long as Satan is able to go about doing mischief. Yet soon, Paul said, Satan's shenanigans will end abruptly, and peace will reign through the mercies of God.

148. Satan and married celibates

The Christians in Corinth lived in a city known for sexual looseness. No wonder Paul had much to say about sexual morality. While he himself preferred the single (and celibate) life, he knew it wasn't for everyone. He took a sensible approach to married life, assuming that physical intimacy was normal. Apparently some of the Corinthian Christians were attempting to be celibate while married, but Paul advised against this: "Do not deprive one another except with consent for a time, that you may give yourselves to fasting and prayer; and come together again so that Satan does not tempt you because of your lack of self-control" (1 Cor. 7:5).

149. Satan's devices

The early Christians took sin seriously, so much so that a backsliding Christian might be temporarily excluded from fellowship. We read of such a situation in 2 Corinthians 2, where Paul spoke of such a man; after the man had been chastised, he was to be received back with warmth and comfort. In fact, they must do so, "lest Satan should take advantage of us; for we are not ignorant of his devices" (v. 11). Put another way, leaving the man outside the fellowship permanently would give the devil a victory; being overly harsh or unforgiving to a brother who repents is something Satan delights in, since it drives the man to despair and makes the other believers spiritually proud.

150. the god of this age

Jesus referred to Satan as the "prince of this world," and in 2 Corinthians Paul refers to him as "the god of this age" (4:4). Paul was contrasting eternity, the age to come, with this present moment. Satan rules—or seems to rule—this world dominated by sin, in which sinners are the majority. But God rules eternally. By calling Satan "the god of this age," Paul was saying "the *temporary* god, who won't last."

151. angel of light

While warning the Corinthian Christians about false apostles, Paul told them to be on guard, because "Satan himself transforms himself into an angel of light" (2 Cor. 11:14). This is in keeping with the idea that Satan is a liar and deceiver, so good at guile that he can even appear to be the opposite of what he really is. In "masquerading," Satan is pretending to be what he once was (the bright angel Lucifer, thrown out of heaven for his pride), and Paul's warning indicates that, yes, Satan is able to deceive some people. This also reminds us that evil does not always appear evil on the surface. Paul may have even been familiar with the old Jewish legend that Satan had appeared to Eve in the form of an angel, entrancing her with his beauty and his angelic singing.

152. thorn in Paul's side

This familiar phrase comes from the apostle Paul, who admitted that he suffered because "a thorn in the flesh was given to me, a messenger of Satan to buffet me . . . Concerning this thing I pleaded with the Lord three times that it might depart from me. And He said to me, 'My grace is sufficient for you, for My strength is made perfect in weakness'" (2 Cor. 12:7–9). Paul may have been referring to some physical ailment, though we can't be sure.

153. the prince of the power of the air

Paul called Satan by this name in Ephesians 2:2: "You once walked according to the course of this world, according to the prince of the power of the air, the spirit who now works in the sons of disobedience." The air was considered to be the dwelling place of demons, those disobedient spirits who oppose the work of God. They and their prince, Satan, now influence sinful human beings, the "sons of disobedience."

154. do not give place to the devil

Paul's letter to the Ephesians is full of reminders about the practical meaning of "love your neighbor." It contains the wise advice "Do not let the sun go down on your wrath," followed by "nor give place to the devil" (4:26–27). Since the devil (Greek *diabolos*) is a slanderer and accuser, "giving place" to him may mean following him in slanderous words—something all of us are inclined to do when angry.

155. the whole armor of God

One of the most quoted passages from Paul's letters concerns the "armor of God." Paul urged believers to be strong, and to "put on the whole armor of God, that you may be able to stand against the wiles of the devil." He went on to say that our spiritual warfare is against not mere mortals but against "the rulers of the darkness of this age, against spiritual hosts of wickedness in the heavenly places." The spiritual armor includes a waistband of truth, a breastplate of righteousness, shoes of peace, the helmet of salvation, the sword of the Spirit, and "above all, taking the shield of faith with which you will be able to quench all the fiery darts of the wicked one" (Eph. 6:10–16).

156. two kingdoms

According to Paul, Christians have been rescued from Satan's kingdom and brought into Christ's kingdom (Col. 1:13). Through the centuries, theologians have emphasized this again and again: There are two choices, and if we do not belong to Christ's kingdom, we belong to Satan.

157. "establish you and guard you"

Paul warned Christians about the evils of the "man of sin," but he was certain that neither that man nor Satan himself need cause believers any anxiety, for "the Lord is faithful, who will establish you and guard you from the evil one" (2 Thess. 3:3).

158. "puffed up" like Satan

In speaking to the young pastor Timothy of the spiritual qualifications for pastors, Paul stated that he must not be "a novice, lest being puffed up with pride he fall into the same condemnation as the devil" (1 Tim. 3:6). The Jews and the early Christians believed that the angel Lucifer (see 131) had become conceited and changed from angel to devil, from Lucifer the beautiful to Satan the liar and destroyer. Paul was aware that, human nature being what it is, giving a new believer too much authority could easily lead to pride.

159. death and the devil

Sin, death, and the devil are all connected, which is why the poet John Milton made the three of them a kind of perverse "anti-Trinity" in his *Paradise Lost*. According to Hebrews 2:14, Jesus' saving work included destroying "him who had the power of death, that is, the devil." From the story of the serpent in Eden, people knew that Satan had brought death into the world (by tempting Adam and Eve to disobey God, which brought death). Through his death on the cross, Christ undid the work of Satan, releasing mankind from sin and from ultimate death.

160. resist, and make the devil flee

The Bible makes it clear that the devil is powerful . . . but so are our own evil impulses. If we can control ourselves, if we can resist rebelling against God, we are well on our way to breaking the devil's power. Note James 4:7: "Submit to God. Resist the devil and he will flee from you." The devil personifies rebellion against God. Submitting to God and resisting the devil amount to the same thing.

161. Satan the roaring lion

In 1 Peter 5:8, the apostle warned the Christians, "Be sober, be vigilant because your adversary the devil walks about like a roaring lion, seeking whom he may devour." Peter used the word *adversary* (which is what the name Satan means in Hebrew). Peter had spoken about persecution, and it is clear that he associated the devil with such persecutions. But Peter also made it clear that this roaring lion can be resisted.

162. "the wicked one"

In a few places the New Testament refers to Satan as "the wicked one" (or "evil one," depending on the translation). The word in the original Greek is *poneron*, a form of *poneria*, meaning "evil" or "wickedness." It is always clear that "the wicked one" is not an individual human person, but the ultimate evil one, Satan himself, the one who opposes God, the righteous One. (See Matt. 13:19; 1 John 2:13–14; 3:12; 5:18.)

163. destroying the devil's work

"For this purpose the Son of God was manifested, that He might destroy the works of the devil" (1 John 3:8). Since the works of the devil are sin (harming the sinner and those around him) and death (ultimate separation from God), Christ destroyed the devil's work by canceling sin's hold on people and granting them eternal life.

164. the devil's children

As the Bible sees it, your "father" is the one you obey. Thus, if you obey God, you are God's son; if you obey the devil, you are the devil's son. This is clear enough in 1 John 3:10: "In this the children of God and the children of the devil are manifest: Whoever does not practice righteousness is not of God, nor is he who does not love his brother."

165. the body of Moses

The brief letter of Jude (tucked in between 3 John and Revelation) refers to a dispute between the devil and the archangel Michael over the body of Moses (Jude 9). What is this about? A long-lost book called the Assumption of Moses told the story of how, after Moses' death, Satan and Michael both claimed it as their own. Michael won, naturally. The Assumption of Moses is one of many Jewish works about Bible characters—works that were, you might say, the "historical fiction" of their time.

166. a synagogue of Satan

The Book of Revelation begins with Jesus' pronounce-ments to seven churches. The message to the church of Smyrna warns against "the blasphemy of those who say they are Jews and are not, but are a synagogue of Satan" (2:9). This probably refers to Jews who refused to accept Jesus as Messiah and who were persecuting those who had done so. The message goes on to warn the faith that "the devil is about to throw some of you into prison, that you may be tested" (2:10). Revelation refers to another "syna-gogue of Satan" harassing the Christians at Philadelphia (3:9). The early Christians were aware that persecution of them had more than a human origin: Satan himself despised the people of God and worked to do them harm.

167. where Satan's throne is

Does Satan have an earthly dwelling place? Jesus' message to the church at Pergamos hints that he does, referring to the town as "where Satan's throne is" (Rev. 2:13). The message may be referring to persecution of Christians in the area. It may also refer to local worship of the pagan god Asklepios, whose symbol was a serpent (the same as Satan's symbol, coincidentally). Apparently the locals were prone to idol worship and sexual immorality, so "Satan's throne" meant Satan was having a field day with these people.

168. the depths of Satan

To the Christians at Thyatira, Christ spoke of those involved in "the depths of Satan" (or "the deep things of Satan" in some translations). This may refer to those initiated in idolatrous worship practices (Rev. 2:24). Christians had to steer clear of the "deep things of Satan" and instead pursue the "deep things of God" (1 Cor. 2:10).

169. accuser of the brethren

The book of Revelation calls Satan by the name "accuser of our brethren" (12:10). This harks back to the book of Job in the Old Testament, where Satan is the spirit who accuses Job of being righteous only because it brings him security. By the time Revelation was written, most Christians saw Satan as the unceasing accuser of the church, the evil one who hoped they would not endure persecution.

170. *drakon*

Our word *dragon* comes from the Greek *drakon*, which can mean "serpent," "dragon," or even "sea monster." The ancient world naturally looked upon snakes or any snakelike creatures as evil, so serpents and dragons were

connected with demonic activity. The dragon was frequently a symbol of chaos and disorder—the opponent of
God, who is the One who brings order to the universe.
The *drakon* is the main image used for Satan in the book
of Revelation (see 171 [dragon of Revelation]).

171. the dragon of Revelation

The beginning of the Bible presents us with the sinister, lying
serpent in the Garden of Eden, who tempted Adam and Eve
to disobey God. The Bible ends with a final battle between
heavenly forces and a dragon. Interestingly, the Greek word
for both dragon and serpent is *drakon* (see 170). There is no
doubt that the author of Revelation intended a connection
between the two, and no doubt that he identified the serpent
in the Garden of Eden with Satan.

Revelation describes the dragon in lurid detail: "a
great, fiery red dragon having seven heads and ten horns,
and seven diadems on his heads" (12:3). In chapter 13,
the dragon is connected with the Beast from the sea.
While commentators know that the dragon is Satan, much
ink has been spilled over deciding who—or what—the
Beast is, or represents. He derives his authority from the
dragon/Satan (13:4), which no doubt means he is drawing on the power of Satan.

The horrible dragon meets a dire fate: "I saw an angel
coming down from heaven, having the key to the bottomless pit and a great chain in his hand. He laid hold of
the dragon, that serpent of old, who is the Devil and

Satan, and bound him for a thousand years; and he cast him into the bottomless pit, . . . so that he should deceive the nations no more till the thousand years were finished. But after these things he must be released for a little while" (20:1–3).

End of the story? Not quite. After the thousand years, Satan goes out to deceive the nations and make war on the saints. "And fire came down from God out of heaven and devoured them. And the devil, who deceived them, was cast into the lake of fire and brimstone where the beast and the false prophet are. And they will be tormented day and night forever and ever" (20:7–10).

172. the dragon and the stars

In the highly symbolic book of Revelation, the dragon is Satan (see 171), described as fiery red, horned, and seven-headed. According to 12:4, "His tail drew a third of the stars of heaven and threw them to the earth." Over the centuries, commentators thought this referred to the rebellion of Satan (originally named Lucifer) and his followers against God. "A third of the stars," they said, referred to a third of the angels, who took Satan's side and were cast out of heaven. But it may simply be a way of impressing us with the size of the dragon; if he is huge enough for his tail to sweep a third of the stars from the skies, he is fearsome—fearsome enough to make war with Michael and the other angels, but not fearsome enough to win.

173. Michael's war with the dragon

Revelation 12 presents us with Satan in the form of a hideous dragon. "And war broke out in heaven: Michael and his angels fought against the dragon; and the dragon and his angels fought, but they did not prevail, nor was a place found for them in heaven any longer. So the great dragon was cast out, that serpent of old, called the Devil and Satan . . . he was cast to the earth, and his angels were cast out with him" (12:7–9). Revelation is probably referring to the battle between the rebel Satan (who was originally Lucifer, one of God's angels) and his followers, who are the losers when they rebel against God and are expelled from heaven.

Demons and Fallen Angels

174. Beelzebub

The name means "lord of the flies" and refers to a god of the Philistine people of Ekron (2 Kings 1:2). (Some scholars question whether the Philistines would actually have worshiped a god with such a name. Perhaps this was the Israelites' slur for a false god.) In the New Testament the name refers to the "prince of demons," Satan. Some of Jesus' enemies attributed His miracles to the power of Beelzebub (Mark 3:22; Luke 11:15). In John Milton's great poem *Paradise Lost*, Beelzebub is one of the fallen angels (that is, a demon), and is second in command to Satan himself.

175. Baal

Anyone familiar with the Old Testament knows that Baal was the fertility god of the Canaanites, and Israel was constantly tempted to worship Baal in addition to the true God. The prophets preached against this idolatry, and a handful of reformer kings tried to eliminate Baal worship, but again and again the Israelites worshiped Baal and other pagan gods. In Christian folklore, Baal (like other gods of the pagans) was thought to be a demon, one of the fallen angels cast out of heaven along with Satan. In his fallen state, Baal was worshiped, thus tempting people to forsake the true God. The name *Baal* means "lord" or "master."

176. Belial

This was, as Paul used it, another name for Satan (2 Cor. 6:15). The name occurs many times in the Old Testament of the King James Version, which refers to wicked or worthless people as "of Belial" (Deut. 13:13; Judg. 19:22; 1 Sam. 25:25). In his classic poem *Paradise Lost*, John Milton described Belial with disgust, for "a spirit more lewd / Fell not from Heaven, or more gross to love / Vice for itself." Milton suggested that among the demons (fallen angels), Belial was the lowest of the low.

177. Moloch

In a sense this pagan god was the "god of hell," for he presided over a horrid place that came to symbolize hell. In the Old Testament, Moloch (his name meant "king") was the bloodthirsty god of the Ammonites. A metal image of the god was heated like a furnace, and live children were sacrificed in it, with their cries being drowned out by drums and symbols. Israel was horrified at child sacrifice, even though some wicked Israelites (including some of the kings) sacrificed their own children to this god. One abhorrent place of Moloch sacrifice was Tophet (see 288) near Jerusalem. This place later became Israel's ever-burning rubbish heap, and because of its old associations with Moloch worship, and the fact that it always burned, it came to symbolize hell (see 286 [Gehenna]).

Like other pagan gods, Moloch appears in Milton's *Paradise Lost* as a fallen angel, one of Satan's cronies who is cast from heaven and becomes a demon. True to his nature in the Bible, he is a bloodthirsty demon, fierce and eager to make war on God and His angels.

178. music therapy

Call it therapy for a troubled mind, or an exorcism of an evil spirit: Either way, David's harp playing had a positive effect on Saul, king of Israel. According to 1 Samuel 16, Saul was troubled by "a distressing spirit," and his advisers suggested bringing in a skilled harpist to soothe the king. When David played, "Saul would become refreshed and well, and the distressing spirit would depart from him" (v. 14–23).

179. the beginning of Jesus' ministry

Many people like to think of Jesus as a great teacher, and the Gospels are indeed full of His words. But to the people of His own time He made an even deeper impression with His deeds. Matthew, after telling of Jesus' birth, baptism, and temptation by Satan, begins the story of His ministry in this way: "His fame went throughout all Syria; and they brought to Him all sick people who were afflicted with various diseases and torments, and those who were demon-possessed, epileptics, and paralytics; and He healed them" (Matt. 4:24). Note that among the ailments being healed is *demon possession*. This was a key element not only in Jesus' own ministry, but in that of His apostles as well.

180. commissioning the twelve disciples

Matthew 10 records the names of Jesus' twelve disciples and how He commissioned them: "As you go, preach, saying, 'The kingdom of heaven is at hand.' Heal the sick, cleanse the lepers, raise the dead, cast out demons. Freely you have received, freely give" (vv. 7–8). Note that casting out demons was part of the gospel outreach. As Jesus stated elsewhere, the flight of the demons meant that the kingdom had come on earth.

181. "my name is Legion"

The Gospels show Jesus as One with power to drive demons out of people. Whether these were actual exorcisms or (as some people prefer to believe) Jesus was merely working "psychology" on disturbed people, He had a reputation as a healer of troubled souls. One of the most famous exorcism stories concerns a near-naked, demon-possessed man who lived among tombs and threatened passersby. According to Mark 5, "Night and day, he was in the mountains and in the tombs, crying out and cutting himself with stones" (v. 5). When he saw Jesus, he ran out, begging Jesus, "Son of the Most High God," not to torture him. Jesus asked the man his name. He—they— replied, "My name is Legion; for we are many" (v. 9). Jesus sent the legion of demons into a nearby herd of pigs—which then drowned themselves in a lake. In a touching scene, the man begged to go with Jesus, but Jesus said, "Go home to your friends, and tell them what great things the Lord has done for you" (v. 19).

182. destruction

The devil and demons are destroyers, not creators. The Gadarene demoniac was controlled by a legion of vile spirits, and no one was able to bind him, even with a chain. Not only was he a threat to others but to himself as well, gashing himself with stones (Mark 5:1–5). When Jesus expelled the legion of demons, they went into a herd of swine, which rushed over a cliff into the sea (Mark 5:11–13). An evil spirit controlling a man leaped on two would-be exorcists and overpowered them, so that they fled the place naked and wounded (Acts 19:14–16). Jesus expelled one demon that was causing a young man to throw himself into fire and water (Matt. 17:14–20). Consider Jesus' words about His mission: "The thief [Satan] does not come except to steal, and to kill, and to destroy. I have come that they may have life, and that they may have it more abundantly" (John 10:10).

183. the Seventy and the demons

Jesus chose twelve men as His close group of disciples, but Luke's gospel also mentions disciples in a larger group, "the Seventy." "The Lord appointed seventy others also, and sent them two by two before His face into every city and place where He Himself was about to go." Apparently they had some success in their ministry: "The seventy returned with joy, saying, 'Lord, even the demons are subject to us in Your name'" (10:1–17).

184. God and mammon

"You cannot serve God and mammon," Jesus said (Matt. 6:24). Many versions translate the Greek word *mammon* as "money," but it really means "material possessions" in general. Jesus said elsewhere that it is difficult for the rich to enter heaven (Mark 10:25). But people who "serve mammon" aren't necessarily rich—even a poor person can be a worshiper of material things. "You cannot serve God and mammon" was His way of saying that deep love for God and an obsession with possessions cannot exist together. In John Milton's classic poem *Paradise Lost*, Mammon is a demon, one of the angels cast out of heaven. Milton mockingly describes Mammon as being materialistic even while in heaven, fascinated by the gold in the streets.

185. open warfare

Jesus stated, "If I cast out demons by the Spirit of God, surely the kingdom of God has come upon you" (Matt. 12:28). Jesus was saying that the exorcisms He (and later His disciples) performed were signs that the kingdom of God and the kingdom of Satan were in obvious and open conflict. With its emphasis on deliverance from demons, the charismatic renewal movement in recent years has brought this important teaching into the open once again.

186. unclean spirits

The New Testament uses the term "unclean spirit" more than twenty times to refer to demons. The word *unclean* doesn't sound so terrible to us, but in the Jewish world, with its horror of impurity, uncleanness was a serious thing. It might be appropriate for translators to use something stronger, like "loathsome spirit" or "vile spirit." At any rate, they were under the rule of Satan and had no purpose other than to afflict human beings in body and soul.

187. exorcism at a distance

Jesus and His followers dealt with many people who were demon-possessed. Most of these exorcisms were "in person," with Jesus speaking directly to the afflicted person. Mark 7 records the story of a Gentile woman who fell at Jesus' feet and begged Him to drive the demon out of her daughter. Jesus was impressed by her simple faith, and He told her to go home, for "the demon has gone out of your daughter" (v. 29). The woman returned home and found that it was so. Clearly Jesus did not have to be present for the exorcism to occur. (A bit of trivia: In the Gospels, whenever Jesus performed a miracle on a Gentile, it was always at a distance, as this one was.)

188. Jesus' warning

The New Testament gives witness to the power of the Spirit seen in many wonders—prophesying, casting out demons, and other miracles. Jesus promised such things. Yet He also gave a stern warning to those who pursue miracles for their own sake: "Not everyone who says to Me, 'Lord, Lord,' shall enter the kingdom of heaven, but he who does the will of My Father in heaven. Many will say to Me in that day, 'Lord, Lord, have we not prophesied in Your name, cast out demons in Your name, and done many wonders in Your name?' And then I will declare to them, 'I never knew you; depart from Me, you who practice lawlessness!'" (Matt. 7:21–23). Signs and wonders are good, but the heart must be right with God.

189. relapsing into demon possession

Jesus and the apostles healed many who were demon-possessed, but were the cures permanent? Not always. Jesus spoke of a demon ("unclean spirit") departing a man, wandering restlessly, then returning with "seven other spirits more wicked than himself." For the poor demon-possessed person, "the last state of that man is worse than the first. So shall it also be with this wicked generation" (Matt. 12:43–45).

190. Mary Magdalene

One of the most appealing women in the Bible, Mary was a prominent character in *Jesus Christ Superstar*. In the Bible she is described as one of Jesus' many devoted women followers, someone from whom He had exorcised seven demons (Luke 8:2). Just what were the "seven demons"? No one knows. According to tradition (but not the Bible itself) she was a reformed prostitute. Perhaps the "seven demons" were physical afflictions of some sort, or perhaps the demons were a force in the immoral life she had led.

191. demon-possessed Jesus?

Jesus was fully aware that His teaching would rile the Jewish authorities and eventually lead to His death. In one of His public statements, He asked the question, "'Why do you seek to kill Me?' The people answered and said, 'You have a demon. Who is seeking to kill You?'" (John 7:19–20). Their response to Him is something like a contemporary question, "What, are You crazy?" or "What's the matter, are You paranoid?"

192. a python spirit?

A python is a type of large snake, but the word pops up in the book of Acts in a strange context. In the town of Philippi, the evangelists Paul and Silas encountered "a certain slave girl possessed with a spirit of divination . . . who brought her masters much prophet by fortune-telling" (Acts 16:16). The Greek text states that the girl had a "python spirit"—the python being associated with oracles of the Greek god Apollo. The original readers of Acts would have understood that the girl was a sort of psychic. Many such people were fakes, but Acts 16 indicates that this girl really did have a spirit working within her. She followed Paul and his companions around, crying out, "These men are the servants of the Most High God, who proclaim to us the way of salvation." (Obviously this spirit was capable of discerning the truth at times.) She became such a nuisance that Paul ordered the spirit, "I command you in the name of Jesus Christ to come out of her." The spirit obeyed, but the girl's owners were not pleased that they had lost a source of income. Paul's exorcism of the python spirit led to the evangelists being flogged and thrown into prison.

193. unsuccessful exorcism

The apostles delivered many people from demons, but not all exorcisms in the Bible were successful. Consider Acts 19, which tells of the seven sons of Sceva, who tried to cast out demons in the name of the Jesus preached by Paul. A demon answered that he knew of Paul and Jesus, but who were these exorcists? Then the demon-possessed man leaped on the would-be exorcists and gave them a sound thrashing (19:11–17). Why did they fail? It is as if the way of exorcism used by Paul was a weapon that had fallen into clumsy hands. Some commentators have suggested that the "seven sons of Sceva" were not sincere believers but merely magicians trying to use Christian exorcism for their own personal gain.

194. deceiving spirits

Paul warned Christians that in the world's last days "some will depart from the faith, giving heed to deceiving spirits and doctrines of demons" (1 Tim. 4:1). He believed that false teaching arose not just from human folly but also from the influence of evil spirits. In our own "tolerant" age, which treats religion as a matter of personal taste, we may hate to "judge" anyone's belief, but Paul had no such fear. He saw these "doctrines of demons" as a real threat to faith in the true God.

195. the man of sin

Paul referred to the "man of sin" (or "man of lawlessness") in 2 Thessalonians 2. He referred to an individual who is the agent of Satan and who will oppose God in every way. Paul did not use the word *Antichrist*, but the same idea is present.

196. no atheist demons

One key theme of the epistle of James is that faith without works is dead. In other words, walk the walk as well as talk the talk. To emphasize this point, James said, "You believe that there is one God. You do well. Even the demons believe—and tremble!" (2:19). Saying that you believe in God is useless in itself, for even those who oppose God (the demons) believe that much.

197. demonic wisdom

According to the epistle of James, the only good wisdom is the wisdom that leads to good conduct, to love of God and one's neighbor. James contrasted this kind of godly wisdom with a selfish, malicious type that is no true wisdom at all: "This wisdom does not descend from above, but is earthly, sensual, demonic" (3:15).

198. Abaddon

This Hebrew word means "destruction" or "ruin." It is found untranslated in Revelation 9:11, where it is the name of the angel of the bottomless pit. But in the Old Testament, it is not the name of an angel but of a place, often translated as "hell" or "destruction." Clearly, with such a name the angel of the bottomless pit is a nasty character. Milton, in his *Paradise Lost*, used the name Abaddon for the bottomless pit itself.

199. Apollyon

Revelation 9:11 speaks of the angel of the bottomless pit. His name in Hebrew is Abaddon (see 198), but in Greek it is Apollyon. In *Pilgrim's Progress*, John Bunyan used the name Apollyon for a fiendish demon, more horrible than any monster in one's worst nightmare.

4

Heaven in the Bible

200. what about Enoch?

The Bible's longest-lived man was the famous Methuselah (969 years—wow!), though Methuselah's granddad, Jared, was close (962 years). But breaking the pattern was Jared's son, and Methuselah's father, Enoch. "So all the days of Enoch were three hundred and sixty-five years. And Enoch walked with God; and he was not, for God took him" (Gen. 5:23–24). This phrase "he was not" has led to much speculation. Did he simply never die? Was he taken into heaven? Since Enoch "walked with God," we must assume he was a good man, so heaven would have been an appropriate reward. Jews and Christians have traditionally believed that he was "translated" into heaven, just as, centuries later, the great prophet Elijah was taken into heaven without experiencing death.

111

Belief in heaven is almost absent from the Old Testament, so the story of Enoch is one of the few Old Testament hints that there is a heaven for the righteous. In the period between the Old and New Testaments, the Jews began to believe more firmly in a heaven, and Enoch became the "prototype" of the righteous man finding his reward there. The Wisdom of Solomon, found in the Apocrypha, speaks of Enoch as the example of a righteous man gaining eternal life.

Several books that did not make it into the Bible are supposed to have been written by Enoch. We can be certain that the Enoch of Genesis did *not* write these, but they are important because they reflect how beliefs about heaven, hell, angels, and demons were developing among the Jews. In the Enoch books, Sheol (which the Jews believed was the place of all the dead) is more like the later concept of hell, a place of punishment for the wicked. Likewise heaven is a real place, the reward for the righteous.

The first Christians, like the Jews, honored Enoch as the first man (or the first that we know of) to enter heaven. The letter to the Hebrews places Enoch in its "faith hall of fame": "By faith Enoch was translated that he should not see death . . . for before his translation he had this testimony, that he pleased God" (11:5 KJV).

201. Sheol

The Old Testament has no doctrine of hell in the sense of a place of eternal punishment. It does refer to *Sheol*, a

Hebrew word found more than sixty times and usually translated as "the grave." The King James Version sometimes translates Sheol as "hell," but this is not accurate. In fact, the Israelites thought of Sheol as the place *everyone* went after death. After the Old Testament period a fuller belief in reward for the righteous and punishment for the wicked developed.

202. no remembrance in the grave

The Old Testament has only the shadiest notion of an afterlife. For the most part the Old Testament authors believed in Sheol (see 201). This is clear in Psalm 6, a prayer of distress in time of trouble: "Return, O LORD, deliver me! Oh, save me for Your mercies' sake! For in death there is no remembrance of You; in the grave who will give You thanks?" (vv. 4–5). In other words: "God, save me in this lifetime, for once I am dead, it is too late for You to save me or for me to thank You."

203. eternal life in the book of Daniel

The Israelites had no clear conception of an afterlife (see 201 [Sheol]). The one exception to this is the book of Daniel, one of the last Old Testament books to be written. "And many of those who sleep in the dust of the earth shall awake, some to everlasting life, some to shame and everlasting contempt. Those who are wise shall shine like the brightness of the firmament, and those who turn many to righteousness like the stars forever and ever." These words from Daniel 12:2–3 are the only explicit mention in the Old Testament of a heaven and a hell.

204. Elijah into heaven

The great prophet Elijah had several confrontations with wicked Queen Jezebel's also wicked husband, King Ahab. He predicted doom for both Jezebel and Ahab, prophecies that came true. Elijah's successor, Elisha, saw his master taken to heaven in a fiery chariot (2 Kings 2).

Elijah became a symbol of Israel's prophets, and since he did not die but was taken to heaven, people began to believe that he (or someone like him) would some day return to turn the people back to God. The prophet Malachi predicted that God would send Elijah before the "day of the Lord" to prepare the people. Jesus said that John the Baptist indeed was (spiritually speaking) Elijah returned (Matt. 11:14).

205. Job and the afterlife

The book of Job is a timeless look at the suffering of a saintly man. Typical of the Old Testament, the book seems to assume that any good that a man possesses is in this life only, not in the hereafter. At one point in the book, Job laments that "man dies and is laid away; indeed, he breathes his last and where is he?" Then he raises the painful question: "If a man dies, shall he live again?" (Job 14:10, 14). Later in the book he makes a stirring affirmation: "I know that my Redeemer lives, and He shall stand at last on the earth; and after my skin is destroyed, this I know, that in my flesh I shall see God" (Job 19:25–26). Raised in a culture that did not have a definite belief in heaven, was Job anticipating one? Perhaps. Certainly his phrase "I know that my Redeemer lives" passed into the Christian vocabulary, being applied to Christ. It is set to beautiful music in Handel's *Messiah*.

206. a whisper of immortality

Psalm 16 is quoted in the New Testament as applying to Jesus' death and resurrection. Consider how the psalm ends: "You will not leave my soul in Sheol, nor will You allow Your Holy One to see corruption. You will show me the path of life" (v. 10–11). While the Old Testament generally regards Sheol as the dreary final resting place of everyone, there are hints—such as this psalm—that God will not leave all righteous people there—that something better is in store. The early Christians applied the psalm to Jesus, whom God did not leave in Sheol (the grave, that is), nor did He allow Him to decay. (See Acts 2:27; 13:35.)

207. the house of the Lord forever

Psalm 23, which begins, "The LORD is my shepherd," is one of the most familiar Bible passages. The "Shepherd

Psalm" is a touching song of praise for God's protection and care. Note the ending: "Surely goodness and mercy shall follow me all the days of my life; and I will dwell in the house of the Lord forever." Is this an affirmation of heaven? Probably not, since the Psalms don't really express any belief in a heaven. The "house of the LORD" is probably the temple in Jerusalem. But Christians have loved this psalm as much as the Jews did, and its final verse has been taken to refer to eternal bliss with the Lord.

208. swords into plowshares

The phrase, used by the prophets Isaiah and Micah, refers to moving from a state of war to a state of God-sent peace. "They shall beat their swords into plowshares, and their spears into pruning hooks; nation shall not lift up sword against nation, neither shall they learn war anymore" (Isa. 2:4; Mic. 4:3). Human nature being what it is, Christians pray for (but do not necessarily expect) this kind of peace to occur in the world. For such a wonderful state of things we have to wait for heaven.

209. "and a little child shall lead them"

Isaiah the prophet envisioned a time and place (clearly heaven, not earth) in which the selfishness and brutality of this present life will be no more: "The wolf also shall dwell with the lamb, the leopard shall lie down with the young goat, the calf and the young lion and the fatling together; and a little child shall lead them . . . The nursing child shall play by the cobra's hole, and the weaned child shall put his hand in the viper's den. They shall not hurt nor destroy in all My holy mountain" (Isa. 11:6–9). Sounds beautiful, doesn't it? These words have inspired numerous artworks, and have been quoted or alluded to countless times (see 709 [Edward Hicks]).

210. "the Lord is there"

Most of Ezekiel's prophecies concern the restoring of the nation of Israel, but many readers interpret the prophecies as applying to the end of time. Consider the end of the book: Ezekiel has been describing a new Israel, but his words seem to apply to a heavenly habitation. Ezekiel's prophecy ends, "and the name of the city from that day shall be: 'THE LORD IS THERE'" (48:35). How close this is to Revelation: "Behold, the tabernacle of God is with men, and He will dwell with them, and they shall be His people. God Himself will be with them" (Rev. 21:3).

WHAT JESUS TAUGHT

211. heaven and hell: a new view

The Old Testament says very little about the afterlife. For the people of Israel, the main goal in life was to live on earth and have a good relationship with God and with other human beings. After death . . . what? Most of the Israelites did not speculate about that. They focused on this life.

But the New Testament makes it clear that God designed human beings for an afterlife—a happy, joyous afterlife with Him (heaven) or an unhappy, despairing afterlife apart from Him (hell). Jesus said a lot about God's love and kindness, but also a lot about what happens to us when we reject that love. By our own choice we can turn to God. Or we can choose to live for ourselves, ignoring God and neglecting our duties to other people.

212. kingdom of God

The "kingdom of God" and the "kingdom of heaven" are mentioned many times in the New Testament, usually by Jesus. Mark 1:15 begins the story of Jesus in this way: "The time is fulfilled, and the kingdom of God is at hand. Repent, and believe in the gospel." But Jesus made it clear that the kingdom is not a place or a political entity. He told Pilate, "My kingdom is not of this world" (John 18:36). "Kingdom of God," as Jesus used it, meant "rule of God"— the condition of God's will prevailing in men's lives. As Jesus put it, "The kingdom of God is within you" (Luke 17:21).

213. "theirs is the kingdom of heaven"

"Blessed are the poor in spirit, for theirs is the kingdom of heaven" (Matt. 5:3). This is the first blessing Jesus pronounced in the series known as the Beatitudes. Some readers puzzle over what "poor in spirit" means. Most likely it is a contrast to pride and ego. People who are proud and self-centered obviously have no place in God's kingdom, while the humble and God-centered will love it.

214. blessed are the persecuted

Through the centuries, one thing has been constant: Good people have been persecuted. Jesus told His followers this would be so. But in the Beatitudes (Matt. 5), Jesus promised that though His people may fail by earthly standards, there is a rich reward in the eternal scheme of things: "Blessed are those who are persecuted for righteousness' sake, for theirs is the kingdom of heaven. Blessed are you when they revile and persecute you, and say all kinds of evil against you falsely for My sake. Rejoice and be exceedingly glad, for great is your reward in heaven, for so they persecuted the prophets who were before you" (v. 10–12).

215. "perfect" Christians

"Therefore you shall be perfect, just as your Father in heaven is perfect" (Matt. 5:48). "Be perfect," you say? Impossible, you say? Perhaps not. The Bible scholars assure us that the word we translate as "perfect" means something more like "whole." Certainly it doesn't mean perfect in looks and such superficial things. In fact, the verse is often quoted out of context. What comes just before it are Jesus' words about loving one's enemies. If we can do that—and the New Testament commands it again and again—then we are well on the way to being perfect, fit for eternal fellowship with God.

216. treasures in heaven

Jesus made it clear that rich people have a hard time entering heaven. He also was aware that many people, rich or poor, are obsessed with money and earthly possessions. "Do not lay up for yourselves treasures on earth . . . but lay up for yourselves treasures in heaven, where neither moth nor rust destroys and where thieves do not break in and steal. For where your treasure is, there your heart will be also" (Matt. 6:19–21). In other words, righteousness endures forever, even beyond the grave, while our earthly possessions do not endure (nor do the people who value possessions above all else).

217. the heavenly banquet

More than once in the New Testament heaven is compared to a grand banquet. Matthew 8 records the meeting of Jesus with a Roman centurion who begs Him to heal his servant. Most Jews despised the Romans (and vice versa), but Jesus was deeply impressed with the man's faith. Jesus said to His followers, "Assuredly, I say to you,

I have not found such great faith, not even in Israel! And I say to you that many will come from east and west, and sit down with Abraham, Isaac, and Jacob in the kingdom of heaven" (vv. 10–11). So, heaven will be full of surprises. Some people who expect to be there will not be, and vice versa.

218. who is the greatest?

God does not see things as human beings do—this is a key theme of the Bible. Jesus made it clear that "greatness" as man normally defined it is not what leads to eternal life. Jesus' disciples asked Him, "Who then is greatest in the kingdom of heaven?" Jesus then called a little child to Him and said, "Unless you are converted and become as little children, you will by no means enter the kingdom of heaven. Therefore whoever humbles himself as this little child is the greatest in the kingdom of heaven" (Matt. 18:1–4). "Become as little children" does not mean "act like spoiled brats." It refers to being simple, humble, not proud or self-assertive.

219. the great promise to Nicodemus

John 3:16 is surely one of the most quoted verses of the whole Bible. People often forget its context: Nicodemus, a Pharisee, visited Jesus by night and began a discussion of eternal life. It resulted in one of the most profound chapters in the Bible. Herewith the famous verse and the one that follows: "God so loved the world that He gave His only begotten Son, that whoever believes in Him should not perish but have everlasting life. For God did not send His Son into the world to condemn the world, but that the world through Him might be saved" (3:16–17).

220. Abraham's bosom

Abraham was spiritually and physically the ancestor of Israel, the "father of the faithful." As Israel began to believe in a blessed afterlife for the faithful, they naturally believed the godly Abraham would be in heaven. The phrase "in Abraham's bosom" (or "at Abraham's side") had the same meaning as "in heaven." Jesus used the phrase in His parable of the rich man and the beggar (Luke 16:22–23). The dead beggar Lazarus ended up "in Abraham's bosom" while the rich man was tormented in a fiery hell.

221. the parable of the lost sheep

Jesus taught the love of God, but He also taught that hell is real. Even so, He made it clear that God desired that everyone would come to Him. Jesus told the parable of a shepherd who had one hundred sheep, one of which had strayed into the mountains. The shepherd left the ninety-nine to seek out the stray. "Even so it is not the will of your Father who is in heaven that one of these little ones should perish" (Matt. 18:10–14).

222. the Sadducees and the resurrection

Among the Jews of Jesus' time, the Sadducees were the aristocratic party, worldly, and in control of the Jewish priesthood. Unlike most Jews, they did not believe there would be a resurrection or a heaven. Knowing that Jesus did, they spun Him a ridiculous riddle about a woman who marries seven brothers in succession, with each one leaving her a widow. In the afterlife, the Sadducees ask, whose wife will she be? Jesus saw this foolish riddle for what it was, but He gave a profound answer: "In the resurrection they neither marry nor are given in marriage, but are like angels of God in heaven" (Matt. 22:30). In other words, the ties that people have to one another on earth will not necessarily apply in heaven. After all, in heaven no one will need to reproduce, and our deepest relationship will be with God.

223. the living bread

The Old Testament records the story of the miraculous manna, bread from heaven that fed the Israelites after their exodus from Egypt. In John's gospel, Jesus spoke of Himself as an even better bread from heaven: "I am the living bread which came down from heaven. If anyone eats of this bread, he will live forever" (6:51). Whereas the manna was only a temporary "fix" for hunger, Jesus Himself is the eternal bread that satisfies man's deepest hunger.

224. losing life to save it

"If anyone desires to come after Me, let him deny himself, and take up his cross daily, and follow Me. For whoever desires to save his life will lose it, but whoever loses his life for My sake will save it" (Luke 9:23–24). These words of Jesus make it clear that Jesus' message was somehow "unnatural"—for people, being selfish by nature, almost always try to preserve their own life in this world. But Jesus had the next world always in sight, and those who would enter His kingdom would do the same.

225. the parable of the good Samaritan

One of the teachers of the Jewish law asked Jesus, "Teacher, what shall I do to inherit eternal life?" Jesus replied by quoting the two basic commandments: Love God, and love your neighbor. When the teacher asked, "And who is my neighbor?" Jesus replied with the famous parable of the good Samaritan. In the story, a man is beaten and robbed and left for dead. The "respectable" religious Jews pass him by, but a Samaritan (the Jews and the Samaritans despised each other) stops and gives the man aid (Luke 10:25–37). Jesus had already stated that to have eternal life we must love our neighbor, and His parable suggests that "love of neighbor" includes showing mercy to those who are our enemies.

226. forsaking all for God

Being a disciple of Jesus wasn't the same as joining a club. His twelve men had to sacrifice much to follow Him. Peter said to Jesus, "See, we have left all and followed You." Jesus replied, "Assuredly, I say to you, there is no one who has left house or parents or brothers or wife or children, for the sake of the kingdom of God, who shall not receive many times more in this present time, and in the age to come everlasting life" (Luke 18:28–30).

227. be prepared

"Be prepared" is the motto of the Boy Scouts, but long before the Scouts, Jesus made it a watchword for those who hope for eternal life. "Take heed to yourselves, lest your hearts be weighed down with carousing, drunkenness, and cares of this life, and that Day come on you unexpectedly . . . Watch therefore, and pray always that you may be counted worthy to escape all these things that will come to pass, and to stand before the Son of Man" (Luke 21:34, 36).

228. *aionios*

This Greek word is used seventy-eight times in the New Testament and is translated "eternal" or "everlasting" or "forever." "Eternal life" is how we translate *zoe aionios*. It means "life of the age to come," but the New Testament makes it clear that this isn't just a postdeath experience, but also something that Christians begin to experience in this life.

229. this is life eternal

John's gospel repeatedly refers to "eternal life," but unlike the book of Revelation, it gives us no visual descriptions of the afterlife (such as golden streets, pearly gates, and harps). But the book of John does tell us some important things about eternal life, notably that it involves being close to God. Consider the words of Jesus' prayer to His Father: "This is eternal life, that they may know You, the only true God, and Jesus Christ whom You have sent" (17:3).

230. the Resurrection and the life

Chapter 11 of John's gospel tells of Jesus' raising His friend Lazarus from the dead. Before He accomplished this grand miracle, He said to Lazarus's sister Martha, "I am the resurrection and the life. He who believes in Me, though he may die, he shall live" (11:25). The fact that He raised Lazarus is proof that his words to Martha were not a vain boast. The raising of Lazarus is a sort of "preview" of what will happen for all who trust in Christ.

231. reward for bearing the cross

Jesus did not preach an easy message: "If anyone desires to come after Me, let him deny himself, and take up his cross, and follow Me" (Matt. 16:24). Obviously this is not a message everyone can accept, but there is a payoff in the eternal sense: "The Son of Man will come in the glory of His Father with His angels, and then He will reward each according to his works" (16:27). For some people, communion with the Father, the Son, and the angels may be worth a life of self-denial.

232. the Transfiguration

Were the saintly men of the Old Testament already in heaven? The Gospels suggest that this was the case. Consider the event known as the Transfiguration: "Jesus took Peter, James, and John his brother, brought them up on a high mountain by themselves; and He was transfigured before them. His face shone like the sun, and His clothes became as white as the light. And behold, Moses and Elijah appeared to them, talking with Him . . . a bright cloud overshadowed them; and suddenly a voice came out of the cloud, saying, 'This is My beloved Son, in whom I am well pleased. Hear Him!'" (Matt. 17:1–3, 5). In Jewish tradition, Moses represented the Law while

Elijah represented the great prophets of Israel. This amazing encounter serves as proof that Moses and Elijah were not just dead-and-buried saints, but also living men.

233. many mansions

"In my Father's house are many mansions: if it were not so, I would have told you. I go to prepare a place for you. And if I go and prepare a place for you, I will come again and receive you unto Myself; that where I am, there you may be also" (John 14:2–3). These words of Jesus' to His disciples are obviously referring to heaven, but just what are these "many mansions"? The Greek word that we translate "mansions" actually means "dwellings" or even "rooms." Jesus' meaning seems to be that there is plenty of room in heaven for those with faith to enter there. It also suggests that there is room for individuality in heaven, as commentator Matthew Henry put it: "Though all shall be swallowed up in God, yet our individuality shall not be lost there," for there are "distinct dwellings, and apartments for each."

234. "My kingdom is not of this world"

Jesus' trial before the Roman governor Pilate is an interesting confrontation: raw earthly power facing the ultimate spiritual power. Jesus' enemies, hoping to be rid of Him, wished to raise Pilate's suspicion by having him think that Jesus was just another Jewish revolutionary, another "king of the Jews." They knew that Pilate would quickly execute such a person. But Jesus truthfully assured Pilate, "My kingdom is not of this world. If My kingdom were of this world, My servants would fight, so that I should not be delivered to the Jews; but now My kingdom is not from here" (John 18:36). Even as he grudgingly consented to Jesus' crucifixion, Pilate knew that this Jesus was no threat to him or to Rome. (See 212 [kingdom of God].)

235. today in paradise

The Gospels tell us that Jesus was crucified between two criminals, one of whom mocked Him as he was dying. But the other one, seeing eternity before him, said to Jesus, "Lord, remember me when You come into Your kingdom." Jesus replied, "Assuredly, I say to you, today you will be with Me in Paradise" (Luke 23:39–43). So the last human being Jesus spoke to before His death was a repentant criminal (see 259 [paradise]). Tradition names the repentant thief Dismas, and Christians point to his last-minute conversion as the classic example of a deathbed repentance.

Later, Christian authors worked to reconcile the "today" of Jesus' words with the New Testament teaching that the final destiny in heaven lies in the future. Some authors explained that paradise refers not to heaven itself but to a happy state where the saved person waits for the Last Judgment, after which he will go to heaven.

236. Jesus or the gardener?

On Easter morning, Jesus' devoted follower Mary Magdalene went to the Lord's tomb and found it empty, with two angels inside. Puzzling over where Jesus' body had been taken, she heard a man ask her, "Woman, why are you weeping? Whom are you seeking?" Mary assumed the man was the gardener, and she asked him where Jesus' body was. "Jesus said to her, 'Mary!' She turned and said to Him, 'Rabboni!' (which is to say, Teacher)" (John 20:11–16). Clearly, Mary did not recognize Jesus' physical appearance at first, though perhaps the familiar tone of His voice did the trick. It bears repeating: Jesus' resurrection body was a new form of His earthly body—similar, yet not the same.

237. the road to Emmaus

One thing is clear from the Gospels: After Jesus was raised from the dead, His body was different from (but still similar to) His earthly body. Luke's gospel records the story of two of His followers making their way from Jerusalem to a village called Emmaus. While walking and talking together, they were joined by a third man, whom they did not immediately recognize as their Master. He joined in their discussion of the recent events (His own crucifixion and resurrection), but they did not recognize Him until He joined them at a supper in Emmaus. "Then their eyes were opened and they knew Him; and He vanished from their sight. And they said to one another, 'Did not our heart burn within us while He talked with us on the road, and while He opened the Scriptures to us?'" (Luke 24:31–32). Clearly, this was the Jesus they had known, and yet different enough that they did not recognize Him during their long walk to Emmaus.

238. "they had seen a spirit"

Gathered in Jerusalem, Jesus' disciples were discussing the story that He had been resurrected. "Now as they said these things, Jesus Himself stood in the midst of them, and said to them, 'Peace to you.' But they were terrified and frightened, and supposed they had seen a spirit. And He said to them, 'Why are you troubled? And why do doubts arise in your hearts? Behold My hands and My feet, that it is I Myself. Handle Me and see, for a spirit does not have flesh and bones as you see I have.'" And when they still doubted, He ate some fish and some honeycomb as a way to show that He was, indeed, raised bodily, not just as a phantom (Luke 24:36–43). Clearly the resurrected body (the "spiritual body," as Paul called it) is similar to, yet different from, the earthly body.

239. doubting Thomas

The phrase "doubting Thomas" has become part of our language. Thomas was one of Jesus' twelve disciples, one who happened to be away from the group when the resurrected Jesus appeared to them. The others told him they had seen the risen Jesus, but Thomas was skeptical: "Unless I see in His hands the print of the nails, and put my finger into the print of the nails, and put my hand into His side, I will not believe." Then, eight days later, all the disciples, including Thomas, were gathered together, and "Jesus came, the doors being shut, and stood in the midst." He was already aware of Thomas's doubts, and He said to him, "Reach your finger here, and look at My hands; and reach your hand here, and put it into My side. Do not be unbelieving, but believing." Thomas was then convinced (John 20:24–28).

The story is interesting for several reasons: For one, Jesus somehow appeared in the room even with "the doors being shut." Was His resurrection body able to pass through closed doors? John's gospel had already reported that the risen Jesus was at first not recognized by Mary Magdalene (John 20:11–16), so clearly He was changed somehow. Yet it is also clear that the wounds from the Crucifixion were still visible, for He showed these to Thomas.

240. the Ascension

All four Gospels report that Jesus rose from the dead and appeared to His disciples afterward. Only Luke reports what became of Him after that: "Now it came to pass, while He blessed them, that He was parted from them and carried up into heaven" (Luke 24:51). In Acts 1:10–11, he adds more detail to this account: "While they looked steadfastly toward heaven as He went up, behold, two men stood by them in white apparel, who also said, 'Men of Galilee, why do you stand gazing up into heaven? This same Jesus, who was taken up from you into heaven, will so come in like manner as you saw Him go into heaven.'" This is known as the Ascension, and it is mentioned several times in the New Testament. The early Christians believed that, just as Jesus had left the earth to ascend to heaven, He would soon return from heaven and take His followers home.

WHAT THE APOSTLES TAUGHT

241. the right hand of God

Several times the Bible refers to Jesus, after His ascension into heaven, as being at "the right hand of God" (Acts 2:33; 5:31; 7:55; Rom. 8:34; Eph. 1:20; Col. 3:1; Heb. 1:3; 12:2; 1 Peter 3:22). Since God does not have a literal right hand, what does this mean? In Bible times, just as today, the "right-hand man" was special. To sit at a host's right hand at a meal was to have the place of honor. "The right hand of God" means that Jesus is next to God Himself in honor.

242. the Sadducee-Pharisee ruckus

Paul the apostle found himself in trouble many times, as the book of Acts tells us. On one occasion, dragged before the Jewish ruling council, he shrewdly managed to turn his trial into a battle. "When Paul perceived that one part were Sadducees and the other Pharisees, he cried out in the council, 'Men and brethren, I am a Pharisee, the son of a Pharisee; concerning the hope and resurrection of the dead I am being judged!' And when he had said this, a dissension arose between the Pharisees and the Sadducees; and the assembly was divided. For the Sadducees say that there is no resurrection—and no angel or spirit; but the Pharisees confess both" (Acts 23:6–8). In the ensuing scuffle, the Roman authorities took Paul away, fearing he would be torn to pieces. Paul saved his skin by proclaiming that he believed in the afterlife.

243. from darkness to light

Called to defend himself before the Jewish official Agrippa, Paul presented in a nutshell the story of his life and conversion to Christianity. He told Agrippa that he received directly from the Lord his commission "to open their eyes and to turn them from darkness to light, and from the power of Satan to God" (Acts 26:18). Paul himself had been blinded by his vision of Jesus, so there was a special meaning when he spoke of turning from darkness to light. Many times in the Bible the works of Satan and the works of God are compared to darkness and light.

244. joint heirs

The Bible teaches that Christ, as the Son of God, is heir to all—that is, He will rule God's dominions and is the chief inheritor of heaven. Romans 8 tells us that just as Christ called God "Father," so can we, for we are spiritually adopted by God. We become His children, "and if children, then heirs—heirs of God and joint heirs with Christ, if indeed we suffer with Him, that we may also be glorified together" (vv. 14–17).

245. whether we live or die

The early Christians had a confident belief in heaven, so much so that heaven seemed as real (or more so) as earth itself. Paul, in Romans, reminds Christians that they are the Lord's, both in this world and the next. "For if we live, we live to the Lord; and if we die, we die to the Lord. Therefore, whether we live or die, we are the Lord's" (14:8).

246. "eye hath not seen"

"Eye hath not seen, nor ear heard, neither have entered into the heart of man, the things which God hath prepared for them that love him" (1 Cor. 2:9 KJV). In these words the apostle Paul spoke of the wonderment of eternity, which could only be described as indescribable.

247. an imperishable crown

The word we translate as "crown" usually referred to the laurel wreath placed on the heads of winners in athletic contests. Paul used the metaphor of such competitions when he spoke of running a race with an imperishable crown as its prize. In other words, the greatest prize of all is not a crown of leaves (which will wither, as will earthly glory), but the Great Prize itself, eternal life (1 Cor. 9:25).

248. hope

The word is used in the usual sense in the Bible, but it also had some deeper meanings. In the Old Testament, Israel's supreme hope was that God would finally deliver the nation from all political oppression and the people would live the holy lives God expected of them. In the New Testament, the key hope is for eternal life. This is not just a wish or dream, but an expectation, based on the promises of Christ. Paul emphasized that even though faith in Christ brought satisfaction in this earthly life, even more important was what lay ahead: "If in this life only we have hope in Christ, we are of all men the most pitiable" (1 Cor. 15:19).

249. as in Adam all die

One extremely dramatic section of Handel's *Messiah* is the musical setting of the words "As in Adam all die, even so in Christ all shall be made alive" (1 Cor. 15:22). The "Adam" section is low and gloomy, but the "Christ" section is loud and triumphant, as if Handel were setting the resurrection to music.

Paul's words have been misinterpreted: "In Christ all shall be made alive" does not refer to the entire human race, but to Christians, which is very clear if you read all of 1 Corinthians 15. The resurrection and heaven are not for all, for all will not put their faith in Christ.

250. the last enemy

"The last enemy that will be destroyed is death" (1 Cor. 15:26). In his famous chapter on the raising of believers to eternal life, Paul claimed that death will finally be destroyed forever. While Christians will still have to face physical death, death has no ultimate power, for just as Christ rose again after His death, so will all believers do so.

251. eat and drink, and nothing more

Paul emphasized again and again that Christ had risen from the dead, and so would all who believed in Him. If this is not so, he said, Christianity is meaningless. "If the dead do not rise, 'Let us eat and drink, for tomorrow we die!'" (1 Cor. 15:32). In other words, if this earthly life is all we have, why bother with morality or faith, since the best thing would be to indulge our hunger for pleasure. But Paul insisted that there is a life after this earthly life.

252. "spiritual body"

This phrase sounds contradictory: How can a body be "spiritual" (nonmaterial), for a body must be material? Paul may have been aware that his phrase sounded non-sensical, but it was the only way of describing something indescribable: the body of Christians after they are resurrected. Jesus, raised from the dead, set the pattern, and the Gospels show that His risen body was like—but also different from—His earthly body. Paul tells us that just as our earthly bodies are like the body of Adam, so our risen bodies will be like the body of the risen Christ. Our earthly body is dust, our new body is heavenly (1 Cor. 15:35–48).

253. in the twinkling of an eye

"Behold, I tell you a mystery: We shall not all sleep, but we shall all be changed—in a moment, in the twinkling of an eye, at the last trumpet. For the trumpet will sound, and the dead will be raised incorruptible, and we shall be changed" (1 Cor. 15:51–52). Stirring words, aren't they? No wonder these words, set to music, are so beautiful a part of Handel's *Messiah*. Paul, in keeping with Jewish tradition, believed that a blast of the trumpet would signal the resurrection of the righteous. (He didn't mention an angel blowing the trumpet, but that is the traditional view.) The fact that Paul spoke of "we" indicates that he himself hoped to be alive on earth when the trumpet sounded.

254. "O death, where is thy sting?"

"O death, where is thy sting? O grave, where is thy victory?" So wrote Paul in 1 Corinthians 15:55 (KJV), near the end of his glorious and triumphant chapter about the resurrection of the dead. He was reemphasizing that Christ had defeated man's final enemy, death, and that death and the grave need no longer fill us with dread. The verse has long been a part of the Anglican (Episcopalian) burial service and has passed into common use in English. It was also set to music in Handel's *Messiah*.

255. from glory to glory

Paul talked about the "unveiling" of the word of God. Paul, raised a devout Jew, came to see, after his conversion to Christianity, that there is a veil (spiritually speaking) over the Jews' hearts, a veil that somehow separates them from God. With Christians there is no veil: "We all, with unveiled face, beholding as in a mirror the glory of the Lord, are being transformed into the same image from glory to glory" (2 Cor. 3:18). In the Old Testament, Moses alone saw God face to face. In the New Testament, thanks to Christ, all believers may draw close to God. Paul implied that we will not have to wait for heaven for this to happen, for it begins now in our own lives.

256. the weight of glory

Life in this world isn't always easy, and Christians bear the burden of sometimes being persecuted for their faith. But Paul had some words of comfort: "Our light affliction, which is but for a moment, is working for us a far more exceeding and eternal weight of glory . . . For the things which are seen are temporary, but the things which are not seen are eternal" (2 Cor. 4:17–18). In the great scheme of things, our afflictions on earth, no matter how burdensome, are "light," while eternity has "weight," for it endures.

257. tent vs. house

Before they had the temple as a house of worship, the Israelites centered their worship on the tabernacle, a large tent. So the tabernacle was only temporary, while the temple was intended to be permanent. Paul had this in mind when he told Christians that our earthly bodies are only "tents," while we have "a building from God, a house not made with hands, eternal in the heavens." While we suffer afflictions in our earthly "tents," we can look forward to a heavenly home that endures (2 Cor. 5:1–8).

258. "out-of-body experiences"

Paul described an anonymous Christian (perhaps himself) who had been caught up in the "third heaven . . . whether in the body or out of the body I do not know" (2 Cor. 12:2–3). While Paul seems to be describing a vision of heaven, some Christians today have claimed to have out-of-body experiences similar to Paul's. Some would call such people "the lunatic fringe," though others might say that if Paul had such an experience, couldn't Christians today?

259. paradise

We use it as a synonym for "heaven," and that is how the Bible uses it. Jesus on the cross promised the repentant thief crucified near Him, "I say to you, today you will be with Me in Paradise" (Luke 23:43). Paul, in 2 Corinthians 12:4, speaks of a man (himself, apparently) who was caught up to paradise and who heard inexpressible things. Paul, it seems, had had a glimpse of heaven. Revelation 2:7 mentions "the tree of life, which is in the midst of the Paradise of God." The word is from the Greek *paradeisos*, meaning "parkland."

260. sowing to the Spirit

The flesh itself isn't evil (since God created it), but Paul often used the phrase "the flesh" to refer to the life of pleasure seeking, living as if this material world is all there is. He contrasted the life of the flesh with the life of the Spirit, and promised that "he who sows to his flesh will of the flesh reap corruption, but he who sows to the Spirit will of the Spirit reap everlasting life" (Gal. 6:8).

261. heavenly places

Paul used "heavenly places" five times in his letter to the Ephesians, and these are the only times it occurs in the Bible. He stated that God has "raised us up together, and made us sit together in the heavenly places in Christ Jesus" (Eph. 2:6). (See also Eph. 1:3; 1:20; 3:10; 6:12.)

262. saint

The Catholic church defines a saint as a person who is in heaven—made official by a church process called "canonization." But the New Testament applies "saint" to all believers, people called to be God's holy ones while living in the sinful world. Some saints are more "saintly" than others, but all believers whose lives are led by the Spirit are destined for eternal life. The New Testament epistles make it clear that saints had to be reminded that they belonged to God and their lives should show it (Eph. 4:1; Col. 1:10; 2 Cor. 8:4).

263. bowing at the name

Christianity, following the words of Jesus Himself, has always made a virtue of humility. Paul's letter to the Philippians is full of praise for Jesus, the divine One who humbled Himself, became fully human, and suffered death on the cross. "Therefore God also has highly exalted Him and given Him the name which is above every name, that at the name of Jesus every knee should bow, of those in heaven, and of those on earth, and of those under the earth" (Phil. 2:9–10). In short, every being in heaven and on earth and under it (commentators disagree on what "under it" means) pays homage to Christ as Lord of all.

264. conversation in heaven

The word *conversation* to us simply means "talk," but when the King James Version of the Bible was being prepared it could have meant "citizenship" or "commonwealth" (as newer translations have it). Paul told the Philippian Christians that "our conversation is in heaven; from whence also we look for the Saviour, the Lord Jesus Christ" (Phil. 3:20 KJV). In other words, we are already citizens of heaven, even before we die.

265. "fight the good fight"

This phrase is a part of our language, even for people who have no idea it comes from the Bible. Paul advised his protégé, the young pastor Timothy, to "fight the good fight of faith, lay hold on eternal life" (1 Tim. 6:12). Earlier in this same letter, Paul told Timothy to "wage the good warfare" (1:18). There is a curious thing about what the Bible tells us about heaven: We receive it as the gracious gift of God, yet we also take an active part in taking hold of it, fighting for it, and working for it.

266. "if we endure"

The life of faith is easy (we have God as our guide and shield) and hard (we face persecution and weariness). The life of faith is not for the lazy, nor for quitters. The New

Testament reminds us frequently that we must "go the distance" if we want eternal life. In Paul's words, "If we endure, we shall also reign with Him. If we deny Him, He also will deny us" (2 Tim. 2:12).

267. preserved for heaven

Poor Paul! In his busy life as an apostle, he made many friends, but also many enemies, and at times he was even abandoned by those he thought were fellow believers. He suffered much, but was always sustained by the belief that something better was ahead: "The Lord will deliver me from every evil work and preserve me for His heavenly kingdom" (2 Tim. 4:18).

268. a high priest in heaven

The Jews had a high priest who once a year entered the Holy of Holies in the temple and made atonement for the people's sin. The letter to the Hebrews tells us that Someone greater has come: We now have a High Priest in heaven, Jesus, One who is making atonement for our sins eternally. We no longer have need of the earthly high priest as the mediator between us and God, for Jesus plays the role of Mediator forever (Heb. 4:14; 8:1; 9:12).

269. the author of salvation

The letter to the Hebrews frequently reminds us of the difference between the eternal and the transitory. It tells us that Jesus is now our eternal High Priest in heaven, so we no longer have need of an earthly priest. According to Hebrews 5:9, Jesus, "having been perfected, He became the author of eternal salvation to all who obey Him." Note the wording: Eternity is for those who obey.

270. the copy and shadow

This material world we live in seems extremely *real* to us, but the letter to the Hebrews turns this view upside down: It is heaven, and the heavenly things, that are really real (since they endure forever, while what we see around us will not endure). According to Hebrews 8:5, the Jewish system of priests and sacrifices is only "the copy and shadow of the heavenly things." The eternal High Priest, Jesus, is the "model" for the transitory priesthood on earth.

271. a better country

The land of God's promise was, in the Old Testament, Canaan. But in the New Testament is the new promise, heaven, which the book of Hebrews calls a "better" country, the "heavenly country" (11:16).

272. cloud of witnesses

Chapter 11 of the letter to the Hebrews is known as the "Faith Hall of Fame," praising the great heroes of faith from the Bible. Chapter 12 identifies these as a *nephos marturon*, a "cloud of witnesses": "Since we are surrounded by so great a cloud of witnesses, let us lay aside every weight, and the sin which so easily ensnares us, and let us run with endurance the race that is set before us" (v. 1). It is as if our predecessors in faith are watching us in a cosmic coliseum as we "run the race" of a faithful life. More than just spectators, they are "witnesses" and role models for us. This is one of a few passages in the Bible that suggest that the saints in heaven are aware of, or even participating in, the lives of the saints still on earth.

273. "a kingdom which cannot be shaken"

The study of history makes us wary of putting our faith in nations or politicians, for an obvious reason: They do not endure. By contrast, the letter to the Hebrews claims that God's people "are receiving a kingdom which cannot be shaken" (12:28). In this world where even the mightiest nations have fallen and crumbled, this promise ought to give us courage.

274. the best inheritance

The New Testament often contrasts eternal treasure with the worthless treasures we pursue on earth. For those who believe in Christ, there is "an inheritance incorruptible and undefiled and that does not fade away, reserved in heaven for you" (1 Peter 1:4).

275. sojourners and pilgrims

While the righteous people of the Old Testament looked to Canaan as their promised land, their inheritance from God, Christians shifted their focus to heaven, something more enduring than Canaan. Several New Testament passages remind Christians that this world is not our true home. In 1 Peter 2:11, believers are called "sojourners and pilgrims"—that is, people just "passing through" on their way to a better place.

276. partakers of the divine nature

In 2 Peter we find a curious promise to Christians: They will become "partakers of the divine nature" (1:4). This idea (if not the exact words) crops up several times in the New Testament. We are reminded that heaven is more than just freedom from pain and earthly burdens, more than just the eternal sensation of pleasure. It is a sharing— partaking—in the nature of God Himself, something that human words and pictures can never fully communicate. We do not "become God," but in some sense we do "taste divinity" in a way that we cannot presently understand.

277. love, the ticket to eternity

Knowledge does not save us; correct beliefs do not save us. Believing is worthless without love. According to 1 John 3:14, "We know that we have passed from death to life, because we love the brethren. He who does not love his brother abides in death." Without goodwill and charity, our "faith" is meaningless and we have no hope of heaven.

278. assurance

This refers to the assurance of being saved, the certainty of heaven after death. The New Testament is clear that believers can have assurance. Paul spoke often of assurance, and so did John in his epistles, where he connected assurance with the working of the Spirit: "By this we know that we abide in Him, and He in us, because He has given us of His Spirit" (1 John 4:13).

279. the keys of Hades and of death

In Revelation 1, John had an encounter with the risen Christ, luminous with unearthly whiteness. Christ assured him that He had died but now lives evermore, and has "the keys of Hades and of Death," meaning that He has the power over them. By dying and rising again, Christ is master over the hostile forces of death (vv. 1:17–18).

280. "blessed are the dead"

Revelation contains many comforting words, including these: "I heard a voice from heaven saying to me, 'Write: "Blessed are the dead who die in the Lord from now on."' 'Yes,' says the Spirit, 'that they may rest from their labors, and their works follow them'" (14:13). In other words, we leave behind the struggles and pains, while the good things (such as capacity for giving, for feeling joy) never end.

281. the marriage supper of the Lamb

Throughout the Old Testament, God's people (the nation of Israel) are portrayed as the bride of God, bound together in a covenant. This changes with the New Testament: The "bride" is no longer Israel but the fellowship of all Christians. The book of Revelation speaks of a future "marriage supper," a feast where the Lamb (Christ) and His bride (Christians) will celebrate their union (19:9). Jesus had referred to Himself as the Bridegroom (Matt. 9:15; Mark 2:19–20; Luke 5:34–35), and spoke of a great banquet in the kingdom of heaven

(Matt. 8:11). Christians at the "marriage supper of the Lamb" are both guests and a marriage partner.

282. pearly gates and streets of gold

People are so accustomed to thinking of heaven as having pearly gates and streets of gold that we wonder, *Is that in the Bible?* It is, indeed, part of a description of the New Jerusalem (heaven) in Revelation 21:21: "The twelve gates were twelve pearls: each individual gate was of one pearl. And the street of the city was pure gold."

283. harps and white robes

The popular image of heaven is of white-robed people playing harps. This image comes from Revelation 15:2, which describes the saints who held harps given to them by God. And the white robes? Note Revelation 7:9: "Behold, a great multitude which no one could number, of all nations, tribes, peoples, and tongues . . . clothed with white robes." White robes symbolize purity, and the harps symbolize the music of peace and harmony.

284. the Tree of Life

It existed in the Garden of Eden, and after Adam and Eve disobeyed God, God was concerned that they might eat its fruit "and live forever" (Gen. 3:22). Whatever the tree was (or represented), God banished the couple from Eden forever. But the Tree of Life is mentioned again much later, in Revelation's description of heaven, the New Jerusalem (22:2). There the faithful are free to eat of its fruit.

5

Hell in the Bible

285. fire and brimstone

People often refer to "fire-and-brimstone preachers" without knowing just what brimstone is. It is an old name for sulfur, an element common in volcanic areas. When Genesis reports that God destroyed the immoral cities of Sodom and Gomorrah with fire and brimstone, it may be referring to a volcano (Gen. 19:24). The book of Revelation says that at the end of the world Satan and all unbelievers will be cast into a lake of fire and brimstone where they will burn eternally (Rev. 14:10; 19:20; 21:8). So "fire and brimstone" is another way of saying "the fires of hell."

286. Gehenna

Why is hell pictured as a place of fire? The Valley of Ben Hinnom outside Jerusalem was noted as a place of slaughter, where children were sacrificed (by burning) to the god Moloch. The good king Josiah put a stop to these horrors, but for years people remembered the site as a place of idol worship and death. In the period between the Old and New Testaments some Jewish writers claimed it was the gateway to hell. The Hebrew name *Ge Hinnom* ("Valley of Hinnom") passed into Greek as *Gehenna*. In the Greek New Testament, Gehenna signified the place of eternal punishment—which we translate "hell." Jesus Himself used the word several times. To Him, and probably to everyone who used the word, it brought to mind the sacrificial fires of the gruesome god Moloch. Also, years later, the site was used as Jerusalem's garbage dump and kept continually burning. Into it was thrown not just garbage but also animal carcasses and the bodies of executed criminals. No wonder Gehenna suggested a horrible place of unending fire.

287. fiery places

The New Testament uses other expressions for hell besides Gehenna: "furnace of fire" (Matt. 13:42); "lake of fire" (Rev. 19:20); and "eternal fire" (Jude 7). The word translated "hell" in 2 Peter 2:4 is *Tartaros*—a word the Greeks used to refer to an underworld place of punishment for the wicked.

288. Tophet

This Hebrew word refers to the same place as Gehenna (see 286), the loathsome site outside Jerusalem where idol worshipers sacrificed their children to pagan gods. The reformer king Josiah made the site unusable for such purposes by heaping it with dead bodies, garbage, and other such matter (2 Kings 23:10). After his time it became the permanent garbage heap of the city, kept continuously burning, no doubt contributing to the place's connection to an ever-burning hell.

The name Tophet may mean "fire place" or "a place to be spit upon," or it may come from the word *toph*, meaning "drum." Drums, cymbals, and other noises had been used during the sacrifice of infants to drown out their screams. As with Gehenna, the name Tophet came to be a synonym for *hell* (Isa. 30:33; Jer. 7:31; 19:6).

289. Isaiah's ending

The book of Isaiah is one of the most read portions of the Old Testament, but it ends on a frightening note. The prophet describes the Lord predicting the end of time, with a dire fate awaiting the wicked: "They [the righteous] shall go forth and look upon the corpses of the men who have transgressed against Me. For their worm does not die, and their fire is not quenched. They shall be an abhorrence to all flesh" (Isa. 66:24). The phrase "their worm does not die, and their fire is not quenched" has been interpreted to refer to the never-ending fire of hell, and if this is so, it is the Old Testament's only reference to an eternal burning hell. Jesus repeated the phrase three times in Mark 9.

290. Christ the Judge

In our "sensitive" and "compassionate" age, the worst thing in the world is to be "judgmental." But earlier times had no problem with the idea of God as Judge, or Christ as Judge. In the Middle Ages, just about every church had a stained-glass window or painting showing Christ at the Last Judgment, receiving the faithful into heaven but casting unrepentant sinners into hell. While the church did teach the compassion and mercy of Christ, they definitely did not neglect His role as Judge of human sin.

291. the narrow gate

Jesus' great Sermon on the Mount includes His words about the way to eternal life: "Enter by the narrow gate; for wide is the gate and broad is the way that leads to destruction, and there are many who go in by it. Because narrow is the gate and difficult is the way which leads to life, and there are few who find it" (Matt. 7:13–14).

292. good fruit, bad fruit

In the Sermon on the Mount, Jesus spoke of producing "good fruit," for our "fruits" tell more about us than our words do. Good trees produce good fruit, and bad trees produce bad fruit. And, "every tree that does not bear good fruit is cut down and thrown into the fire" (Matt. 7:19). A threat of hell? Possibly. Certainly it is a stern reminder to watch what kind of "fruit" we are bearing.

293. the winnowing fork

This was a farm tool used to toss grain into the air so as to let the wind separate the grain from its chaff. The good grain was collected and kept, while the chaff was burned. The Bible uses "the winnowing fork" as an image of judgment: God will separate the righteous from the unrighteous, like grain from chaff (Isa. 41:16; Jer. 15:7). John the Baptist spoke of Jesus as the One who came with His winnowing fork in His hand, to burn the chaff in "unquenchable fire" (Luke 3:15–17).

294. everlasting life, or wrath

The "wrath of God" is an unpopular topic these days, but Jesus had no problem with it. Consider John 3:36: "He who believes in the Son has everlasting life; and he who does not believe the Son shall not see life, but the wrath of

1001 Things ... Angels, Demons, & Afterlife

God abides on him." Could any statement about dividing the human race into saved and unsaved be more direct?

295. "weeping and gnashing of teeth"

Several times in the Gospels, Jesus speaks of the torments of hell. One phrase He used to express the agony of eternal torment is "weeping and gnashing of teeth" (Matt. 8:12; 22:13; 24:51; 25:30; Luke 13:28). Perhaps more than any images of fire and brimstone, the weeping and gnashing of teeth suggests pain, regret, and eternal sorrow of an earthly life wasted.

296. outer darkness

In the New Testament, light is good and dark is bad, obviously. While Jesus used the image of fire to refer to hell, He also spoke of it as "outer darkness," presumably a place where one would be excluded from light eternally (Matt. 8:12; 22:13; 25:30). Artists who have attempted to picture hell have faced the challenge of making it dark and gloomy, yet showing it as a place of fire.

297. blasphemy against the Spirit

This deadly serious sin is mentioned in the gospels of Matthew, Mark, and Luke. In Mark's gospel, Jesus stated,

"I say to you, all sins will be forgiven the sons of men, and whatever blasphemies they may utter; but he who blasphemes against the Holy Spirit never has forgiveness, but is subject to eternal condemnation" (Mark 3:28–29). Millions of sensitive souls have agonized over this, wondering, *Have I committed the unpardonable sin?* Most people have no clear idea of what "blasphemy against the Spirit" is. But the Gospels make it clear: Jesus' words in Mark follow an accusation by His enemies that His power to cast out demons came from Satan. In other words, they attributed His holy power to the power of darkness—calling Jesus a servant of Satan. They called good *evil*, something the Bible heartily condemns (Isa. 5:20).

298. the parable of Lazarus and the rich man

Luke's gospel is notable for its sympathy for the poor, and this is clear in 16:19–31, which tells the story of a wealthy man and a beggar named Lazarus. Both died, and Lazarus was at Abraham's side (meaning heaven) while the rich man was tormented in hell. The rich man begs for relief, but Abraham reminds him that his earthly life was happy, while now the tables are turned and Lazarus was happy. The rich man pleaded for someone to warn his family of the danger of hell, but Abraham replied that they (the parable is obviously referring to the Jews) had the Law and the Prophets to guide them—in fact, Abraham said, they would not change their ways even if someone rose from the dead. The parable is a slap to the Jewish religious establishment, which rejected Jesus, while outsiders (such as Lazarus) have a home in heaven.

299. the parable of the dragnet

A dragnet in the water will probably net some good, edible fish—along with all sorts of other vile creatures. Jesus compared His kingdom to a dragnet, "which, when it was full, they drew to shore; and they sat down and gathered the good into vessels, but threw the bad away. So it will be at the end of the age. The angels will come forth, separate the wicked from among the just, and cast them into the furnace of fire. There will be wailing and gnashing of teeth" (Matt. 13:48–50).

300. "brood of vipers"

John the Baptist, a relative and the forerunner of Jesus, was an outspoken wilderness prophet, preaching repentance of sins and baptizing those who sought a new, more moral life. "But when he saw many of the Pharisees and Sadducees coming to his baptism, he said to them, 'Brood of vipers! Who has warned you to flee from the wrath to come?'" (Matt. 3:7). John, like Jesus, had a low opinion of most Pharisees and Sadducees, for he saw past their "respectable" religion and knew their hearts weren't right. Calling them a "brood of vipers" suggests that John doubted their sincerity in seeking baptism. The "wrath to come" refers, of course, to the judgment of God, in which those whose hearts were not right would receive the ultimate punishment.

301. Pharisees and hell

Will being religious keep a person out of hell? Not necessarily.

Matthew 23 is a long tirade by Jesus against the "respectable" Jewish authorities, the scribes, and the Pharisees. They practiced what we might call an "outward-directed" religion, while neglecting genuine love for mankind and for God. Jesus could be extremely harsh to such people: "Serpents, brood of vipers! How can you escape the condemnation of hell?" (Matt. 23:33). The scribes and the Pharisees no longer exist, of course, but Jesus' words against "outward" religion still apply.

302. hypocrites in hell

Jesus directed some of His harshest words to religious hypocrites, people who appear spiritual on the outside but who are lacking in love for God and man. In Matthew 24:51 He refered to a person being assigned a place in hell "with the hypocrites." In Matthew 23, which contains His long list of "woes" against hypocrites, He warned that they "shut up the kingdom of heaven against men; for you neither go in yourselves, nor do you allow those who are entering to go in" (v. 13). In the same speech He spoke of the irony of hypocrites who "travel land and sea to win one proselyte, and when he is won, you make him twice as much a son of hell as yourselves" (v. 15).

303. hate equals murder

Jesus made it clear that our inside needs to be as clean as our outside—that is, our attitudes and thoughts are important, not just our acts. Thus it is possible to commit adultery in our hearts (Matt. 5:28), and murder as well. In 1 John we read that "whoever hates his brother is a murderer, and you know that no murderer has eternal life abiding in him" (3:15). Does this mean that being peeved at someone will keep us out of heaven? Of course not. It does mean that the attitude of hate is inappropriate in someone who expects eternal life. Love is the attribute of heaven, and hate is the attribute of hell.

304. body and soul in hell

Jesus, teacher of God's love and mercy, clearly believed in hell also. "Fear not them which kill the body, but are not able to kill the soul: but rather fear him which is able to destroy both soul and body in hell" (Matt. 10:28 KJV). Some readers believe that the "him" here refers to Satan, but in fact it is clearly referring to God. Jesus had just told His listeners that they would face persecution in this world, and then He told them that there is a worse fate (after death) than persecution on earth. By way of tempering this stern warning of hell, however, Jesus reminded His people that God values them highly.

305. the gates of hell

"Thou art Peter, and upon this rock I will build my church; and the gates of hell shall not prevail against it"—so said Jesus to His disciple Simon, after Simon exclaimed that Jesus was "the Christ, the Son of the living God" (Matt. 16:16–19 KJV). What are the "gates of hell"? It is clear from the context that Jesus was referring to hell in the sense of the forces of evil, forces that will oppose the church but never triumph over it.

306. "if your right eye causes you to sin . . ."

Many people gladly accept Jesus as a good man and as a religious teacher, but have trouble accepting His belief in hell. But there it is in the Bible, as clear as the light of day. Jesus spoke of God's love and mercy—but also judgment and punishment. He said in Matthew 5:29: "If your right eye causes you to sin, pluck it out and cast it from you; for it is more profitable for you that one of your members perish, than for your whole body to be cast into hell." Jesus wasn't suggesting self-mutilation, of course, but merely emphasizing that sin is serious enough that it can lead to eternal damnation.

307. the eye of a needle

"It is easier for a camel to go through the eye of a needle than for a rich man to enter the kingdom of God" (Mark 10:25). When Jesus said this He knew that His listeners were familiar with the bulk of the camel (as opposed to the smallness of a needle's eye). While Jesus made it clear that it *was* possible (but rare) for the wealthy to enter heaven, the New Testament consistently states that people in love with possessions cannot be in love with God.

308. no other way of salvation

Are Christians the only ones who will make it to heaven? In our tolerance-obsessed age, even Christians are tempted to say, "Well, it's kind of hard to say . . ." The book of Acts in the New Testament does contain this statement from the apostle Peter: "Nor is there salvation in any other, for there is no other name under heaven given among men by which we must be saved" (Acts 4:12). Harsh? Intolerant? Perhaps, but not something that can be easily ignored.

309. Paul and hell

The word *hell* (in the Greek, *Gehenna*) never occurs in any of Paul's writings, but the idea is certainly present. In Romans 2, Paul saw a great divide in the human race:

"Eternal life to those who by patient continuance in doing good seek for glory, honor, and immortality; but to those who are self-seeking and do not obey the truth, but obey unrighteousness—indignation and wrath, tribulation and anguish, on every soul of man who does evil" (vv. 7–9).

310. Paul's list of exclusions

Paul the apostle enjoyed speaking about the joy of salvation and faith in Christ, but he definitely did not believe that everyone would be saved. (As a missionary and evangelist, of course, he did everything in his power to save as many people as possible.) In three places in his letters Paul lists specific types of people who will not enter the kingdom of God. Note 1 Corinthians 6:9–11: "Do you not know that the unrighteous will not inherit the kingdom of God? Do not be deceived. Neither fornicators, nor idolaters, nor adulterers, nor homosexuals, nor sodomites, nor thieves, nor covetous, nor drunkards, nor revilers, nor extortioners will inherit the kingdom of God. And such were some of you." There is a similar list in Galatians 5:19–21: "Now the works of the flesh are evident, which are: adultery, fornication, uncleanness, licentiousness, idolatry, sorcery, hatred, contentions, jealousies, outbursts of wrath, selfish ambitions, dissensions, heresies, envy, murders, drunkenness, revelries, and the like; of which I tell you beforehand, just as I also told you in time past, that those who practice such things will not inherit the kingdom of God." And, finally, Ephesians 5:5: "For this

you know, that no fornicator, unclean person, nor covetous man, who is an idolater, has any inheritance in the
kingdom of Christ and God."

311. turning to the Gentiles

Would people reject an offer of everlasting life? Of course.
In the city of Antioch, the evangelists Paul and Barnabas
preached the gospel to the Jews. But some of the Jews
stirred up trouble, and the two apostles spoke out boldly:
"It was necessary that the word of God should be spoken
to you first; but since you reject it, and judge yourselves
unworthy of everlasting life, behold, we turn to the
Gentiles" (Acts 13:46). The Gentiles (non-Jews) were
glad, and many of them believed the apostles' message of
eternal life.

312. "without excuse"

Is Christ the only way to heaven? Will people who have
never heard the Christian gospel go to hell? In his letter
to the Romans, Paul hints at the answer. In chapter 1,
Paul speaks of how God's invisible qualities are present in
the created world, which everyone can see. In other
words, even without hearing the gospel or knowing the
Bible, people have some sense that there is a God, "so that
they are without excuse" (Rom. 1:18–20).

313. the wages of sin

Paul's letter to the Romans is Christian doctrine "in a nut-shell." One of the most-quoted verses of the New Testament is 6:23: "The wages of sin is death, but the gift of God is eternal life in Christ Jesus our Lord." Paul was reminded the Christians at Rome that if they had been left in their sins, they would suffer eternal death. But through the work of Christ, they became the servants of God, not the slaves of sin.

314. better to marry than to burn

In the King James Version, 1 Corinthians 7:9 reads, "It is better to marry than to burn." Many readers have assumed this means that it is better to marry than to burn in hell. But the verse has nothing to do with hell, but with the flame of passion. Newer translations are more accurate: "It is better to marry than to burn with passion." Paul was telling Christians that celibacy is good, but not everyone can control the sexual impulse for long, so it is better to marry and give the sexual drive a moral outlet.

315. God desires all to be saved

Is there a hell? Yes, according to the Bible. Does God take any pleasure in people going there? No, indeed. Paul told

Timothy that God "desires all men to be saved and to come to the knowledge of the truth" (1 Tim. 2:4). Believing this, Paul urged Timothy to pray for all men.

316. the wrath to come

Judgment and wrath belong together, and the early Christians felt both relief and joy that when Christ returned to earth as Judge, they would not experience His wrath. Paul spoke of Jesus, "who delivers us from the wrath to come" (1 Thess. 1:10).

317. backsliding

The word does not occur in the New Testament, but the concept of a believer slipping back into sin—and even losing his hope of heaven—is there. During Jesus' earthly ministry His own disciples, notably Peter, were guilty of backsliding (Matt. 26:56, 69–75), and the New Testament refers to Christians who forsook their faith (2 Cor. 12:20–21; Rev. 2:4). The early Christians believed that this relapse into the sinful life grieved the Holy Spirit (Eph. 4:30). But the Spirit was also the "seal" of the believer's eternal union with Christ (Eph. 1:13–14), so there is hope for the wayward Christian. On the other hand, see 318 (crucifying Christ again).

318. crucifying Christ again

Can a Christian fall away from the faith and be eternally condemned? A lot of ink has been spilled over this issue of backsliding (see 317), particularly the stern words of Hebrews 6:1-8. This passage speaks of those "who were once enlightened, and have tasted the heavenly gift, and have become partakers of the Holy Spirit." What happens when they "fall away"? According to this passage, they cannot be renewed to repentance, for in so doing they "crucify again for themselves the Son of God." Does this mean that a saved person can become unsaved? Some interpreters would say no, if the person falls away, he was never saved to begin with—he only *appeared* to be a true Christian. Others would take the Hebrews passage at face value and say yes, God gave us free will, and though He will not let go of us, we can let go of Him.

319. a tongue from hell

The brief letter of James contains some wise words about the need to control the tongue. James noted that though it is a small part of the human body, it is powerful and destructive. "And the tongue is a fire, a world of iniquity. The tongue is so set among our members that it defiles the whole body . . . it is set on fire by hell" (3:6). The word we translate as "hell" is the Greek word *Gehenna*, which occurs only in the Gospels and this one verse in James. Does James mean that hell literally sets the tongue on fire? Of course not. No doubt he does mean, though, that hell (the place of destruction, the place of Satan and demons, of opposition to God) figuratively inflames the tongue, which explains why so much harm can be done (both to others and to ourselves) by what we say. In other words, the tongue can be a hellish force in our lives.

320. Sodom and Gomorrah and hell

The letter of Jude refers to the sinful cities of Sodom and Gomorrah, which God destroyed with fire and brimstone (Gen. 19:24). They suffered this fate because they had "given themselves over to sexual immorality and gone after strange flesh" and thus suffered "the vengeance of eternal fire" (Jude 7). Since the fire that fell on the sinful cities wasn't itself eternal, we can only assume that Jude was referring to the fires of hell.

321. the fate of the false

The main point of the brief letter of Jude is, "Beware of false teachers." In no uncertain terms Jude made it clear that these selfish and misguided ones will suffer "the blackness of darkness forever" (v. 13). When Jude referred to the false teachers as "wandering stars," he may have been referring to the book of Enoch, which describes "wandering stars" as fallen angels, destined for eternal punishment.

322. the winepress of hell

One popular image of hell in the Middle Ages and even later was that of an enormous winepress, with agonizing sinners squeezed together like grapes. This image comes from the Bible, which speaks in several places of God's anger against sin being like a winepress, "the great winepress of the wrath of God" (Rev. 14:19; see also Isa. 63:2; Lam. 1:15; Joel 3:13). From these same passages, the writer of the "Battle Hymn of the Republic" drew the image of God "trampling out the vintage where the grapes of wrath are stored."

323. "the books were opened"

The book of Daniel contains a vision of God in majesty: Daniel calls Him the "Ancient of Days," seated on a throne, with "ten thousand times ten thousand" (of angels, we assume) standing before Him. And then "The court was seated, and the books were opened" (7:10). Commentators believe that "the books" refer to the records of men's deeds, the basis of God's judgment, and of their destiny in heaven or hell (see 324 [Book of Life]).

324. the Book of Life

In Revelation, an important part of the Last Judgment of mankind is the Book of Life. All the dead stand before

God, and the record of every person's deeds on earth is the basis of judgment. Those whose names are in the Book of Life are taken into heaven, while those whose names are not there are thrown into the lake of fire (Rev. 20:12–15; 21:27). Several other passages in the Bible refer to, or hint at, this Book of Life (Ps. 69:28; Dan. 12; Luke 10:20; Phil. 4:3).

325. the second death

In Revelation this phrase occurs four times (2:11; 20:6, 14; 21:8) and refers to the "lake of fire," which is the final destiny of those who are not found in God's Book of Life. God's faithful ones are assured that the second death has no claim on them. We can assume that the "first death" refers to the normal physical death of a person. Because the souls of the unrighteous would seem to be destroyed in the lake of fire, some Christians argue that hell is not eternal, but is the annihilation of the soul (see 28 [anni-hilationism]).

6

The End Times and the Bible

326. eschatology

This is the study of "the last things," for the Greek word *eschaton* means "end" or "last." Many parts of the Bible speak of "the day of the Lord" and Jesus' return to earth sometime in the future. Eschatology is the attempt to harmonize these different parts of the Bible and make sense of them all. The book of Revelation is important in eschatology, and so are Paul's statements in 1 Corinthians 15, 1 Thessalonians 4:13–5:11, and 2 Thessalonians 2:1–12. Jesus Himself spoke of the end times, notably in Mark 13, Matthew 24, and elsewhere. From the Old Testament, Daniel chapters 7 through 12 are studied. (See 328 [the Second Coming]; 338 [Rapture]).

327. parousia

This Greek word meant "presence" or "coming." Specifically, it referred to the visitation of a king or a god. Such an occasion would signal to people, "Look your best, get everything shipshape, someone important is going to be looking us over." The New Testament used *parousia* to refer to the second coming of Jesus (see 328), something more dramatic and final than the visit of any earthly king. Jesus has already come to earth once, but His coming in glory, His *parousia,* will be more dramatic and final, for it will decide the ultimate fate of all people: heaven or hell.

328. the Second Coming

The early Christians knew Jesus had ascended to heaven, and they expected that He would return from heaven for His people, as angels told the disciples (Acts 1:11). We refer to this expected event as the second coming of Christ, although the term is never used in the Bible. Jesus foretold His return but made it clear that no one could predict the time (Matt. 24–25; John 14:3). Paul referred to the great hope many times: 1 Corinthians 15:23; Philippians 3:20; Colossians 3:4; 1 Thessalonians 4:15–17; and other passages. The New Testament authors clearly expected the event to occur in their lifetimes. Just as clearly, the event has not yet occurred. No doubt the New Testament authors would repeat their message: Stay alert.

While many people in our day are skeptical about the Second Coming, the early Christians believed in it so strongly that they made it a part of all the major creeds (the Apostles' and Nicene Creeds, for example). (See 338 [Rapture]; 329 [day of the Lord]; 906 [Last Judgment].)

329. day of the Lord

The prophets used this phrase to refer to a future time when God would intervene to punish sin and deliver His righteous ones. "The day of the LORD is great and very terrible; who can endure it?" (Joel 2:11). (Some other examples from the prophets include: Isa. 2:12; 13:9; Jer. 46:10; Ezek. 13:5; Joel 3:14; Amos 5:18; Zeph. 1:7; Zech. 14:1; Mal. 4:5.)

The New Testament adds a new element: the return of Christ, who will judge all men. Paul referred to the "day of the Lord Jesus" (2 Cor. 1:14). According to 2 Peter 3:10, the day will catch people by surprise and will be dramatic: "The day of the Lord will come as a thief in the night" (see 330 [thief in the night]).

330. "a thief in the night"

More than once the New Testament uses this expression to refer to the return of Jesus to earth. The idea is that it will catch people unaware, thus the faithful must be alert at all times. According to Paul, "The day of the Lord will come like a thief in the night" (1 Thess. 5:2 NIV). Peter elaborated on this return: "The day of the Lord will come as a thief in the night, in which the heavens will pass away with a great noise, and the elements will melt with fervent heat" (2 Peter 3:10). A widely used evangelistic film of the 1970s was titled *A Thief in the Night.*

331. the judgment seat of Christ

Christ as Judge of all men is a key theme of the New Testament. When He appears gloriously at His second coming (see 328), He will judge the living and the dead. This is stated succinctly by Paul: "We must all appear before the judgment seat of Christ, that each one may receive the things done in the body, according to what he has done, whether good or bad" (2 Cor. 5:10). This raises an interesting point: While all people have either heaven or hell as their final destination, the Bible has no idea of "total equality," for it is clear that there are degrees of reward in heaven, based on what we have done or not done in our earthly lives.

332. the sheep and the goats

The parable of the sheep and the goats in Matthew's gospel is a picture of the Last Judgment. Jesus depicted Himself as a shepherd separating a flock—sheep on one side, goats on the other (Matt. 25:31–46). He thanked the sheep (the righteous ones) for giving Him food, clothing, and hospitality. The sheep were surprised, asking when they ever did those things for Him. He replied, "Inasmuch as you did it to one of the least of these My brethren, you did it to Me." Then He said to the goats, "Depart from Me, you cursed, into the everlasting fire prepared for the devil and his angels . . . inasmuch as you did not do it to one of the least of these, you did not do it to Me." The goats learned that loving God involves everyday acts of kindness to human beings.

333. the wheat and the tares

In Jesus' parable, a man sowed wheat in his field, but at night his enemy sowed tares (weeds), which grew among the wheat. The man who sowed the wheat chose to let the wheat and tares grow together till harvesttime, when the tares would be rooted up and burned. The wheat represents the children of the kingdom, the enemy is the devil, the tares are the children of the devil, and the harvest is the end of the world. The "reapers" are the angels, who separate good from bad (Matt. 13:24–30, 36–43).

334. the parable of the talents

A "talent" in New Testament times was a unit of money. In Matthew 25:14–30, Jesus told His parable of the talents. A wealthy man distributed his money among his three servants before going on a journey, giving different sums to each one. When he returned, he found that two of the servants had invested wisely. He praised them and promised a greater reward. But one servant had buried his money in the earth, and his master called him wicked and slothful for not making better use of the money. Jesus clearly intended this to be a parable of the Last Judgment, with this meaning: Each of us is given different "talents" (a fortunate choice of words, isn't it?), but each of us must wisely use what we have. If we do not put our talents to use, we are worthless servants and do not deserve an eternal reward.

335. angels and trumpets

Trumpets in olden times were used to signal something important. Jews and (later) Christians naturally believed that at the Last Judgment there would be a global blast of the trumpet, and of course, angels accompanying the appearance of God. An old Christian tradition holds that the angel Gabriel will blow the trumpet signaling the end of time. In fact, the Bible does not name any angelic trumpeter, though Jesus Himself said that angels would sound the trumpet and gather God's people together (Matt. 24:31). Paul spoke of the Rapture with these words: "The Lord Himself will descend from heaven with a shout, with the voice of an archangel, and with the trumpet of God. And the dead in Christ will rise first" (1 Thess. 4:16). (See 338 [the rapture].)

Seven angels with trumpets played an important role

in the book of Revelation. The first six angels sounded their trumpets in succession, announcing six horrible plagues on mankind. Finally, the seventh angel with a trumpet announced that the world belongs to Christ, and (as Handel's *Messiah* has it) "He shall reign forever and ever" (Rev. 8–11).

The only time the Bible actually uses the phrase "last trumpet" is in 1 Corinthians 15:52 (see 253 [twinkling of an eye].)

336. "perilous times will come"

Writing to his protégé Timothy, Paul said, "know this, that in the last days perilous times will come." He went on to describe the selfishness and evil that will characterize the end times (2 Tim. 3:1–9). What Paul described is, of course, the state of humanity in all times—self-centered, opposed to a life lived in love with God and man. But Paul and the other New Testament authors were sure of one thing: Before Christ returned to earth, evil would increase even more—would "pull out all the stops," making earth as hellish as possible until Christ finally broke evil's power forever.

337. the Tribulation

Jesus Himself predicted that in the end times "there will be great tribulation, such as has not been since the beginning of the world until this time, no, nor ever shall be"

(Matt. 24:21). The book of Revelation, the great book of the end times, addresses this issue, depicting (in a symbolic way) the suffering of the saints under the powers of evil. Revelation 7:14 speaks of the period of persecution as "the great tribulation," and so the phrase passed into the Christian vocabulary.

While it is possible—even likely—that the worst persecution still lies ahead, every day since the time of the apostles Christians have been tortured and killed on some part of the globe. It would be an injustice to say to the martyred dead that "the Tribulation has not yet happened." (See 328 [Second Coming]; 339 [the Millennium].)

338. the rapture

The Rapture refers to Christians being united with Christ at His second coming. The idea is based on Paul's words in 1 Thessalonians 4:16–17: "The Lord Himself will descend from heaven with a shout, with the voice of an archangel, and with the trumpet of God. And the dead in Christ will rise first. Then we who are alive and remain shall be caught up together with them in the clouds to meet the Lord in the air."

Jesus' classic statement on the Rapture is probably Matthew 24:39–41: "Two men will be in the field: one will be taken and the other left. Two women will be grinding at the mill: one will be taken and the other left."

The word *Rapture* supposedly comes from the Latin *rapio*, meaning "caught up," but obviously the normal meaning of *rapture*, "a state of intense emotional excitement," is present also. (See 328 [Second Coming].)

339. the millennium

It means "a thousand years," and is important in Christian thought because of Revelation 20, which speaks of a thousand-year reign of Christ and His saints on the earth. During this period Satan will be "bound," and Christ and His saints (including those who have died) will exist in a golden age, after which Satan will be released, but then will be defeated forevermore.

With its visions full of symbols and hidden meanings, Revelation has puzzled people for centuries. People who study it disagree about the timing of the Millennium. There are "premillennialists," "postmillennialists," and "amillennialists." The "pre" people believe Christ will return before the Millennium, while the "posts" believe He will return after it. Amillennialists take the "thousand years" symbolically, referring to the period between Christ's days on earth and His final return. Much ink has been spilled over the matter of the Millennium.

340. the first millennium

As A.D. 1000 approached, many Christians believed that Christ would return to earth for the Last Judgment and take His people home to heaven. After all, they reasoned, there had been a thousand years of Christianity, so after this thousand-year reign of Christ on earth (or so they imagined it), He would return. Thousands of hymns, poems, and sermons spoke of the "Day of the Lord," which would inevitably come with the year 1000. At the beginning of the 900s, a church council officially decreed that the final century of history had begun. A Latin phrase came into wide use: *adventante mundi verspero*—"since the evening of the world is near." But it didn't happen. The lesson we learn: As Christ told us, no one knows the day or the hour when He will return (Matt. 24:36).

341. "those who have fallen asleep"

The earliest Christians took the Second Coming seriously, and most of them eagerly expected to be alive when Christ returned. As years passed without Christ returning, some grew anxious, wondering what would become of Christians who had already died. Paul addressed this pressing question in 1 Thessalonians: "I do not want you to be ignorant, brethren, concerning those who have fallen asleep, lest you sorrow as others who have no hope. For if we believe that Jesus died and rose again, even so God will bring with Him those who sleep in Jesus" (4:13–14). Note his use of "sleep"; Christians who have died are not really "dead," for the dead do not awaken, but those who are only "sleeping" will awaken.

342. Jude and Enoch

The writings known as the book of Enoch were never offi-cially accepted as inspired by most Christians, but Enoch was widely read anyway. The letter of Jude (vv. 14–15) quotes it: "Behold, the Lord comes with ten thousands of His saints, to execute judgment on all, to convict all who are ungodly." While Enoch isn't considered inspired Scripture, Jude is, and this quotation certainly expresses the Bible's view of the Last Judgment.

343. the crown of glory

Jesus is referred to as the Chief Shepherd in 1 Peter 5:4, which states that when He appears (at the Second Coming, that is) Christians "will receive the crown of glory that does not fade away."

344. God's two witnesses

Revelation 11 tells of two witnesses from God who will be persecuted and killed by the Beast near the end of time. Though dead, they will be brought to life again by God, who will take them into heaven. An old Christian tradi-tion says that the two witnesses are Elijah and Enoch, the two Old Testament men who never died but were taken into heaven. Another tradition says they are Elijah and Moses, the two men who appeared with Jesus at His transfiguration (Mark 9:4–5).

345. Gog and Magog

In Ezekiel 38:2–3, Gog is mentioned as being prince in the country of Magog. But in Revelation 20:8, Gog and Magog refer to two nations (or perhaps forces) that will war against the people of God at the end of time.

7

All About Guardian Angels

346. guardian angels

Ideas and beliefs go in and out of fashion, just like clothes. While for years angels were seldom discussed (even among most Christians), they are a hot topic today. Books and magazines discuss guardian angels, including how to get in touch with one's own. What does the Bible say about guardian angels, in the sense of one special angel guarding each person?

Not much. While angels' protection of us is mentioned many times (Ps. 91:11–12, to name one important reference), there are only two passages that hint that each of us has his own particular angel. Matthew 18:10 quotes Jesus as saying, "See that you do not look down on one of these little ones. For I tell you that their angels in heaven always see the face of my Father in heaven" (NIV). Jesus had just spoken to His disciples about being humble like a little child, then told them the seriousness of leading a "little one" astray. While His words in 18:10 suggest that angels watch them, there is nothing said about one angel per little one.

Acts 12 tells of Peter's deliverance from prison by an angel (see 112 [Peter and the angel]). When free, he went to the home of Christian brethren, surprising the servant girl who heard his voice. His friends told the girl, "It must be his angel." Some commentators say that the friends believed that Peter's guardian angel had appeared in Peter's place. Apparently some Jews of that time believed that a person's guardian angel could appear exactly as that person. Acts gives no indication that this is so.

In short, the Bible gives us no definite teaching on whether each person has a particular angel. But there are definitely angels (plural) guarding us (plural). Theologian John Calvin, who insisted on basing his theology on the Bible, affirmed that angels do watch over us, but to speculate whether each of us has one is a waste of time.

347. the little ones' angels

In God's eyes, no one is worthless or insignificant, and His view of a person's worth may be vastly different from our own. Consider Jesus' words in Matthew 18:10: "Take heed that you do not despise one of these little ones, for I say to you that in heaven their angels always see the face of My Father who is in heaven." Bible scholars interpret this passage in various ways, but one meaning seems clear enough: We need to heed what we say or do to anyone, for even if no one else witnesses our deeds, the angels always do.

348. chariots of fire

The great prophet Elijah did not die, according to 2 Kings 2. He was with his successor, the prophet Elisha, when "suddenly a chariot of fire appeared with horses of fire, and separated the two of them; and Elijah went up by a whirlwind into heaven" (v. 11).

Chariots of fire appeared for Elisha in another incident. He was wanted by the king of Aram, who sent a mighty force to capture him. Elisha's servant saw the Aramaean troops coming and was terrified. Elisha said to him, "Those who are with us are more than those who are with them." And then the Lord opened the servant's eyes and he saw that "the mountain was full of horses and chariots of fire all around Elisha." This story is one of the Bible's most vivid reminders that there indeed are angels who protect God's people (2 Kings 6:8–18).

349. the angels of the seven churches

The book of Revelation opens with messages from Christ to seven churches in Asia (the area we now call Turkey). The seven separate messages each begin "To the angel of the church of . . ." The early Christians seemed to believe that each fellowship of Christians had its own angel, a sort of guardian angel for the group (2:1, 8, 12, 18; 3:1, 7, 14).

350. *agathodaimon*

This Greek word means "good demon" or "good spirit." In the pre-Christian period, many Greeks believed that each person had an *agathodaimon* who watched over him throughout his life. When Christianity came along with its belief in God's good angels, it was easy for believers in the *agathodaimon* to believe that God had given each individual a guardian angel.

351. genius

We use this to refer to a brilliant intellect, but the Latin word *genius* had a different meaning for the Romans. It referred to a kind of guardian spirit, one attached not only to people but also to places and things. A *genius* of a person was essentially the same as a guardian angel. As many Romans became Christians, they translated their belief in the *genius* to belief in a guardian angel.

352. Feast of Guardian Angels

The Catholic church officially celebrates October 2 as the Feast of Guardian Angels. It falls only three days after the more important feast day celebrating the angels Michael, Gabriel, and Raphael. The Guardian Angels feast has been celebrated officially since 1518.

353. Opus Sanctorum Angelorum

This is a Catholic group, given official approval by the pope in 1968. Its Latin name means "work of the holy angels," and its members work to encourage belief in guardian angels and to encourage humans to work with the angels for the glory of God and the good of mankind.

354. good angel and bad angel?

Movies and sitcoms get an easy laugh by showing a character listening to his good angel and bad angel, often shown perched on the character's shoulders, pulling the person's conscience in different directions. Does the Bible support this? Hardly. While there may be something to the belief that each person has a guardian angel (a good one, that is), the Bible says nothing about one angel and one devil per person. The belief is very old, though, for in the 1500s theologian John Calvin knew of it. He chalked them up to "vulgar imagination." *The Screwtape Letters* by C. S. Lewis show that Lewis believed each human had a tempter demon assigned to him.

355. do only believers have guardian angels?

Are there guardian angels for Christians only, or for everyone? Most of the early theologians stated that guardians were for Christians only, while a few said no, everyone on earth has an angel. Generally, Christians have believed that everyone has a guardian angel, which does not mean that every person will make it to heaven.

356. can guardians withdraw?

We assume that our guardian angels will always "be there for us." Some of the Christian saints have disagreed. While our guardians naturally work to move us to think and do right, when we sin or err in some way, the angel may withdraw for a time. The great Ambrose, bishop of Milan in the 300s, believed an angel might withdraw in protest at the person's sin, though he would return when the person repented.

357. "the Bible only"

Generally speaking, Catholics have a rich belief in angels, with many Catholic pronouncements dealing with guardian angels, angels in worship, and so on. Protestants do not reject angels, but since the Protestant Reformation of the 1500s was a "back to the basics" (meaning "back to the Bible") movement, much of Catholic belief and practice was swept away. This included the multivolume theology of Thomas Aquinas, who wrote hundreds of pages about angels. The basic Protestant attitude has been that Christians should be content with what God has revealed in the Bible. Anything beyond that is mere speculation and can lead us into trouble. So, for example, while Catholicism officially teaches that we have guardian angels, Protestants have no official position on this, since the Bible is unclear on the subject. One thing is for sure: Where people are allowed to speculate about the nature of angels, almost anything goes. Could the first Protestant leaders see the spate of New Age books on angels and "spirit guides," they would no doubt say, "See, we told you to stick with the Bible."

358. Simeon Stylites (390–459)

Simeon was a "pillar saint," who spent the last thirty-seven years of his life atop a sixty-foot pillar. His disciples—and he had many—used buckets and ropes to send him the small amounts of food and drink he needed. Odd as it seems to us, the pillar-sitters believed they were protesting against worldliness by showing how little of the world they required. Simeon was sought out by many as a spiritual guide. Witnesses claim he was visited often by his guardian angel, who also foretold the time of his death.

359. Gemma Galgani (1878–1903)

In her short life this Italian woman, now a saint of the Catholic church, had visions of Christ and encounters with both demons and angels. She recorded these encounters in her diary and letters, and witnesses also observed her in conversation with angels (hearing only her voice, not the angels'). When she felt assaulted by demons, she would call upon her guardian angel, whom she believed was like a brother to her.

360. angels and purgatory

Christian folklore has it that the guardian angel guides the righteous person's soul to heaven. What if the person must go to purgatory before entering heaven? Catholics believe that the guardian angel will visit and comfort the soul in purgatory, then, when that soul has "done its time," guide the soul on to heaven.

361. national guardians

Many Christians believe that individuals have guardian angels, but some believe that nations and even cities might have their own guardians. Acts 16:9 reports Paul's vision of "a man" of Macedonia, begging Paul to come and preach the gospel to the Macedonians. Some believe "the man" was the guardian angel of the Macedonians, eager for his people to become Christians.

362. ethnarch

The word means "ruler of a nation." Jewish folklore holds that each nation has its own guardian angel, its ethnarch. Taken as a whole, the ethnarchs play the role of trying to keep the whole world as peaceful as possible. Since the Jews were often persecuted by other nations, they developed the idea that other nations' ethnarchs were not necessarily good angels. Obviously the evil empires of history have very bad (or at least ineffective) ethnarchs.

363. *psychopomps*

Most religions have a tradition that the soul of a person who has just died needs some sort of escort to the afterlife. Religion scholars call this a *psychopomp*. Officially, neither Christian nor Jews have any firm belief in this, but Jewish and Christian folklore both have a place for angel guides who conduct the soul to heaven or hell. In most versions of the story the psychopomp is, appropriately, the person's guardian angel.

364. Aquinas on guardians

Thomas Aquinas (see 606), the Catholic church's premier theologian, taught that each person has a guardian angel who comes at the moment of birth. When a person enters heaven, he will be given angelic companions, not the same as his guardian angel on earth. In hell, on the other hand, each condemned soul will have its own demon to punish it eternally.

365. Bernard of Clairvaux (1090–1153)

Bernard was one of the best-loved saints of the Catholic church, a fierce preacher against heresy, but also the author of hymns and devotional guides. Bernard believed strongly in guardian angels and believed Christians should show great respect and gratitude toward the holy angels. But, in keeping with the official Catholic position, he insisted that angels should be honored—but not actually worshiped.

366. Pius XI (1857–1939)

Long before he became pope, he had believed strongly in guardian angels and prayed to his own throughout the day. In his meetings with the many officials of the church, Pius would pray to his angel, asking him to work in concert with the angels of those persons he was meeting. He claimed that his own angel's interactions with those of other men aided him in the delicate negotiations required in being pope.

367. Pius XII (1876–1958)

Faced with a changing world that was more and more skeptical of traditional teaching, Pope Pius issued an encyclical in 1950, insisting that angels are real beings and that their existence should not be questioned by any Catholic. He liked to remind people that guardian angels are an "equalizer" in the church, for even the poorest, humblest believer has one.

368. John XXIII (1881–1963)

The beloved man known as "Good Pope John" insisted that Catholics faithfully remember their guardian angels as well as those of any persons they dealt with. In his radio addresses to Catholics, he urged them to recall their own guardians and to teach their children that they were ever under the protection of guardian angels.

369. caretaking angels

The early theologian Clement of Alexandria believed that infants born prematurely were under the guardianship of "caretaking angels." Later, Christian writers claimed that the caretakers also watched over illegitimate children.

370. angels in the Talmud

The Talmud, the ancient collection of commentary on the Jewish Law, has a high regard for guardian angels. Each Jew is attended throughout life by eleven thousand of them. All creation benefits from guardians—in fact, every blade of grass has an angel, telling it, "Grow."

371. New Age angels and mantras

In that vast web of beliefs called the New Age movement there is serious interest in angels. Many New Agers accept the idea that each individual has a guardian angel. Some New Age gurus claim that the person can chant a mantra (a particular word or phrase, repeated to help the person "focus") to help summon the guardian angel. Once this angel is given a name, that name can be used as the mantra for summoning it.

372. spirit guides

In the New Age movement, getting in touch with one's spirit guide is a popular pastime. While some New Agers call them angels, some do not (since many New Agers avoid words that even faintly suggest Christianity). Spirit guides perform many of the same functions as guardian angels, except that (the New Age movement being so concerned with tolerance) the spirit guides seldom scold a person for sin. Spirit guides, quite unlike the angels of the Bible, can aid in contacting the dead.

373. Eularia and the UN

The belief in guardian angels for individuals and even for nations is very old. The New Age movement has had a field day with guardian angels, and one book even claims the United Nations has its own guardian. The book *Ask Your Angels*, published in 1992, claims that the UN's guardian angel is named Eularia. (People who are suspicious of the UN may well wonder if Eularia is a demon instead of an angel.)

8

Encounters, Real and Imaginary

374. the third heaven

Paul referred to a man (possibly himself) who was caught up in the third heaven (2 Cor. 12:2). This reflects a belief of the Jews that there were three distinct heavens: (1) the air, the atmosphere around the earth; (2) the firmament, the location of the stars and the planets; and (3) the heaven of heavens, the habitation of God, home of the Redeemer and the redeemed. In saying "third heaven," Paul was speaking not of floating in the atmosphere, but of seeing a vision of God's abode itself. (See 258 [out-of-body experiences].)

375. Moody's vision

Evangelist D. L. Moody (see 619), when he was believed to be near death, said that "earth recedes, heaven opens before me." He told the people near him, "This is no dream. It is beautiful, it is like a trance. If this is death, it is sweet." Moody revived and related that he had been permitted to see into the unseen world, into the gates of heaven, where he saw faces of loved ones long since gone. He told his friends that when they read in the papers that D. L. Moody was dead, "Don't you believe a word of it. At that moment I shall be more alive than I am now."

376. Corrie ten Boom

The saintly Dutch woman who authored *The Hiding Place, Tramp for the Lord*, and other Christian classics relates her own experience with angelic protection. In her book *A Prisoner—And Yet*, she relates how she and her sister were taken to a Nazi prison camp during World War II. Corrie, hiding a Bible under her dress, prayed to God for angelic protection as guards searched all the women. Somehow—and Corrie attributes it to the angels—her Bible went unnoticed, even while the guards searched other women and found them hiding objects.

377. Kenneth Hagin (b. 1917)

As author Hagin reports in *I Went to Hell*, he literally did: In 1933, during one ten-minute period his vital signs failed three times, each time leading him to see hell. This resulted in his conversion and, a year later, he was healed of his ailments. The former invalid was baptized in the Spirit in 1937 and began a Pentecostal ministry.

378. Anthony the hermit (c. 300)

Anthony, a wealthy Egyptian, experienced a spiritual crisis when he heard a sermon on Jesus' command to the rich young ruler: "If you want to be perfect, go, sell what you have and give to the poor" (Matt. 19:21). Anthony gave away his land and donated his money to the poor. He lived a simple life, sleeping on the ground and existing on one meal a day (bread and water). He lived for years in an abandoned fort, yet he attracted followers, who believed Christianity had become worldly and materialistic (it had).

The Egyptian wasteland was wild and desolate, but not empty, for Anthony claimed it was filled with demons. He spoke about how he did battle with all sorts of ghastly devils. Thanks to the popularity of the *Life of Anthony*, and thanks to the challenge of painting a saint afflicted by monstrous demons, Anthony has been the subject of thousands upon thousands of paintings.

The life of self-denial and resisting demons must have been healthy. Anthony lived to be 105.

379. Monica (332–387)

She was the mother of Augustine (see 596), one of the great Christian authors. Long before Augustine's conversion to

Christianity, Monica prayed for him and rejoiced when he converted. Mother and son had many discussions about the afterlife. While talking one day, both shared a vision of heaven. Shortly afterward, Monica died. Both believed that heaven was far greater than any earthly pleasures.

380. Girolamo Savonarola (1452–1498)

In the Renaissance era, the city of Florence in Italy was notoriously worldly. For a brief time there was a religious and moral revival due to the preaching of Savonarola, a monk who preached boldly against corruption and immorality. He spoke with authority, and people responded. He believed angels spoke to him, warning him that the events in the book of Revelation were to come to pass. The Antichrist, Satan's agent, ruled Italy, but Christ would soon return. Sadly, Savonarola made the mistake of defying a corrupt and immoral pope, who had him executed.

Savonarola's preaching on divine judgment was a powerful influence on the painters Michelangelo (see 698) and Botticelli (see 699).

381. Teresa of Avila (1515–1582)

She is one of the Catholic church's most popular saints, well known for her devotional writings and her visions of divine ecstasy. Teresa, like many saintly persons, was painfully aware of her own failings. Her prayer life was so rich that she feared the devil was trying to deceive her and make her proud. But she had more pleasant dealings with angels, notably a vision known as the "transverberation." She claimed that an angel appeared to her in bodily form—unusual, because earlier she had never seen an angel, but had only been aware of them spiritually. This angel, who did not identify himself, was fiery and beautiful. He held a golden spear with a fiery point, and he plunged it deeply into her heart several times. The pain was, oddly, sweet. Teresa claimed that after experiencing this sweetness, the soul would never want anything but God.

The sculptor Bernini produced a famous statue of the saint being pierced by the angel's spear. It is called *The Ecstasy of St. Teresa*, and is probably the world's most famous sculpture of an angel.

382. near-death experiences

This term has entered the American vocabulary, and many people, religious or not, are fascinated by NDEs. One interesting and often overlooked aspect of these experiences: They aren't all pleasant. People who don't believe in hell have taken some pleasure in hearing all the glowing reports of people who died and had visions of heaven. But researchers in this area have come to realize that some people who clinically "died" had negative, "hellish" near-death experiences. Of course, the reports on NDEs do not prove there is a hell any more than they prove there is a heaven. It is a fact, however, that many people who have had NDEs are spiritually and morally transformed after the experience. This is true not only of the ones who believe they had glimpses of heaven but also of those who had a preview of hell.

383. Raymond Moody

In the past, few people ever talked about their near-death experiences, but this is no longer true. One who helped bring about the change was Moody, a physician who published the groundbreaking book *Life After Life* in 1975, following it up with several other successful books. Moody and other researchers described common traits of the experiences (NDEs), such as the tunnel ending in bright light, meeting dead relatives and friends, having one's life reviewed, meeting angel-like figures of brilliant light, and so on. (See 382 [near-death experiences].)

384. Maurice S. Rawlings

Rawlings, a heart specialist, had no real religious beliefs, but he changed when a man he was trying to revive screamed out, "Don't stop! Don't let me go back to hell!" This led Rawlings to suspect that not all near-death experiences (see 382) are pleasant glimpses of heaven. In his book *Beyond Death's Door,* he told of thousands of people who had experienced hell while clinically dead. Some, he found, were horrified to see deceased friends and relatives among the dead in hell.

QUESTIONABLE, BUT INTERESTING

385. *St. Brendan's Voyage*

The real Brendan was an Irish saint living in the sixth century, but like Ireland's more famous saint (Patrick), he was the center of many legends. *St. Brendan's Voyage*, written probably in the tenth century, tells of the voyage of a boatload of Irish monks. Far out in the Atlantic they encounter various demons and people being punished for their sins. They even encounter the condemned Judas, who spends six days a week in hell but has certain Sundays off. The story is told with a certain lightheartedness, and it is obvious that people of the Middle Ages did not always take hell with total seriousness.

386. *The Vision of Alberic*

Alberic, an Italian monk, had an illness that left him in a coma for nine days. While comatose, he had a vision of hell, and when he finally awakened, he dictated this vision, which circulated in book form around 1125. Guided by St. Peter and two angels, Alberic described such hellish sights as a frozen valley, a cauldron of pitch, a sulfurous oven, a lake of blood, a lake of fire, and a gigantic chained dragon holding on to such notorious sinners as Judas and Herod.

387. *Thespesius*

The Greek author Plutarch was best known for his *Parallel Lives*, widely read biographies of famous Greeks and Romans. Plutarch also wrote *Thespesius*, a strange vision of a journey through both hell and heaven. Thespesius finds his own father in hell because he had lived such a wicked life. Thespesius is determined to warn people to live virtuous lives so they will find bliss, not torment, after death. Though Plutarch was not a Christian, the journey is very close to what Christians believed about the afterlife.

388. Osanna of Mantua (1449–1505)

Beginning at age five, Osanna had visions of heaven. In some of these visions she met great men of the Bible and was even embraced by God Himself. She learned that in heaven the feast days of saints are celebrated just as they are in the Catholic church.

389. Basil of Caesarea (329–379)

Basil was a bishop and an influential theologian. One story about him relates that he had a vision of the Virgin

Mary reigning as queen of heaven, surrounded by legions of angels and seated on a stunning jeweled throne. Basil was one of many Christian authors who helped the cult of devotion to Mary gain strength.

390. New Harmony, Indiana

In the early 1800s, a German Christian group settled New Harmony, Indiana, along the Wabash River. Called the Rappites (after their leader, "Father" Rapp), they expected Christ to return to earth soon. New Harmony prospered as a kind of Christian commune, but members grew restless when Christ did not appear as expected. Father Rapp claimed he had encountered the angel Gabriel in the forest, and to this day there is an "angel footprint" (or something resembling it) on a stone slab in New Harmony.

391. Tundal the monk

Many Christians have written books or painted pictures depicting the horrors of hell. Perhaps none are more vivid than the writings of the Irish monk Tundal, who lived in the twelfth century. Tundal claimed to have had visions of hell. In the center of it, he said, Satan was fastened with red-hot chains to a burning gridiron, but his hands were free to grab hold of sinners. With his teeth he crushed them, afterward swallowing them down his burning throat. Other demons plunged hell's inhabitants into fire then into icy water, or beat them into flatness on an anvil. To make the fiery place even more repugnant, sulfur added its foul stench to the air. Hell was full of fire, yet the fire gave no light, so the people suffered in thick darkness. While the Catholic church authorities sometimes questioned such visions (realizing that it was easy to go overboard and emphasize hell more than heaven), descriptions such as Tundal's had a great effect on people's imaginations. *The Vision of Tundal*, written around 1149, was translated into at least fifteen languages, and some of the copies were lavishly (and frighteningly) illustrated.

392. Joan of Arc (1412–1431)

The French peasant girl who rallied her country's armies and booted the English out of France had angelic inspiration. She claimed to be inspired by heavenly voices, one of which was the archangel Michael. She fell into the hands of the English, but not before making a name for herself as one of the most amazing women who ever lived.

In 1431 the Catholic church had Joan burned at the stake for witchcraft. In 1920 the Catholic church declared her a saint.

393. Emanuel Swedenborg (1688–1772)

The son of a Swedish bishop, Swedenborg gained world fame as a brilliant scientist, an amazing man whose mind encompassed mathematics, physics, anatomy, astronomy—and also religion. While in his fifties he published his best-known book, *Heaven and Hell*. In it, writing in cool, unemotional (downright "scientific") language, he described heaven and hell, angels and demons, as if he were a travel writer describing lands he had toured. Heaven and hell, he said, have their own geography just as this visible earth does. There are several hells, with the most unpleasant ones being reserved for the worst sinners. Like writers of the Middle Ages, Swedenborg went into great detail about the physical horrors of hell. He firmly believed that God had called him to view and report on the unseen worlds of heaven and hell.

Swedenborg lived and died believing himself a good Christian. He never intended to start his own religious movement, but after his death some followers started the New Jerusalem Church, which is small but active throughout the world, including the United States.

394. Moroni and the Mormons

Joseph Smith was the founder of the religious group known as the Latter-day Saints (more commonly known as the Mormons). According to Smith, on the night of September 21, 1823, an angel appeared to him in the form of a man. He hovered above the floor, dressed in white robes, and had a face like lightning. This angel was Moroni, who had once been a human. He identified his father as Mormon, a descendant of the biblical Jacob. Moroni told Smith about the Book of Mormon, written on gold plates and buried in a hillside in upstate New York. Then Moroni ascended back into heaven, but the same night appeared to deliver the message again, then a third time. Smith went and found the place as Moroni had told him.

A statue of the angel Moroni is atop the Mormon Temple in Salt Lake City, Utah. He is depicted in flowing robes and is blowing a trumpet, but has no wings. He has become a worldwide symbol of the Mormon faith.

395. Charles Lindbergh (1902–1974)

"Lucky Lindy" was the first man to fly solo across the Atlantic. This historic 1927 event, taking just under thirty-four hours to fly from New York to Paris, may have been aided by angels—or so Lindbergh thought. In *The Spirit of St. Louis*, published in 1953, and his *Autobiography of Values*, published after his death, Lindy revealed that while flying over the Atlantic he slipped into a peculiar state of consciousness, not quite awake, not quite asleep. While in this state he believed that the plane's fuselage was filled with humanlike ghostly presences, weightless and transparent. They spoke in friendly voices, giving him advice on his flight. Lindbergh almost believed he had died and was having conversations with the dead. His landing in Paris convinced him that he was alive and that these "emissaries from a spirit world," as he called them, had aided him. His experience did not turn him into a Christian by any means, but did convince him that there was a "new and free existence" beyond death.

396. Hildegard (1098–1179)

She was an abbess (head of a convent) and widely loved for her warmth and her spiritual insight. In her book *Scivias* she wrote of some of her visions, in which she saw both heaven and hell. She saw the saints dressed in lovely silks, with the splendor of each robe in keeping with the good deeds carried out on earth. Nine concentric circles of angels were arranged around the throne of God. The best part of heaven, she said, is being able to behold the face of God.

397. Gertrude (1256–1302)

An orphan girl raised by nuns in Germany, Gertrude had heavenly visions from an early age, even more so as she saw her death approaching. In one vision she saw the souls of her deceased sisters escorted to heaven by angels. In another vision, Jesus told her that when she entered heaven there would be a grand celebration, as there is over any newcomer to paradise.

398. Clovis and Clothilda

Clovis, king of the Franks, was married to a Christian named Clothilda. With the Frankish army facing the cruel Huns, Clovis asked Clothilda to pray to her God for victory. The Franks won, and Clovis became a Christian. He was baptized (babtized nude—see 639), and during the ceremony (so the story has it) angels descended from heaven bearing three lilies and gave them to Clothilda as a sign of heaven's favor. Thus the lily flower—the *fleur-de-lis*—became the emblem of France for many centuries. Clothilda died in 545 and was later declared a saint.

399. Crispin (c. 300)

Crispin and his brother Crispinian were martyred during one of the Roman persecutions of Christians. Both men had been simple shoemakers, and both made dazzlingly beautiful shoes from (so legend has it) material delivered to them by angels. The shoes fetched amazing prices, and the two brothers used the profits to aid the poor.

400. Christina (1150–1224)

Does sin have an odor? Christina thought so. She died (or so it appeared) after an epileptic seizure, but during her funeral she leaped from her coffin, clung to a beam of the church, and refused to come down. She finally did, saying she had died and had a vision of hell, purgatory, and heaven, and that she could no longer abide the smell of human sin. She became a nun and was noted for her kindness, but throughout her life she claimed that humans "smelled of sin."

401. Catherine of Siena (1347–1380)

An Italian girl who was extremely devout from her youth, Catherine heard heavenly voices that gave her comfort and advice. At age eighteen she had a vision of Jesus asking her to become His betrothed. In a kind of mystic marriage ceremony, Mary, saints, and heroes of the Old Testament were witnesses. Catherine was so highly regarded that she even advised popes on spiritual matters. She is one of the Catholic church's most popular saints.

402. Chad (c. 630–668)

Most people who believe in heaven hope they will be reunited with loved ones there. Chad, an English monk who died of the plague, had a vision just before his death of his beloved brother. Surrounded by angels singing beautiful hymns, the brother told Chad that he looked forward to their reunion in paradise.

403. Afra (d. 304)

Afra died during the persecution of Christians by Roman emperor Diocletian. Burned at the stake, she saw a vision of heaven in which the clouds parted and the saints opened their arms to welcome her home.

404. Godkin's vision

Most near-death experiences are heavenly, but surely not all. One of the most publicized was back in the 1940s, when George Godkin, a Canadian farmer with long-term health problems, died (at least temporarily). He reported being in total blackness, so thick it felt like pressure upon him. He recovered, reported the vision, and stood by his story.

405. Drithelm (d. c. 700)

The positive side of fearing hell is that it sometimes turns bad people into good. Drithelm was a selfish nobleman in England. While ill, he became comatose for several hours, during which he had visions of hell and purgatory. When he regained consciousness, Drithelm was a changed man, so much so that the Catholic church later made him a saint.

406. Bridget of Sweden (1302–1373)

Here was a common phenomenon of the Middle Ages: an extremely saintly person who experienced visions of hell. Bridget was widely loved for her warmth and devoutness, but she had blood-chilling visions of hell and reported them in the hope that all would seek to avoid eternal torment. She also had pleasurable visions of heaven. She was and is the patron saint of Swedish Catholics.

407. the Venerable Bede (673–735)

Bede was an Anglo-Saxon theologian and historian, best known for his *Church History of the English People*, written in Old English. Much of the work is straight, objective history, but Bede also reported the visions of hell experienced by certain people. Being so widely read, Bede helped popularize "hell visions," an important part of literature in the Middle Ages.

408. Benvenuto Cellini (1500–1571)

One of the great artists of the Renaissance, Cellini wrote a highly readable autobiography, which is a tribute to his amazing ego. Even so, it includes a curious story of how, when he had been put in prison for stealing the pope's jewels (yes, really!), he attempted to commit suicide, but was stopped by an "invisible power." Later this power appeared in his dreams as a "most lovely youth," who scolded him for trying to destroy himself, God's handi-work. The angel urged him to trust in God's goodness and guidance. Cellini said these words enabled him to endure imprisonment. The angel's influence didn't stick, apparently: Cellini later dabbled in calling up demons.

409. the angels of Mons

During World War I, an amazing incident occurred during the Battle of Mons in Belgium (August 26–27, 1914). British and French troops were surrounded by Germans and expected to be massacred. Many were killed, but fewer than expected, and the British and French—and even some of the Germans they captured—claimed to have seen angelic troops coming down to battle the Germans, along with Saint George (England's patron saint) on a white charger. Most reports said the angels were in the form of archers, who rallied the British and French and led them to assault the Germans in the trenches. Some reports said that the angels were seen by the Germans' horses, who stam-peded in terror. This story made its way into various English and French newspapers, and was a great morale booster. Fact or fiction? Hard to say.

410. Michael on Gargano

In the year 490 the archangel Michael supposedly appeared to a Catholic bishop on Mount Gargano near Naples, Italy. A shrine was built in the cave where he appeared, and it drew many Christian pilgrims. In 663 a victory of Christian forces over the Muslims was attributed to Michael, and the popularity of the shrine increased. The Sanctuary of St. Michael is still a much-visited shrine. The nearby town is Monte Sant'Angelo, "Mount of the Holy Angel."

411. the angel at Fatima

At Fatima, Portugal, in 1917 occurred an appearance of the Virgin Mary that the Roman Catholic Church has approved as real and valid. Three children were paid visits by an angel who called itself the Angel of Portugal. Then Mary appeared to the children several times, instructing them to pray the rosary daily. A devotional cult to the Angel of Portugal sprang up, with Catholic approval.

412. Lawrence (d. 258)

Lawrence was a deacon in the Church of Rome and was martyred during the persecutions under Emperor Valerian. Lawrence was first tortured by being stretched on a rack, during which a booming angelic voice told him that harsher pains awaited him. Not only did he hear the voice, but so did people nearby, including one of the Roman soldiers, who later converted to Christianity. The angel's prophecy proved true: Lawrence died while being slowly roasted on a gridiron.

413. Vincent Ferrer (1350–1419)

He was a noted preacher in his native Spain and throughout Europe, where he converted many Jews and Muslims to Christianity. Vincent was widely renowned for his saintly life. As he lay on his deathbed, witnesses claimed that beautiful white birds gathered about him, vanishing suddenly at just the moment he died. Some believed these were angels, who took his soul away to heaven.

9

Folklore, Legends, & Other Tales

SATAN HIMSELF

414. the devil and idleness

For generations parents have warned their children, "An idle mind is the devil's workshop." (In a variant form, "An idle mind is the devil's playground.") It does seem to be true of most people that if they have nothing to do, they naturally incline to mischief or downright wickedness.

415. speak of the devil

"Speak of the devil and he will appear"—so says an old proverb. It is for this reason that many people in times past would never refer to this sinister being as "devil" or "Satan" for fear he might put in an appearance. Hence he was given many nicknames, some noted in the following entries.

416. Old Nick

This nickname for the devil has been around since at least the 1600s. Some say it derives from the old German word *nickel*, meaning "goblin." Others say it derives from the cynical Italian author Niccolò Machiavelli, who wrote *The Prince*, a manual for politicians on the use of slyness and hypocrisy to rule well. Machiavelli's portrait certainly strikes many people as devilish enough.

417. Old Scratch

This old American folk name for the devil is derived from the Scandinavian word *skratta*, meaning "goblin." In the famous story "The Devil and Daniel Webster," Stephen Vincent Benét gives the name Mr. Scratch to the devil.

418. the Deuce

"The deuce you say" was a mild substitute for "the devil you say." How did Satan become "the Deuce"? Long ago *deuce* could mean "rotten luck," so naturally it became a name for the source of the worst luck, Satan himself.

419. Scotch Satan

The Scots speak English, but with enough of their own colorful Celtic words thrown in to make it sound almost foreign. Scotland's most famous poet, Robert Burns, addressed Satan in one of his poems: "O thou, whatever title suit thee, / Auld Hornie, Satan, Nick, or Clootie." *Auld* means "old," and of course, since Satan is depicted with horns, we understand "Auld Hornie," but Clootie is still a puzzle. For an explanation of Nick, see 416.

420. Merlin, son of the devil

In the King Arthur tales, Merlin is a wise wizard who uses his power for good. But, the legends say, he started his existence in an unpromising way: His father was the devil, who impregnated an unwilling woman. When the baby was born, the mother rushed it to a priest for baptism. Because of this, Satan had no power over his son, yet Merlin inherited from Satan supernatural powers, which he used for good.

SOME DEMONIC FOLKLORE

421. incubus and succubus

In a prescientific age, a baby born with some horrible birth defect was regarded with terror. Some said that a deformed child could only result from a human's having had relations with a demon. So in the Middle Ages many people believed that a male demon (called an incubus) could impregnate a woman, leading (obviously) to a monstrous-looking child, while a female demon (a succubus) could have relations with a sleeping man, flying off to some other place to bear her hideous offspring. Since demons can deceive, an incubus or succubus might take on the form of the person's spouse, then suddenly, after the act was consummated, reveal what had happened. Prior to the twelfth century, the church took the official position that demons could not have sexual relations with humans, but popular pressure led to a change in the church's attitude.

422. devil's tattoo

Not a tattoo on the skin, but the beating of drums. Drumming with one's fingers, as in boredom or irritation, is called the "devil's tattoo." The idea is that a person bored or irritated is calling the devil forth, since such a person is ripe for falling into sin. (See 414 [the devil and idleness].)

423. the devil's books

This name was applied to playing cards in times past. Many Christians frown on gambling, and some have taken the strict view that since cards are associated with gambling, it's best not to play cards at all, not even for fun. Centuries ago, people called playing cards "the king's books" (since there are four kings in a deck of cards), but some ministers stated that, no, these were the devil's books.

424. Abezi-Thibod

This cumbersome name is given to a demon in Jewish folklore. The Bible tells us that Pharaoh's heart was hardened against Moses, and that two of Pharaoh's magicians opposed Moses. It was Abezi-Thibod who acted as the evil spirit behind Pharaoh and his magicians. The Jews saw him as a sort of "patron demon" over Egypt. His name means "father lacking counsel."

425. Lilith

Not in the Bible, but a prominent character in Jewish folklore, Lilith was a demon and the wife of Adam before God created Eve. Through her union with Adam she gave birth to all the demons on the earth. She deserted Adam and haunted the night and all wild places and ruins. She was a sort of vampire character, considered especially threatening to children. The Hebrew word *lilith* is used in the Old Testament to refer to some wild "night creature," sometimes translated "screech owl" or even "night hag" (Isa. 34:14), but some translations actually use the word *Lilith*.

426. Astaroth

The Old Testament many times mentions Ashtoreth (or Asherah, or Astaroth), a fertility goddess of the Canaanites. Like Baal (see 175), she received worship from the Israelites, even though the Hebrew law prohibited worshiping pagan deities. Hebrew folklore turned this pagan goddess into a demon, a former angel who had joined in Satan's rebellion and been expelled from heaven. In the folktales, she (sometimes "he") is shown riding a dragon and holding a viper in her hand.

427. Samael

This malicious fallen angel is mentioned frequently in folklore, but never in the Bible. Some legends say he, not Satan, was the serpent who tempted Eve, and that he, not Adam, was the father of Cain (thus explaining why Cain was evil).

428. the scapegoat

We use "scapegoat" to refer to someone who takes the blame and/or punishment for another's wrong. In the Bible the scapegoat was a literal goat. In the annual Day of Atonement ritual described in Leviticus 16, a goat was brought to Israel's high priest, who placed his hands on the goat, symbolically placing on it the sins of Israel. The goat was then driven into the wilderness. The ritual symbolized taking Israel's sin away and expelling it. The Israelites associated the wild places and deserts with demons. In Hebrew, the scapegoat is *azazel*, a word that can also refer to a desolate region or a demon. (See 429 [Azazel]).

429. Azazel

This is the Hebrew word that we translate "scapegoat" (see 428). Because of the ritual of sending the goat into the wilderness, symbolically carrying Israel's sins, the name Azazel came to refer to a demon inhabiting desolate places. In Jewish tradition, Azazel is usually thought of as hideously ugly, with seven serpent heads and twelve bat-like wings. Folktales say that he taught men aggression by teaching them to make swords, and he taught women vanity by giving them cosmetics.

430. Rimmon of Russia

The Bible mentions Rimmon, who was a kind of storm god of the Syrians (2 Kings 5:18). In folklore of the occult he is, for some reason, the devil's ambassador to Russia.

431. Solomon the exorcist

Solomon, son of David and king over Israel, was so wealthy and wise that thousands of legends grew up about him. Many legends say he was skilled at driving out demons, while others say he ruled over demons almost like a king. The legends indicate that people were dangerously near turning the "wise" king into a sort of sorcerer or magician.

432. Solomon's demons

One story about Solomon tells that he asked God for aid in building the temple in Jerusalem, whereupon God sent him a ring, delivered by the angel Raphael. The ring turned out to be magical, with an engraving that gave him the power to subdue all demons. Using the ring, Solomon was able to enlist demons as "slave labor" in building the temple.

433. Asmodeus

This vile demon plays a prominent role in the book of Tobit in the Apocrypha (see 498 [book of Tobit]). His name means "creature of judgment," and the book of Tobit refers to him as a "raging fiend." Besides appearing in the Apocrypha, Asmodeus figures in many Jewish legends. One legend says it was he who made Noah drunk. Another legend says that in hell Asmodeus is in charge of all of the gambling houses. Wherever he appears, he plays the role of the devil of impurity. Many authors throughout the ages have used his name for demons in works of fiction and the theater.

434. Walpurgis Night

In German tradition, a witches' sabbath is held the night before May 1 on the Brocken, the highest peak in Germany's Harz Mountains. There the witches consort with Satan and his demons. If you saw the movie *Fantasia*, you might recall the film's last musical sequence. In it, the music of "A Night on Bald Mountain" is played as grisly demons and witches frolic lustfully in their Walpurgis celebrations, though they scatter as a church bell tolls at sunrise.

435. northern devil

Isaiah's description of the proud Lucifer quotes him as saying, "I will exalt my throne above the stars of God; I will also sit on the mount of the congregation on the farthest sides of the north" (14:13). Jewish and Christian traditions identify Lucifer (see 131) with Satan, who had been an angel but who rebelled against God and was expelled from heaven. Isaiah 14:13 hints that Satan's new place of habitation is "the north," and so the Bible and folklore speak of the north as a place of demons and evil.

436. Behemoth and Leviathan

The book of Job mentions two awesome creatures named Behemoth and Leviathan (40:15–41:34), which the Lord points to as part of the creation He controls. Some commentators try to identify these beasts with real animals (Behemoth being a hippopotamus, and Leviathan being a crocodile). But it's quite possible that the author of Job was referring to mythical monsters. Jewish folklore interpreted Job in this way, saying that Behemoth and Leviathan were dragonlike monsters who would wreak havoc on humanity until finally, at the end of time when the Messiah came, they would be destroyed. Sound familiar? The book of Revelation, with its fiery dragon who is finally destroyed at the end of time, comes to mind.

437. can animals sense evil?

Folk wisdom has it that animals can see, or sense, things humans can't—such as the demonic. One episode of the old *Twilight Zone* TV series dealt with animal sensitivity. In "The Hunt," a man dies while out hunting with his coon dog. He comes to a gate, which a man tells him is the gate to heaven. The hunter can enter, but must leave his beloved dog outside. He refuses, and farther down the road meets an angel, who tells him the gate guardian was, in fact, a demon. The demon would not let the dog enter for fear it would warn the hunter that the place was evil.

438. Adrammelech

In 2 Kings 17:31, we read of him as a god to whom children were sacrificed. The Jews were horrified by child sacrifice, so in Jewish folklore Adrammelech (which means "king of fire") is a horrible demon, usually in the shape of some animal. He appears as a character in *Paradise Lost* and in Klopstock's *The Messiah*.

439. Rahab

In the book of Joshua, Rahab is the name of a harlot who aids the Israelites. But elsewhere in the Bible, it is the name of a demon or monster (Ps. 89:10; Isa. 51:9). Jewish folklore held that this monster Rahab was a demon, a fallen angel. He ruled over the seas, and Jews who dabbled in the occult believed he could be called upon for assistance at sea. One legend held that God destroyed Rahab, who had attempted to chase the Israelites across the Red Sea while it was parted.

440. angelic progeny

Tradition says that good angels do not (and cannot) reproduce, but fallen angels (that is, demons) are able to do so. In the many Jewish and Christian folktales of angels, there is no mention of any good angel being the child of another, yet there are demons who are the offspring of other demons.

441. flooded, but not exterminated

Jewish folklore attributes many evils to the "sons of God" who mated with human women (Gen. 6:1–4). But since all their offspring were destroyed in Noah's flood, they are no longer a problem, right? Wrong. The legends tell us that though these wicked ones were exterminated, their spirits still haunt the earth, working mischief everywhere.

442. weapons from below

Many Jews believed the "sons of God" who mated with mortal women (Gen. 6:1–4) were fallen angels. Among the horrible things they gave to man were weapons of destruction. An interesting legend, but considering that Cain killed Abel (Gen. 4) without aid from fallen angels, we can assume that man needs no aid in finding ways to kill.

443. Azrael

In both Jewish and Muslim folklore, Azrael was the angel of death. As such he was an inevitable fixture in human life, but not a welcome one. Some legends describe him as hideously ugly, the very embodiment of evil. Some people might recall that the wicked Gargamel of *The Smurfs* had an equally wicked cat named Azrael.

444. demons and feminine allure

In ancient Christian folklore, it was the fallen angels (demons, that is) who invented all the accoutrements that men find attractive on women—necklaces, bracelets, rouge, makeup for the eyes.

445. fairies

Fairies, called by many names, are a feature of folk religion throughout the world, a reminder that people have long believed that supernatural creatures (good and bad) are all around us. Our modern age has largely sanitized fairies, making them cute and benevolent, but folktales contain both bad and good ones. (Think of Maleficent, the evil fairy in Walt Disney's *Sleeping Beauty*.) As Christianity spread through Europe, the missionaries were more inclined to view the fairies as demons than as angels, for even "good" fairies could turn on humans and do them harm.

ANGEL TALES

446. angel food

As Moses led the Israelites out of Egypt to their promised land, God miraculously provided the food called manna. No one has ever been quite sure what manna really was, and the Bible tells us nothing more than that it was good to eat and was provided by God. An old Jewish legend says that manna was a kind of heavenly bread, ground by angels on a mill in the third heaven.

447. name that angel

Folklore and superstition are overflowing with names for various angels and demons. But in fact, in the angelic encounters of saints in the Bible and in Christian history, the angels hardly ever name themselves. The Bible names only two, Michael and Gabriel (or three, counting Raphael in the Apocrypha). To discourage the vogue for naming angels, the Catholic church officially prohibits using proper names for angels, except for Michael, Gabriel, and Raphael.

448. Michael in legend

The archangel Michael is mentioned a few times in the Bible, but Jews and Christians have both had a field day creating stories about this most famous of the angels. One ancient story is that it was Michael who appeared to Moses in the burning bush. Another story is that Michael was the angel who stayed Abraham's hand when he was about to sacrifice Isaac. One tale is that he was the mighty angel who destroyed the 185,000 men of Sennacherib's Assyrian army. Still another tale is that after Adam and Eve were expelled from Eden, Michael taught Adam how to farm.

449. angel author

In Jewish tradition, the archangel Michael wrote (or inspired) Psalm 85. The psalm is a lament for the sufferings of Israel. Since Michael was regarded as Israel's guardian angel, it is appropriate that he is the psalm's "author."

450. Melchizedek

This mysterious character appears in Genesis as a priest-king. The patriarch Abraham is blessed by him and pays tithes to him (Gen. 14:18–20). Melchizedek is not mentioned again until Psalm 110:4, which speaks of "a priest forever according to the order of Melchizedek." The letter to the Hebrews quotes this psalm and applies it to Christ, who is a priest forever in heaven. The letter notes that Melchizedek was "without father, without mother, without genealogy, having neither beginning of days nor end of life, but made like the Son of God, remains a priest continually" (Heb. 7:3). These verses have puzzled commentators. Might it mean that the Melchizedek of Genesis was actually Christ, putting in an appearance before His birth in Bethlehem? Some have thought so, and the book of Hebrews suggests this. But there are also Jewish and Christian legends to the effect that Melchizedek was an angel. In the third century there was a sect named the Melchizedans, who claimed that Melchizedek was a power greater than Christ. Some occult groups even said that Melchizedek was the Holy Spirit.

451. Raphael

This angel appeared not in the Old or New Testament but in the Apocrypha. There, in the book of Tobit, he was companion and guide to Tobit's son Tobias. At the end of a journey, the angel revealed himself as "one of the seven angels" that attend the throne of God. The weavers of Jewish and Christian legends had much to say about Raphael. He was, some said, the guide of souls to Sheol (the afterlife, neither heaven nor hell). One Jewish legend is that he was one of the three angels who visited Abraham (Gen. 18), the other two being Michael and Gabriel. On a more trivial note, legend credits Raphael with healing Abraham after his circumcision. Since his name means "God has healed," Raphael is associated with all manner of healings in the Bible. Some Christians identified him with the angel who stirred the waters of the healing pool at Bethesda (John 5).

452. Uriel

Though not mentioned in the Bible or the Apocrypha (only Michael, Gabriel, and Raphael are), Uriel is one of the most-mentioned angels in Jewish lore. His name means "fire of God," and one legend says he was the cherubim who guarded the gate of Eden with a flaming sword (Gen. 3:24). He has also been identified as the messenger who warned Noah of the Flood, as the angel who wrestled with Jacob, and as the death angel who destroyed 185,000 men in the Assyrian army. In John Milton's *Paradise Lost*, Uriel is described as "the sharpest-sighted spirit of all in Heaven."

453. Gadreel

Mentioned in the widely read book of Enoch, Gadreel was the demon who took the form of a serpent and tempted Eve. Naturally, artists have always depicted him in the form of a snake with a humanlike head.

454. Sandalphon

Jewish tradition (but not the Bible itself) has it that the prophet Elijah, who was taken into heaven in a fiery chariot, now resides in heaven as the angel Sandalphon. Elijah-Sandalphon is one of the most popular angels in Jewish legend. One legend is that he takes the prayers of the Jews and weaves them into crowns, which float through the air to wherever God is. American poet Henry Wadsworth Longfellow wrote a poem about this angel whom he called "Sandalphon, the angel of glory, the angel of prayer."

455. Moses an angel?

The Bible tells us that Moses died, but no one knows his burial place (Deut. 34:6). This led to speculation in folklore that he was taken to heaven without dying, as occurred with Enoch and Elijah. The three are now angels.

456. ministering angels

Did you know that angels can serve as waiters and cooks? In Jewish folklore, three "ministering angels" roasted meat and cooled wine for Adam and Eve while they were in Eden.

457. multilingual angels?

Jewish legend has it that the angels know only one language—Hebrew, what else? Thus, legend says, it is useless for anyone to try to contact them in another language. But another Jewish legend is that the angel Gabriel understands all human languages.

458. Hebrew or tongues?

Jewish folklore has it that the language of the angels is Hebrew. But another folk tradition is that the language of the angels is what we call "speaking in tongues" or "glossolalia." Following this belief, a human who speaks in tongues is not just uttering gibberish but is speaking "angelspeak." If this sounds far-fetched, note the apostle Paul's words in 1 Corinthians 13:1: "Though I speak with the tongues of men and of angels . . ." Clearly Paul believed that the "tongues of angels" meant something besides normal human speech, and it is clear elsewhere in 1 Corinthians that he himself had spoken in tongues.

459. Gabriel and the fetus

Because it was Gabriel who announced the birth of Jesus to the Virgin Mary, one old bit of Christian folklore holds that Gabriel guides the soul from paradise to the womb, and instructs it in the womb for the nine months prior to birth.

460. Jacob and Esau, in utero

Genesis tells us of the twin sons of Isaac and Rebekah, the very different twins named Jacob and Esau. Genesis also tells us of the strained relations of the two brothers, and how Jacob was the ancestor of the Israelites while Esau was the ancestor of the Edomites, two nations frequently at war. An old Jewish legend holds that the two fought while still in the womb. According to the tale, the unborn Esau was on the verge of killing his twin, but the archangel Michael intervened on Jacob's behalf, thus ensuring that he would be born and be father of the Israelites.

461. the angels protesting Moses

The Bible relates that Moses received the Hebrew law
(the Torah) from God on Mount Sinai. Later legends
embellished this story: While on the mountain, Moses was
taken into heaven, where he would receive the Torah.
When some of the angels saw Moses in heaven, they
protested to God that a mortal was among them. God
told them Moses had come to receive the Torah, and the
angels again protested that the Torah had existed from all
eternity, and how could such a treasure be given to a mere
man. God replied that the purpose of the Torah was
always to be a gift to man.

462. Abdiel

Not mentioned in the Bible, the angel Abdiel was a
prominent figure in Jewish folklore. The legends say that
he was a mighty warrior fighting against Satan's rebel
angels, and he appears in Milton's *Paradise Lost* in that
role. Abdiel's name means "servant of God."

463. sin begets angel

In the collection of old Jewish traditions called *Pirke
Aboth*, one of the rabbis stated that "every sin begets an
accusing angel." Put another way, every time we sin,
someone reports the sin to God.

464. Adam

Adam an angel? Not in the Bible, certainly, but since the book of Genesis said so little about the first man, imagination said a lot. In several of the pseudepigrapha (written between the Old and New Testaments), Adam is called "the bright angel," and it is said that when first created, he reached from "earth to the firmament." One story says that he was taken to heaven by the archangel in a fiery chariot. An old Christian story states that he was fetched from hell by Jesus and transported to heaven. Another story has it that when Adam died he was buried by four angels, including Michael and Gabriel.

465. Achtariel

The Old Testament mentions "the angel of the Lord" several times, and it sometimes appears as if this is referring to the Lord Himself. While the "angel of the Lord" has no name in the Bible, Jewish tradition names him Achtariel. Some tales claim that this is actually the "real name" (in heaven, that is) of the Lord Himself.

466. Saint Cecilia

She is the patron saint of music, though her story is probably a mixture of fact and legend. It is fairly well established that she was a Christian martyr, but there are other tales that say she sang hymns so beautifully that angels came down to hear her. Some say she invented the organ, and in art she often is shown seated at the organ, either on earth or in heaven, with angels hovering nearby.

467. the zodiac angels

There are Christians who read the Bible *and* their daily horoscope. If they thought hard about it, they would surely realize that astrology has no place in Christian life. Even so, the two have existed side by side for centuries, and some people with vivid imaginations have connected all twelve signs of the zodiac with angels. None are connected with the angels of the Bible, except Aquarius, whose "patron angel" is Gabriel. Some have said that the twelve angels mentioned in Revelation 21:12 correspond to the twelve zodiac angels.

468. planetary angels

The Bible says nothing whatsoever about angels being connected with planets, though there are hints that some people have connected heavenly bodies with the angels (Job 38:4–7; Rev. 12:4). Folklore, crossing over from Christianity to the occult, assigned angels to the heavenly bodies: Michael to the sun, Gabriel to the moon, Raphael to Mercury, and various nonbiblical angels to the other planets. Supposedly, these angels guide these bodies in their movements through the heavens.

469. sweet perfume

If an angel had a smell, it would no doubt be pleasant. In ages past, people who claimed to have angelic encounters said the angel left a sweet perfume in the air. Demons, on the other hand, are reputed to carry the vilest smells with them, though when they deceive humans they can also mimic the odors of heaven.

470. angel wreaths

Do angels sleep on pillows? Consider this bit of folklore from America's Ozark mountains: Sometimes inside a feather pillow one finds feathers formed into a ring, or wreath. This is an "angel wreath," and when found in the pillow of someone who has just died, that means the person was a saint and has gone to heaven. Obviously, the wreath is similar to a halo and to the crown promised to the saints (1 Cor. 9:25). While this bit of Americana strikes some people as silly, it is still taken seriously by many, a sign that their loved one is in heaven. (An alternative superstition: The angel wreath was put there by Satan and should be destroyed.)

471. angels of destruction

The Bible never uses this phrase, but it is clear that angels sometimes have destructive work to do, as in the destruction of the Assyrian army of Sennacherib (2 Kings 19:35). Tradition says that Gabriel was sent to destroy wicked Sodom and Gomorrah. One tradition says that the angels of destruction are angels from hell, with their power used by God on occasion to punish the wicked.

472. Anpiel

Jewish tradition names him as the angel who protects birds. He resides in the sixth heaven and is sometimes said to be the angel who took Enoch to heaven. (For an explanation of the concept of "multiple" heavens, see 932 [seventh heaven]).

473. Ariel

The name means "lion of God" and appears in the Bible, though not as the name of an angel. Isaiah 29 uses it as an alternative name for Jerusalem. In Jewish folklore, Ariel is the name of an angel, sometimes called one of the seven ruling angels. In the world of occult and magic, Ariel is described as being lion-headed, based on the meaning of his name in Hebrew. Shakespeare used the name Ariel for the servant sprite in The Tempest.

474. angel of death

There is no "angel of death" mentioned in the Bible, but he certainly appears in Christian folklore. Harsh as the name sounds, he was not a "killer angel," but rather the guide of the Christian's soul to eternity. (See 363 [psychopomp].) Old pictures sometimes show an angel taking hold of a dying person's soul (which might have the form of a naked babe emerging from the person's mouth or ear). Some said the archangel Michael was the angel of death, while others said Gabriel played this role. Many Jewish folktales are centered on the angel of death visiting a person to tell him his time has come to die.

475. Ezra

The book of Ezra is one of the least-read parts of the Old Testament, but the scribe Ezra became an important figure in Jewish tradition. According to legend, after death, he was taken to heaven, where he was made an angel and the scribe of God.

476. angelolatry

This refers to the worship of angels. Given the renewed interest in angels in recent years, it may be that some people are dangerously close to worshiping angels, or at least guilty of giving them more attention than they deserve. (Christian tradition is that we worship God alone, not human beings, not things, not even angels.) Colossians 2:18 quotes Paul warning the Christians at Colossae not to worship angels, so apparently this was a temptation in the earliest days of Christianity.

477. the oaks of Mamre

The book of Genesis tells of three angels visiting Abraham under the oaks of Mamre (Gen. 18). Because of this divine encounter, people were visiting the site centuries later, worshiping the tree and idols of the three angels. (This is ironic, considering how the Bible is so strongly opposed to idolatry.) The site was still being used for idolatrous worship as late as the year 300, even after the "sacred oak" was long gone. Jews and Christians went there because of the associations with Abraham, and even Greeks who had no connection with the God of the Bible honored the site because of its association with angels.

478. Isaac the angel

When Isaac was born, his parents Abraham and Sarah were both old—*very* old. (Abraham was one hundred, and Sarah was well past child-bearing age.) So amazing was this birth (which God had promised them), that Jewish legend held that Isaac was more than amazing—he was an angel from heaven. Isaac was the "angel of light," existing before the world began.

479. Jael and Zarall

The Old Testament describes the ark of the covenant, with the two cherubim figures stretching their wings toward each other. The Bible doesn't name the cherubim (why would it?), but someone's fertile imagination added the names Jael and Zarall to Jewish folklore.

480. Mastema and Moses

Exodus 4:24–26 records a story that gives Bible readers fits: Moses, the man God has chosen to lead the Israelites out of Egypt is almost killed—by God. "The LORD met him and sought to kill him"—though this never happens. No one has yet explained that odd interlude. But someone's imagination bestowed a name on the "killer": He was an angel named Mastema. Jewish legend holds that Mastema was a kind of divine executioner, doing harm at God's command.

HEAVENLY FOLKLORE

481. Saint Peter at the gate of heaven

In popular images of heaven, Saint Peter is usually the gatekeeper, the "official" whom one must pass to enter eternal bliss. Is this based on the Bible? Sort of. After Peter exclaimed that Jesus was "the Christ, the Son of the living God," Jesus replied, "You are Peter, and on this rock I will build My church . . . And I will give you the keys of the kingdom of heaven, and whatever you bind on earth will be bound in heaven, and whatever you loose on earth will be loosed in heaven" (Matt. 16:13–19). The phrase "keys of the kingdom" has been associated with Peter ever since, and so as the "keeper of the keys," he can lock or unlock the gate to heaven.

482. Elijah and the angel of death

The Bible tells us that the great prophet Elijah was taken into heaven, never having to die. A Jewish folktale relates that this offended the angel of death, who complained to God that everyone must die, even Elijah. God told the angel that Elijah was special, and could even replace the angel. Elijah and the angel of death confronted each other, but God held back Elijah from destroying the angel.

483. Elijah, Enoch, or both?

The Old Testament speaks of two men, Enoch (Gen. 5:24) and Elijah (2 Kings 2:11), who were taken into heaven without having to die. One old Jewish tale says that Elijah *was* Enoch, who had come back to earth for a time to serve as prophet, then returned to heaven. The Bible certainly never says so, but note something interesting: It never mentions Elijah's parents, which is something the Old Testament authors believed important. It is as if he is "parentless," and the amazing events of Elijah's life hint that he is almost supernatural in origin.

484. Gan Eden

Jews in the postbiblical age became much more detailed in their view of heaven (which is hardly hinted at in the Old Testament). Heaven, called *Gan Eden*, is a garden with every physical and spiritual delight. Wine flows freely, and the air is sweet with perfumes. There is a continuous banquet, with God Himself present, and the supreme joy is beholding His face.

485. Luz

Genesis mentions Luz as the place where Jacob had his famous dream of angels on the ladder to heaven (Gen. 28:19). Jacob renamed the place Bethel, meaning "house of God." Jewish folklore has it that Luz still exists as a secret city where the inhabitants remain immortal so long as they don't venture past the city gates.

486. Metatron

It sounds like the name of some high-tech machine, but, in fact, it is the name that Jewish legend gave to the Enoch of the Genesis story. According to Genesis, Enoch never died, for "God took him" (Gen. 5:24). The legend is that when he entered heaven, Enoch became an angel with the name Metatron. More than just acquiring a new name, Enoch/Metatron became the top-ranking angel.

487. "queen of heaven"

Revelation 12:1 describes a woman "clothed with the sun," with the moon beneath her feet and a crown of twelve stars on her head. Commentators have had fierce disagreements over who, or what, the woman symbolizes. Traditionally, Catholics have identified her with the Virgin Mary, and based on this passage in Revelation, Mary is often shown in art as the "queen of heaven," with a crown of stars on her head.

488. Michael and Mary

The Bible tells of Gabriel's announcement of Jesus' forthcoming birth to the Virgin Mary. It says nothing whatsoever about Mary and the archangel Michael, but Catholic tradition says it was Michael who announced to Mary her approaching death and who carried her body to heaven.

489. upper Gehenna

An old Jewish belief was that after a person had died he had a period of one year to walk the earth (unseen, normally) and visit the places and people he knew. Some referred to this state as "upper Gehenna." Some of the early Christians held a similar belief, and in some ways resembles the state of purgatory, the idea being that the person had some "unfinished business" on earth, so he couldn't pass directly on to heaven.

490. Legend of the Ten Martyrs

This much-loved Jewish legend from centuries ago has an interesting perspective on heaven: To get there, one must not only lead a good life, but must also firmly *believe* in heaven. Put another way, the only people in heaven will be those who hoped for it.

491. Merkabah

A long tradition of Jewish mysticism is known as the Merkabah, which means, in Hebrew, "God's Throne-Chariot." The name refers to the visions of the prophet Ezekiel, who saw the glowing cherubim and God's throne-chariot in the sky. The Merkabah tradition, like most forms of mysticism, goes "off the deep end" with its talk of bizarre journeys through the seven heavens to the "throne world" while being assailed by evil spirits.

492. Avalon

Among the ancient Celts, Avalon was paradise, the Fortunate Isle, a place of feasts, music, and eternal celebration. The great King Arthur of English legend was said to have been carried there at his death, and he now awaits the souls of all the righteous. Some Christian authors have used the name Avalon as a synonym for *heaven*.

IMAGINING HELL

493. volcanoes

Though it was never officially taught by the church, many Christians believed that volcanoes—since they emitted smoke, rumblings, and sometimes lava—were the openings into hell. The rumblings were supposed to be echoes of the moanings of the people in hell. Even a wise pope like Gregory the Great could argue that the crater of Mount Etna was growing wider so as to receive the growing number of people who were condemned to hell.

494. Saint Patrick and the pit

There really was a Saint Patrick, the great apostle of Ireland, but his real history is mingled with a thousand legends. One story about him concerns his preaching about hell and purgatory to the pagans. When some doubted, he ordered that a deep pit be dug, and the monks who descended into it came back with vivid tales of what they had seen in the nether regions. The actual pit—whether or not Patrick had been connected with it—existed for years and attracted religious pilgrims. It was closed in 1497 by order of the pope.

495. seven-story hell

According to many of the rabbis, hell (like heaven) was divided into seven stories, with degrees of torment. Of the Jews themselves only the worst ones would go there, but not forever, for hell's punishments were long, but not eternal. Some rabbis said there were three sorts of persons who might spend eternity there: one who commits adultery, one who shames another person in public, and one who gives another a bad name. (See 489 [upper Gehenna].)

496. the harrowing of hell

In Christian tradition, this refers to Jesus' descent into hell, or Hades, after His death and before His resurrection (see 640 [Jesus' descent into hell]). The nonbiblical *Gospel of Nicodemus* relates that the souls in Hades (the underworld for all people, good and bad) saw a bright light, which terrified the evil souls but caused the righteous to rejoice. Christ broke down the gates of hell, took Adam by the hand, and led the righteous to paradise. Though not part of the Bible, this story fascinated artists and authors in the Middle Ages, and there are many paintings called *Harrowing of Hell*. Odd as the story seems to us today, it does answer a logical question: What is the eternal fate of the righteous people who lived before Christ? The answer: Christ rescues them from Hades and takes them to heaven.

THE APOCRYPHA

497. the punishment of Heliodorus

In the Apocrypha, 2 Maccabees 3 tells the story of a nasty character named Heliodorus, who tries to confiscate the funds of the temple in Jerusalem. When he arrives, he is confronted by a horseman clad in gold, along with two other young men in radiant attire. The two men flog him mercilessly until he finally collapses, enveloped in thick darkness. Curiously, the author of 2 Maccabees never identifies the three mysterious visitors as angels, but he makes it clear that this was a divine visitation, the power of God protecting His temple.

498. the book of Tobit

The Apocrypha (accepted as divinely inspired by Catholics but not by Protestants) contains the charming book of Tobit. Somewhat like the book of Ruth in the Old Testament, Tobit is a domestic story, but quite unlike Ruth, Tobit involves both angels and demons. Tobit, a righteous Jew in exile in Nineveh, is old and blind. A relative of his, Sarah, has problems of her own: She has married seven men in succession, and on her wedding night each groom was killed by the demon Asmodeus. God sends the angel Raphael, who brings Tobit's son Tobias to Sarah, whom she marries. Raphael knows a way to repel the demon Asmodeus: burn the entrails of a fish. The stench disgusts Asmodeus so much that he hightails it all the way to Egypt. Raphael pursues him there and shackles him. The book of Tobit is responsible for popularizing the angel Raphael.

One bit of trivia: The book of Tobit is the only part of the Bible that mentions anyone having a pet dog.

10

Dealings with
(and Against) the Demonic

CONFRONTING THE DEMONS

499. demon-possessed Christians?

Ever hear the word *daimonizomai*? This Greek word in the New Testament Gospels is often translated "having a demon" or "demon-possessed." But some scholars suggest that it means something more like "demonized" or "afflicted by a demonic power." Note the difference: If we say a person is "possessed," this suggests that the demon dwells in the person and controls him. But if he is "afflicted by a demon," the demon is simply causing trouble, but not necessarily in full control. Can a Christian be demon-possessed? The Bible's answer seems to be no, because they are under Christ's lordship. But can a Christian be afflicted by a demon? Definitely. This is why the New Testament speaks often about guarding against demonic influences.

500. spiritual warfare

Christians use this expression to refer to the ongoing battle between the forces of good (God, Christ, the angels) and the forces of evil (Satan, the demons). On an individual level, each person, no matter how saintly, is a battlefield where good and evil meet, clash, and clash again. What takes place in the individual takes place in the world at large—Christ versus Satan.

501. not the world's weapons

The good fight of faith is tough, because Satan and the demons are formidable opponents. Nonetheless, Paul gave a comforting reminder: "Though we live in the world, we do not wage war as the world does. The weapons we fight with are not the weapons of the world. On the contrary, they have divine power to demolish strongholds" (2 Cor. 10:3–4 NIV).

502. deliverance ministry

In a broad sense this term can refer to deliverance from demons, sickness, depression, and so on. But generally speaking, a person with a deliverance ministry has demonstrated some ability in casting out demons. It has been neglected through the centuries, particularly since modern thought leads many people to believe that Satan and demons are simply not real. To the credit of the modern charismatic movement—and to people's sense that there really *are* demonic forces in the world—believers are now more open to seeking divine help in deliverance from demons.

503. *Jesus and the Kingdom*

George Eldon Ladd, a professor at Fuller Theological Seminary in California, published this book in 1964. He concluded after intense study of the New Testament that Jesus is the King and Christians are His subjects, and that the King equips His subjects with the power to preach, drive out demons, and heal the sick. The book was a key influence on John Wimber, his Vineyard Christian Fellowship, and the broad renewal movement.

504. pandemonism

The New Testament accepts demons as real and dangerous. So do many Christians, and casting out demons is still a vital part of Christianity. *Pandemonism* refers to the habit of "seeing devils everywhere"—that is, attributing everything unpleasant to the work of demons, including minor personal faults and mishaps. (Spilled a glass of milk? Could have been caused by a demon.) While many Christians connect demonic power with serious illness (inward or outward), most Christians do not believe that *all* of life's minor inconveniences are caused by the powers of darkness.

505. possession: a definition

Back in the 1970s, the book (and then the movie) *The Exorcist* caused a surge of interest in demonic possession. While the movie was essentially a horror film with a religious veneer, it did raise the question: What does it mean to be "possessed"? Christianity generally defines *demon possession* as a condition in which one or more demons inhabit a person's body and take control. The demon's personality eclipses the victim's personality, and the demon manifests his personality through the victim's body.

506. possessing the innocent

The Exorcist presented us with an innocent young girl made loathsome by the demon who inhabited her. Has this happened in real life? Yes, but rarely. The Gospels speak of a boy who was possessed from his childhood (see Mark 9:21), but in most possession cases the person has of his own accord yielded to temptation and sin, weakening his own will and making himself susceptible to an invading spirit.

507. some characteristics of possession

Based on the New Testament and on centuries of experience with possessions, we know there are several definite symptoms: (1) unusual physical strength; (2) fits of rage; (3) disintegration or splitting of the personality; (4) resistance to spiritual things; (5) super-mental abilities, such as clairvoyant powers or the ability to speak in a language the person never learned; (6) alteration of voice. Christians who have dealt with possession know that some of these characteristics can indicate mental illness—but not all of them at once. A mentally ill person might have fits of rage or increased physical strength—but not clairvoyant powers or the ability to speak in a language he has never known.

508. preparing for exorcism

Just as a surgeon washes up before surgery, so a person involved in expelling demons must "wash up" spiritually. An exorcist does not have to be perfect (only Jesus was), but does have to be in a right relationship with God, repenting of any sin, praying, and preparing to draw spiritually on the power of Christ. Some people involved in deliverance claim that fasting also helps them. Obviously a deep knowledge of the Bible is helpful, heightening our knowledge of God's power and of how the demons operate and how believers can assume authority over them. Putting on the "whole armor of God" (Eph. 6:10–18) is essential, of course.

509. exorcism in Jesus' name

We assume that "taking God's name in vain" means cursing, but it also means using God's (or Christ's) name as a kind of magic formula—calling Him "Lord" when the person may not honor Him as Lord. Acting "in Jesus' name" means "on His behalf" and "with Jesus' authority." Any act "in Jesus' name," including exorcism, means the serious business of acting as Jesus' representative. While the old rituals for exorcism involve many repetitions of the names Lord and Christ, Christians involved in exorcism claim that this is unnecessary, for a barrage of words is not what gets the demon's attention.

510. do we need the demon's name?

According to the Bible, no. Jesus and the disciples never asked a demon to name itself. In the case of the Gadarene demoniac, Jesus asked the man (not the demon) what his name was, with the famous answer, "My name is Legion" (Mark 5). Holding a conversation with the demon is *not* part of exorcism. The exorcist commands the demon, in Jesus' name, to depart the person. This is an authoritative order, not a dialogue.

511. the gift of discernment

Jesus Himself had the gift of discerning of spirits and used it on several occasions. "He knew what was in man" (John 2:25). Likewise, the Spirit gives some Christians a special gift of reading people's insides, distinguishing between hypocrisy and reality, between the influence of good and evil spirits (1 Cor. 12:10). The Spirit gives some a keen ability to distinguish between what comes "from above" and what comes "from below." Those who minister to the demon-afflicted do well to have this gift.

512. binding and loosing

Jesus promised His followers that what they bound and loosed on earth would be bound and loosed in heaven (Matt. 16:19). Thus any Christian, any member of the body of Christ, has the authority to act on behalf of Christ to loose the power of the demonic over a person. How is this done? Is there a "correct" formula for casting out a demon? Persons experienced in dealing with the demonic recommend something like this: "In Jesus' name, I [or we] command you, evil spirit [here the spirit is named], to come out of this person and never enter him again."

513. specialized exorcists?

In the early days of Christianity, there was no distinction between clergy and laypeople. But one developed, and soon there were several classes of clergy—bishops, priests, even exorcists. Some churches, including the Roman Catholic Church, still have people who are specially designated "exorcists," but most Christians with experience in dealing with demon possession say there is no need to be "specialized." Any Christian can, in theory, aid in casting out demons, as we see clearly in the New Testament.

514. *ekballo* and *exorkizo*

We take our word *exorcism* from the Greek *exorkizo*—but that word is never used in the Bible. The Bible uses the Greek *ekballo*, meaning to "cast out" a demon. To *exorkizo* a demon implies the use of conjuring and magical formulas, which is not what Jesus and the apostles did. There was no incantation or magic, just an authoritative command for the demon to leave at once.

Incidentally, the various acts that accompany the command to the demon—laying hands on the person, making the sign of the cross, applying holy water—are unnecessary. The movie *The Exorcist* suggested that casting out demons is a long and involved procedure, but most often it is not. In most cases, the demon either departs quickly or not at all. The person casting out the demon may need further preparation, such as prayer.

515. energumen

This peculiar word refers to a person possessed by a demon. In times past, rituals and manuals for exorcism used it (since it is easier than saying "the demon-possessed person").

516. *exsufflatio*

This Latin word refers to part of the infant baptismal service in times past. In the Middle Ages, the Catholic church mandated that all infants be baptized as soon as possible after birth. During the service, there was a ritual of exorcism: The priest breathed three times on the face of the infant, saying, "Depart from him, unclean spirit, and give place to the Holy Spirit." This was Catholic practice for centuries, and this ritual form of exorcism, or some form of it, was also included in Lutheran services and services of other Protestant denominations. The *exsufflatio* did not mean that people believed infants to be demon-possessed. The rite was simply a symbol that the infant was being "claimed for Christ," casting out any evil influence.

517. demons in the cities

Cities have a centuries-old reputation for being more wicked than small towns or rural areas. Evangelist Lester Sumrall, noted for his ministry of delivering people from demon possession, has written that demons like to dwell in human bodies, and so naturally they are drawn to cities, where human bodies (potential "homes" for the demons) are more numerous.

518. territorial demons

Are demons attached to certain locations? The question is not a silly one. C. Peter Wagner researched the subject at length and concluded that some evil spirits are apparently tied to certain locations, as evidenced by missionaries' encounters with them. Wagner's views have not been accepted by everyone, but he made a good case for them in his 1991 book *Engaging the Enemy: How to Fight and Defeat Territorial Spirits*.

519. "vice demons"

The great theologian Origen (see 29) believed that there were "vice demons," demons in charge of a particular moral vice (such as gambling, drunkenness, and so on). While this strikes some modern readers as foolish, evangelists such as Lester Sumrall agree, believing that there are, for example, demons of pornography, drug addiction, and other modern vices that plague mankind.

520. weather demons?

People are more prone to complain about bad weather than to praise God for good weather. Many Christian teachers, including the influential Thomas Aquinas (see 606) believed that bad weather and other natural catastrophes were brought about by demons. Wind, storms, and "rains of fire from heaven" could be caused by demons, or by humans using demonic power to go after their enemies.

521. "criminal tampering"

Christianity has always had a dim view of magic and the occult, mostly because the occult connects people with the worship of demons or pagan gods. The theologian Augustine called magic "criminal tampering with the unseen world." He believed any form of magic, even when called "white magic" and felt to be harmless, was a dangerous dabbling in the demonic.

522. do I really need a demon?

Can we sin without promptings from Satan? Of course. Human beings are quite capable of sinning on their own, through weakness, selfishness, and so on. While the Bible speaks of Satan in connection with human sin, it also assumes that humans do much of Satan's work for him.

Flip Wilson's old line "The devil made me do it" is not in keeping with the Bible, since Satan can only tempt, not *make* us do anything.

523. idols

People in America and Europe collect statues, masks, and amulets from Africa and Asia, hanging them on their walls as mementos and artworks. Harmless as this seems (and often it is), Christians experienced in exorcism know that there is a real connection between demonic activity and idols (and the statues and amulets were originally made as idols, even if the purchaser just wants them as decorations). Missionaries abroad know that possession of such objects is an invitation for evil spirits to exercise their powers. When such objects are brought home as curios, they may exert some sinister powers. For all the faults in the movie *The Exorcist*, its connection of a demon possession with an Assyrian idol is rooted in actual cases.

524. dualism

When speaking of religion, this term refers to a religion of two gods—one opposed to the other. Inevitably this means Bad God vs. Good God, and in most dualistic religions the good god is expected to triumph ultimately over the bad god. Christianity, since it believes in only one God, is considered a *monotheistic* ("one God") faith, not dualistic. But as the New Testament relates: While there is never any doubt that God will triumph in the end, there is also no doubt that Satan and his demons are very powerful and are putting up a serious fight. The words of Jesus and the apostles are clear enough: Satan is the "ruler of this world" (John 12:31; 14:30) and even the "god of this age" (2 Cor. 4:4).

525. the wounded lion

Church growth expert C. Peter Wagner has had experiences around the globe with demonic influences. He claims that Satan is doomed to defeat, but will not cease to threaten man until finally destroyed at the end of time (Rev. 20:10). Until then, Wagner says, Satan is like a mortally wounded lion—at his most dangerous in the time between being shot (the first coming of Christ) and dying (Christ's return and triumph).

526. witch doctors and missionaries

Missionaries from America and Europe encounter an odd phenomenon in Third World countries: Many of their converts, even after years of being Christian, still consult with witch doctors and other dabblers in the occult. Why? The converts chalk it up to the bias Christians have against the supernatural. Most American and European Christians, being "sophisticated," don't give much attention to demonic influences. When Third World converts to Christianity feel they are being assailed by demons, they may find more sympathy with the local witch doctor than with a Christian pastor. This situation is changing. The Third World can teach us a few things about the reality of the demonic.

527. *Christianizing the Roman Empire*

What won people to Christianity in the early days? Eloquent preaching? A good music program? Hardly. The compassion of Christians was a big factor, and so was their certainty about their faith. But there was also the power factor: The early missionaries (as we can see in Acts) could drive out demons, just as Jesus did. Yale University historian Ramsay MacMullen, in *Christianizing the Roman Empire*, concluded that in the Roman world, where most people believed in the supernatural (including the demonic), Christianity could not have succeeded through just preaching or charity. Many people were won to the faith because they saw evidence that the true God was more powerful than false gods and demons.

528. occupying the pagan ground

Critics of Christianity sometimes point out that December 25 was originally a pagan holiday, which the Christians adopted as Jesus' birthday. It's absolutely true. This was deliberate: The first Christians had to show the pagan world that the true God had come to earth and was conquering the old pagan gods and demons. One way to show this was to build churches on the sites of pagan temples. Another way was to "baptize" pagan holidays, making them celebrations of Christ. The Christians' message was "Move over, false gods, the Son of God has come and is taking over."

529. *Rituale Romanum*

For many centuries this was the Catholic church's manual for religious rituals, including casting out demons. Naturally it cataloged various symptoms of demonic activity and witchcraft—and many of these supposed symptoms are exactly what the earliest Christians called "gifts of the Spirit." In other words, the manual condemned the very spiritual gifts that might be useful in casting out demons.

530. "psychological factors"

When there is no physical cause for disturbing behaviors, we chalk it up to "psychological factors." Some things never change: In the 1700s, evangelist John Wesley wrote that when doctors could not give a proper diagnosis, they blamed "nervous" factors. Wesley was willing—and Christians today should be willing—to consider the demonic as a possible explanation for "psychological" problems.

531. James I and *Daemonologie*

King James I of England will forever be associated with the version of the Bible first published in 1611, a project that he had encouraged and that was dedicated to him. James was himself an author, and one of his books was *Daemonologie*, concerned with witchcraft and demons. James was a firm believer in evil spirits and witches, and he also employed a professional angelologist to consult with. His fascination with witchcraft may have been one reason William Shakespeare wrote the play *Macbeth*, in which three witches play a prominent role.

532. *Malleus Maleficarum*

"The Witch Hammer" is what this Latin title means. It was published in Germany in 1486, the work of two prominent members of the Catholic Inquisition. It was a manual on witchcraft for inquisitors tracking down people dabbling in satanism. The book went into great detail about how demons work their many evils upon man. It described how witches cast spells, how they conjure up demons, and how evil spells may be broken. On the legal side, the book told of how to bring witches to trial and how to obtain evidence via interrogation or torture.

533. Anna Ecklund

One of the many odd and frightening stories of demon possession concerns this woman of Wisconsin. Her father, angry that she would not engage in incestuous relations with him, somehow acted to bring about her possession by a demon calling itself Beelzebub. The demon possessed her in 1908 and did not leave her until 1928, exiting with a roar and leaving a foul stench behind.

DALLYING WITH DEMONS

534. the occult

People are incurably religious, and if they don't accept Christianity, they often accept a substitute—sometimes even the occult, with its link to the demonic. Ouija boards, astrology, séances, levitation, fortune-telling, tarot cards, automatic writing, calling upon various "spirits"—all these and more fall under the broad heading of occult. (Much of what today goes by the respectable name "New Age" used to be called "occult," or even "satanism.")

Christians and psychologists who have dealt with demon-possessed persons know that there is a definite connection between the occult and possession. For many people, the occult opens a window by which demons enter, sometimes leading to total possession. The main problem: The occult is a means to bypass God and our dependence on Him. It is a way of obtaining knowledge (whether false or true) or exercising power, making our-selves godlike (the original sin of Adam and Eve, Gen. 3). Dabbling in the occult is a way of saying to God, "I don't need You, and I prefer to take charge of my own destiny." But in the world created and governed by God, this quest can only lead to harm.

535. Aleister Crowley (1875–1947)

How did one shock upper-class Englishmen in the early 1900s? By being a satanist, of course. Crowley was a poet and an author of books on magic and the occult, and he enjoyed his reputation for wickedness as he celebrated the rituals of black magic. To show how his mind worked, one of his books was titled *The Diary of a Drug Fiend*. He was probably not nearly as wicked as he professed to be, but his life and labors did much to introduce satanism to people who might never have considered it.

536. the Church of Satan

In the wacky 1960s, there arose the Church of Satan, headed by a man with the unlikely name of Anton Szandor LaVey. He declared that 1966 was the beginning of the Satanic Age. Back when satanism could still shock the American public (how long ago that seems!), LaVey, who died in 1998, set out to overturn Christianity and "Middle American" virtues. His own church, LaVey said, promoted other "virtues": indulgence, gratification of one's impulses, revenge. He overlooked an important fact: These impulses come naturally to people, so who needs a church to promote them? The young, whom he hoped to attract, were following his "if it feels good, do it" philosophy without bothering to join his church. He probably had much less influence on youth than did such rock acts as Alice Cooper and Black Sabbath, who managed to make satanism look hip. More recently, the most visible member of the Church of Satan is shock-rocker Marilyn Manson. Whether Manson, or his fans, takes his satanic connections seriously is anybody's guess.

537. the prohibition on contacting the dead

The occult has always held a fascination for man, but the Bible strictly prohibits contacting the dead. Why? Probably the main reason is that God wants us to steer clear of contact with evil spirits. Satan and the demons can and do lie, and there is a danger that they could disguise themselves as deceased loved ones in order to lead us astray. Séances are, most of the time, just plain phony. There probably are cases where some spirit really has appeared at a séance, but we need not assume that the spirit is who it claims to be.

538. the witch of Endor

Israel's law prohibited occult activity, and 1 Samuel 28:3 relates that Saul, Israel's first king, expelled the mediums and occultists from the land. Ironically, before a fateful battle with the Philistines, Saul consulted a medium (called "witch" in older translations) in the village of Endor. At his request she called up the spirit of his dead mentor, Samuel. (She seemed genuinely surprised that Samuel came, which suggests her previous "channelings" had been faked.) Samuel's spirit, not pleased, asked Saul, "Why have you disturbed me by bringing me up?" (v. 15). Poor Saul explained that he wanted Samuel's advice, since God appeared to have abandoned him. Samuel stated that Saul's kingdom would be handed over to David, and "tomorrow you and your sons will be with me" (v. 19)—that is, dead. As Samuel predicted, Saul and his sons died the next day.

Readers of the Bible are puzzled by this passage. Did the witch somehow manage to call him from heaven? Unlikely. Certainly the great man was not in hell. So was he in some kind of "holding place" before passing on to heaven? This is one of those "puzzlers" that must, for the time being, remain unanswered.

539. the Hellfire Club

The 1700s was an age of widespread religious skepticism. In the 1750s a group of English aristocrats formed the Hellfire Club, dedicated to mocking Christianity and conventional morality. The club claimed that Satan was its master, and members defiantly announced that they were eager to go to hell after death, where they would have good company. Club members met in a former monastery, where they held mock religious ceremonies with pornographic pictures, inverted crosses, and smutty parodies of prayers. They were heavy drinkers who delighted in orgies. In time the novelty wore off (and members aged). Most likely the members weren't genuine satanists but just enjoyed the shock value of it all, much as today's teens with their satanic look.

540. Isobel Gowdie (c. 1610–1665)

Witch-hunts have rounded up real or suspected Satan worshipers, but Isobel Gowdie came out and confessed her own dealings with the demonic. This Scottish farm wife claimed to have had sexual relations with Satan and to have been taken as his guest to hell. She said she had renounced Christ, joined a coven, and used weapons from hell to slay Christians. We aren't sure if she was executed after her confessions, just as we aren't sure if she was telling the truth or was simply a pathetic and deluded soul.

541. satanic rock

Certain teens have always been attracted to whatever would shock and disgust parents. Thus the satanic look has been an established part of rock, beginning in the 1970s with such acts as Black Sabbath, KISS, Alice Cooper, and others. The group Iron Maiden chose a corpse named Eddie as its logo, with Satan also appearing on their album covers. (Their fans are known as "Hell Rats.") More recently, shock-rocker Marilyn Manson, looking gaunt and sinister, had a best-seller with the album *AntiChrist Superstar*. Many parents have been shocked to learn that song lyrics and record covers feature Satan, devils, skulls, human sacrifice, and other occult signs and symbols. Music videos via MTV bring the Satan look into homes around the clock. Harmless fun? For some kids, yes. A doorway into something horrible for many other kids? Sadly, yes.

542. Dungeons & Dragons

In 1974 the world had its first exposure to Dungeons & Dragons, and the role-playing game became quite the rage. While some players enjoyed it as a harmless pastime, the game became an obsession for others, who took its demons, wizards, and witches way too seriously. It was linked to at least one grisly murder in the 1980s, raising some questions among parents as to whether such games are harmless after all.

543. *misophaes*

This word means "haters of light," and is sometimes used in Christian literature as a name for demons. The idea is rooted in the Bible, where Satan and the demons are those who hate the light (truth, goodness), while God and Christ are light, and Christ's followers are told to be the "light of the world."

544. Satan and crime

People persecuted as witches have sometimes been harmless eccentrics—but not always. Back in the heyday of witch-hunts, some satanists really did commit horrible crimes, including grave robbing, vandalism of church property, animal sacrifice, even sacrifice of humans. Occasionally people claiming to be Satan-influenced still do horrible things, such as Charles Manson and his "family." A North Carolina teen who recently murdered his father and attempted to murder his mother was an addict of Dungeons & Dragons, and many teen suicides have been linked to obsessions with Satan and hell.

545. agrippa books

Heinrich Cornelius Agrippa was a philosopher of the 1500s, notorious for dabbling in the demonic. Supposedly other devotees of the occult used enormous books called agrippas—thick, five-foot-tall volumes with pages made of human skin. The agrippas supposedly contained the names of the demons of hell and the spells that would bring them forth. The books themselves were supposed to be so evil that they had to be wrapped in chains and kept in empty rooms so their evil would not escape.

546. the Luciferans

In the 1200s this German group claimed to worship Satan as creator and ruler, teaching that he would overcome the Christian God. Initiates had to kiss a toad on its mouth or backside, and the Luciferans practiced all manner of perversions and anti-Christian acts.

547. requiem for the living

In Catholic practice, a requiem mass is celebrated on behalf of a person who has died. In the past, and even today, a satanist may perform a requiem for a *living* person. Thus, the words of the requiem "Give him eternal rest, O Lord" become a kind of death curse upon the person. Over the centuries there have been many cases of perverted people trying to use Christian rituals in such a sinister fashion.

548. black mass

For serious satanists, black mass is *the* ritual. Essentially it is a perverse parody of the Catholic mass. Satan is praised, God and Christ are cursed, the cross is inverted and spat upon. The ritual leaves out the Catholic confession of sins (naturally) and all Alleluias (since these are praise of God). Black, not white, candles are burned. Instead of wine in Communion, satanists use water, urine, or even blood. Sex has always been a key element, and at times the body of a naked woman is used as an altar. The rite often degenerates into an orgy of promiscuous sex.

549. devil's mark

Those people who have made a pact with Satan or a demon are often said to bear some kind of mark or scar on their bodies, the "devil's mark." The devil's mark was a sort of brand, Satan's way of reminding the person, "Remember, you belong to me."

550. hellbroth

Shakespeare's *Macbeth* has its famous scene of the three witches concocting their horrible brew in a cauldron, tossing in eye of newt and other delicacies. It was widely believed that dabblers in satanism and the occult would prepare a magical broth, the hellbroth, for use in their satanic rituals.

551. John Dee (1527–1608)

Dee was a "scientist" (in the days when science wasn't too scientific) and served as a court astrologer to England's

Queen Elizabeth I. As an astrologer, Dee naturally dabbled in the occult, hoping to tap into the power of angels and communicate with spirits of the dead. Dee kept notes in his *Spiritual Diaries*, describing his encounters with angels. Most of the dialogues he claimed to have had with angels were just recycled gibberish from his occult library. He feared demons and was afraid that some of his angel encounters were really meetings with demons in disguise.

552. *daimon*

This Greek word is the source of our word *demon,* but to the Greeks a *daimon* wasn't necessarily good or bad. It was simply a spirit that might sometimes help, sometimes harm, human beings. The universe was full of them, and humans had to take care lest they unwittingly offend a *daimon.* Socrates, Plato, and the other major Greek philosophers all believed in *daimons.* By the time the great theologian Augustine began writing (in the early 400s), belief in these spirits was on the wane, and Augustine could state with authority that spirits were good angels or bad demons, but not neutral *daimons.*

553. the devils of Loudon

In the 1600s in France occurred a curious case of nuns claiming to be bewitched by the demon Beelzebub. Two priests (both notoriously immoral) were implicated in the strange possessions, and the two were executed for witch-craft. The case made a disturbing 1971 movie, *The Devils*.

554. the Inquisition and Beelzebub

The Inquisition was the Catholic church's spiritual court, set up to try cases of heresy and witchcraft. In dealing with many cases over the centuries, the court found that Beelzebub (see 174) was frequently mentioned as the demon with which witches supposedly cavorted. (Satan himself was often mentioned, naturally.) Supposedly witches would deny Christ in the name of Beelzebub, and some women were accused of having carnal relations with the demon.

555. the Haizmann diary

Christopher Haizmann was a German artist who kept a diary of a deal he made with Satan. In exchange for nine years of happiness, Haizmann would have to give the devil his soul. However, the nine years weren't all happy, for Satan would show up periodically to check on the artist, who left us vivid descriptions of Satan's appearance. As the nine years drew to a close, Haizmann panicked and wondered if the deal could be broken. He had priests attempt exorcism, but to no avail. Later he claimed that the Virgin Mary somehow broke the infernal contract. Even so, Haizmann was trou-bled with visions of hell until his death in 1700.

556. Charles Manson (b. 1934)

The leader of the murderous, drugged-out "Family" that shocked America in 1969 was affected by the Bible . . . and also by the Beatles, Scientology, LSD, and environmentalism, among other influences of the time. Manson claimed (sometimes) that he was Christ—and sometimes Satan. His followers believed that Manson/Christ/Satan was going to bring about the final world battle in which the Family would emerge to rule. Manson read the book of Revelation and connected it with—strangely enough— the Beatles. Manson believed the group's *White Album* was sending him messages about how to launch the world revolution. According to Manson, chapter 9 of Revelation correlated with the song "Revolution No. 9" on the *White Album*. The four angels of Revelation 9 were the four Beatles, the "breastplates of iron" were the Beatles' electric guitars, and so on.

557. government approval, 1999

In 1999 the Pentagon approved pagan chaplains for the U.S. military. For the first time in U.S. history, the government has put witchcraft on the same religious footing as Christianity and Judaism.

558. voodoo

In the Middle Ages, a group known as the Waldensians took their Christianity seriously, but were persecuted as heretics by the Catholic church. The Waldensians were also known as the Vaudois, and because they were wrongly suspected of many evils (including satanism), the name Vaudois became corrupted into *voodoo*. The mishmash of beliefs known as voodoo today are mostly rooted in Africa but are particularly connected with the troubled land of Haiti. Many Americans and Europeans have become unhealthily fascinated by voodoo in recent years.

11

~

Ideas and Thinkers, Mostly Sensible

559. heaven without hell?

This is what many people today claim whenever they are polled: Most believe in heaven, only a dwindling percentage believe in hell. Yet C. S. Lewis wrote that he had never truly met anyone with a deep, life-enhancing belief in heaven who did not also believe in hell. Put another way: Part of the joy of heaven (and our expectation of it) is the joy of escaping hell.

560. emotional to the max

Heaven, to many people, sounds blah and emotionless. There is no reason to think it is, for Christianity is (or should be) a highly emotional religion, filled with the joy of being in a right relationship with God and our fellow-man. The Greek philosophers, and philosophers in general, may imagine a kind of cool, passionless heaven, but this is not in keeping with the Bible or Christian tradition. The Bible says nothing about leaving our emotions behind when we live with God.

561. the "dark night of the soul"

Just as many Christians have had experiences of being tempted or tormented by demons, some Christians have had painful visions of the torments of hell. The Spanish mystic John of the Cross spoke of the "dark night of the soul," the horrible experience of feeling separated from God, or of being in (or having visions of) hell itself. John's friend the saintly Teresa of Avila claimed to have experienced the torments of hell, but said it was a sort of purification process. The "dark night of the soul" is anguish-filled, but has the benefit of making the person draw nearer to God in time.

562. physics and the Resurrection

For two centuries we have watched the battle of Christianity versus science, and Christianity seemed to be losing. Things are changing, partly because science is constantly updating itself, finding new data. The field of physics is making intelligent people more and more open to the possibility of miracles—including the resurrection of the human body. Our flesh feels solid enough, but physics is now pretty certain that flesh consists of innumerable electrical particles, held together by an energy we have yet to understand fully. Some scientists say that Jesus' resurrection may have had something to do with nuclear disintegration and reintegration. Jesus promised His followers that they would be raised as He had been—into what Paul called the "spiritual body." Thanks to our new understanding of physics, "spirit" and "body" may not be so different as we once thought. Author Russell Kirk wrote that "it is now more rationally possible to believe in the Resurrection than it was in St. Paul's time."

563. hell and class-consciousness

Are poor (and less educated) people more inclined to believe in hell than sophisticates? Definitely. In 1991, *U.S. News & World Report* ran a cover story on hell. A notable tidbit from the story: Christian ministers in upper-class churches do *not* preach on hell. One minister described her church as composed of "upper-middle-class, well-educated critical thinkers" who would be "stunned to hear a sermon on hell." The article quoted such "critical thinkers" as believing that hell is the sorrow we experience here on earth (such as, one assumes, having the Lexus break down, or watching the stock market fall). Whether a certain class believes in hell has nothing to do with hell being a reality.

564. justice or mercy?

The English devotional writer Jeremy Taylor (1613–1667) wrote that "If we refuse mercy here, we shall have justice in eternity." He was echoing a basic Christian belief: God in His mercy forgives us, not giving us the justice (eternal separation from Him) that we really deserve. If we refuse to show mercy for others, God will not show mercy to us. (Matt. 5:7; Mark 11:26; James 2:13).

565. forgive—or else

"We must all forgive our enemies or be damned." So wrote C. S. Lewis (see 718), the English lay theologian who took hell seriously. Mercy—even to one's enemies—is required of those who hope and expect (through God's mercy) to enter heaven (see Luke 6:27–35; James 2:13).

566. "enjoyment of His beauty"

Meeting in response to the Protestant Reformation, the Catholic Council of Trent in the 1560s issued many statements of official Catholic teaching. On the subject of heaven, the council decreed that man's reward in the afterlife is "the vision of God and enjoyment of His beauty." In other words, the chief joy of heaven is God Himself.

567. "the chief end of man"

Calvinist theology is often considered solemn and joyless, but it has its pleasant side. The Westminster Catechism, compiled by the English Puritans in the 1600s, is a basic statement of Calvinist beliefs, and it does not leave out joy. The Cathechism asks the question: What is the chief end [purpose] of man? The answer is: The chief end of man is to glorify God and enjoy Him forever.

568. theocentric

The word means "God-centered," and it describes the more traditional Christian view of heaven, with nearness to God being the greatest joy. Today most people, including many Christians, have a more anthropocentric ("human-centered") view, the main joy being reunion with friends and loved ones. The New Age view presented in many books and movies has little use for God in heaven.

569. God the Governor

Evangelist D. L. Moody (see 619) preferred to convert people with happy images of heaven than with the fires of hell. But he believed strongly in hell and scolded ministers who did not. Those who teach that all will be saved, Moody noted, claim that God is too merciful to condemn anyone. But what if God were the governor of a state,

Moody asked, and He decided to be "merciful" and release all the criminals to run amok in society? Is that merciful—or is it a cruelty to the decent people in that state? That "merciful" governor would likely be booted out of office. Just as we do not allow the wrong people to run loose in society, so God will not allow the sinful and rebellious to disturb the peace and joy of heaven.

570. *sic transit gloria mundi*

This Latin phrase means "thus passes away the glory of the world." The phrase is older than Christianity, but many Christian authors through the centuries have quoted it, since it expresses a clear teaching of the Bible. We find it stated eloquently by John: "The world is passing away, and the lust of it; but he who does the will of God abides forever" (1 John 2:17).

571. hell or Hell?

It is customary not to capitalize *heaven* or *hell*, though some books do not follow this practice. No one knows exactly why publishers, over the years, have chosen to lowercase the two words. Contemporary author Ralph de Toledano argued with an editor over this practice, and noted that he preferred that Hell be capitalized. When the editor asked why, the author replied, "Because it's a real place. You know, like Scarsdale." He has a point. If publishers believe that heaven and hell do really exist (and if they are *eternal*, then they exist in a fuller sense than any place on earth, right?), then maybe we ought to try capitalizing the two words from now on.

572. righteous remnant

Throughout the Bible is the idea that the human race as a whole is sinful, but there is a always a "righteous remnant" that God wishes to preserve. Consider the saving of Noah and his family from the great Flood. Later, Israel was supposed to be God's holy, righteous nation, but the nation as a whole was never very righteous. Israel's prophets saw this clearly and spoke of a remnant that would be preserved by God. Isaiah mentioned the righteous remnant dozens of times, as did most of the other prophets. Zephaniah predicted a time when "the remnant of Israel shall do no unrighteousness and speak no lies, nor shall a deceitful tongue be found in their mouth: for they shall feed their flocks and lie down, and no one shall make them afraid" (Zeph. 3:13).

After the coming of Jesus, the "remnant" was applied to Christians, the minority of people in this sinful world who would be saved from destruction and given eternal life.

573. a sabbath rest

The Sabbath, the seventh day of the week, was to be a day of rest for God's people, recalling that God rested from creation on the seventh day. In the ancient world, where most people labored hard, the Sabbath had a deep significance—a brief respite from toil, and one that recurred weekly. The letter to the Hebrews speaks of a "rest for the people of God," connecting this rest with Israel's Sabbath (Heb. 4:1–10). Clearly this is referring to heaven—a kind of "eternal Sabbath," an everlasting rest from the world's woes. After life in this world, facing toil, sorrows, and persecution, the believer looks forward to a Sabbath that will never end.

574. new vs. old

"Do not remember the former things, nor consider the things of old. Behold, I will do a new thing" (Isa. 43:18–19). So said God to Israel. It is human nature to wish to hold to the past, even to romanticize it, forgetting the bad times and recalling the good. But the idea of newness is important in both the Old and New Testaments. Jesus spoke of new wine versus old wine, hinting that too many prefer the old—that is, they hold to the past for its own sake, while the new is better (Luke 5:37–39). At the Last Supper He spoke of a "new covenant" (or "new testament"), not based on the old Law and sacrifices but on individual faith in God. Paul mentioned newness frequently, contrasting each person's "old man" with the "new man," remade in Christ's image (2 Cor. 5:17; Eph. 4:24; Col. 3:10).

Near the Bible's end, in the vision of the New Jerusalem (heaven), God said, "Behold, I make all things new" (Rev. 21:5).

575. names written in heaven

People who believe in an "impersonal" immortality, an afterlife where individuals are "absorbed" into a Cosmic One, are definitely at odds with the Bible. (They are at odds with human nature too: Most people have no desire to lose their individuality after death.) The Bible is clear enough: We will be changed in some way after the resurrection, yet we will still be the individual personalities that we were on earth. Our names (not necessarily our worldly titles, which have no meaning in heaven) are still our own, and we should rejoice, Jesus said, because our names are written in heaven (Luke 10:20).

576. the beatific vision

Beatific means "blessed," and the beatific vision refers to the blessing of seeing God. As the Bible makes clear, hardly anyone sees God face to face. Jacob did (Gen. 32:30) and Moses did (Ex. 33:11), but it was generally considered dangerous to see God "up close and personal." Even so, Paul promised Christians that in heaven they would see God face to face (1 Cor. 13:12). Yet many Christians have hoped to see God, or at least heaven, while still on earth, and there are many stories of saints who have had, at least briefly, the beatific vision. The poet Dante ended his masterpiece, *The Divine Comedy*, with a stunning description of the beatific vision, with the saints and angels arranged like a cosmic rose around the throne of God.

577. gaps in the celestial court

The great theologian Augustine (see 596) and many other Christian authors taught that the rebellion of Lucifer (who became Satan) and his followers left gaps in heaven's court. In other words, after Satan and his followers were cast from heaven, there was "space" available in heaven. God desires to fill this "space" with saints.

578. eternal regrets

While artists and authors have had a field day depicting the torments of hell, some authors have suggested a less picturesque alternative: People in hell are tormented by memories of their lives on earth, knowing nothing can be undone, and that it is too late to repent. While this view of hell doesn't lend itself to painting, it does indeed sound horrible enough, knowing there is no rest from painful memories.

579. adoption

God has no children, genetically speaking. People may *become* sons and daughters of God, so every child of God is an adopted child. God only has spiritual children—that is, those who obey Him as a Father. Paul several times referred to Christians as being "adopted" by God: "You received the Spirit of adoption by whom we cry out, 'Abba, Father'" (Rom. 8:15). While Christians are already children of God, the "full" adoption occurs after death: Believers "groan within ourselves, eagerly waiting for the adoption, the redemption of our body" (Rom. 8:23).

580. "we shall be like Him"

What will we be like in heaven? The New Testament gives us some hints: We will have "spiritual bodies," a condition we find hard to comprehend. In fact, the Bible authors give us only hints because they are describing the indescribable. But consider the words of 1 John 3:2: "It has not yet been revealed what we shall be, but we know that when He is revealed, we shall be like Him." As Christ had a new and different post-Resurrection body, so shall we. We will put on immortality and be free of the sin nature that plagues us now.

IDEAS ABOUT ANGELS

581. light, light, and more light

Angels, the Bible tells us, can appear as normal human beings at times. Yet many times they are both white and bright—creatures of light, unearthly light. This is appropriate: The Bible associates darkness with error, sin, and lostness. Light is truth, awareness, and heaven. Even though Satan can masquerade as an angel of light (2 Cor. 11:14), this mock light is not the true light of heaven. Consider bright light in the New Testament: Jesus at His transfiguration (Mark 9:3); Jesus as the Light of the World (John 8:12); the angels at Jesus' tomb (Matt. 28:2; Luke 24:4), the heavenly light that blinded Saul (Acts 9:3); the light of Peter's angelic deliverer (Acts 12:7); the New Jerusalem that needs no lamp or sun or moon to light it, for God is its light (Rev. 21:23).

582. dual baptism

The influential author Origen (see 29) taught that when a person is baptized, two baptisms are taking place simultaneously: The person's body is being immersed in water by the minister, and the person's soul is being immersed in the Holy Spirit by the angels.

583. christophany

The word *theophany* means "manifestation of God." Likewise, *christophany* means "manifestation of Christ." In the 1500s many Christian theologians, including Martin Luther and John Calvin, insisted that Christ was found throughout the Bible, even in the Old Testament, which does not mention Him by name. Luther and Calvin claimed that the many references to the "angel of the Lord" in the Old Testament refer to Christ, interacting with mankind in an angelic form long before He was born as a human infant in Bethlehem. So the many *theophanies* in the Old Testament were at the same time *christophanies.*

584. angelspeak

Some say that when humans speak in tongues they are speaking the language of angels (see 458). Yet Thomas Aquinas, the main theologian of the Middle Ages, taught that angels do not speak at all among themselves. They read one another's thoughts. They do not engage in speech with God, either: They contemplate His will and "read" it.

585. co-citizens

Augustine and other Catholic theologians taught that the City of God (heaven, that is) is populated by two types of citizens: angels and redeemed human beings. While on earth, people of faith should strive to behave in such a way that their words and deeds would not be out of place among the angels. While believers strive to be "co-citizens" with the angels, the angels aid men in their journey to heaven. The theory is that the more we become like angels here on earth, the more ready we are for heaven.

586. unnecessary angels

John of the Cross (1542–1591), a popular Spanish saint of the Catholic church, believed in angels and their protective role in human life. John was a mystic, a believer in meditation and the contemplation of God. In the many devotional books he wrote, he suggested that angelic aid is mostly for those immature in the faith. As people progress in their spiritual lives and draw closer to God, they have less and less need of angels' assistance. They can, in time, "dial direct" and rely completely on God.

IDEAS ABOUT DEMONS

587. pride and envy—but nothing else

The Catholic church has taught for centuries that Satan and the demons labor to lead man into all forms of sin. Yet, the theologians taught, the demons themselves have no interest in sinning. They are guilty of only two sins, the two that got them booted from heaven: pride (Lucifer thought too highly of himself, rebelled against God, and was expelled) and envy (the rebel angels envied God's power, and they envied the attention God was lavishing upon His newly created humans).

588. "where I am, hell is"

The Catholic church in the Middle Ages taught that the demons (fallen angels) might sorrow over their wickedness, but they could never repent. As such, they never experience joy (or any positive emotion), and in fact exist always in torment. In the words of Satan in Milton's *Paradise Lost*, "Which way I fly is Hell, myself am Hell."

589. "the actual temple of the devil"

From the very beginning Christianity had a low opinion of the theater, not surprising in view of the lewdness of so many plays in the Roman Empire. Many actresses were, or had been, prostitutes, and the immorality of traveling actors was notorious. Even as late as the 1500s the Church of Scotland issued a decree that the theater was "the actual temple of the devil, where he frequently appeared clothed in a corporeal substance and possessed the spectators, whom he held as his worshipers." An exaggeration? Perhaps—or perhaps not. One wonders what the first Christians might think of the movies and TV sitcoms of today.

THINKERS: THE ANCIENT CHURCH

590. Justin Martyr (100–c. 165)

As his name implies, he died as a martyr for the faith. He was also a noted theologian, a former pagan who finally found the ultimate truth in Christianity. Justin was probably the first author to suggest that the "angel of the Lord" mentioned often in the Old Testament was Christ in the guise of an angel. In other words, before Christ's birth in Bethlehem, He existed in a spiritual state (which John 1 makes clear), and He sometimes appeared in angel form to the Old Testament saints.

591. Irenaeus (d. c. 194)

The great theologian was bishop of Lyons in Gaul (what is today France). In his day a serious threat to Christian belief was the broad set of beliefs known as Gnosticism (see 872). Irenaeus wrote his famous books *Against Heresies*, aimed mainly at the Gnostics. The Gnostics generally despised the flesh and emphasized spirit, and they said only spirit can enter heaven. Irenaeus followed the Bible's teaching that body and soul are both saved. He believed, as did many Christians of his time, that after death the Christian entered an intermediate state called Hades while awaiting the second coming of Christ.

592. Methodius (d. c. 311)

The bishop of Olympus in the Roman province of Lycia, Methodius was not only a noted theologian but also a martyr for his faith. Methodius opposed the common idea of his time that the body decayed in the grave but the soul was saved. He insisted (following the Bible) that man is saved body and soul. In fact, he took his idea of bodily resurrection to such an extreme that he claimed that resurrected sinners have to have teeth, since Jesus said that there would be gnashing of teeth in hell (Matt. 8:12).

593. Gregory of Nyssa (330–c. 395)

Gregory was a noted theologian as well as bishop of the town of Nyssa (in what is now Turkey). Gregory was a calm, gentle soul who taught that a key goal in life was *apatheia*, freedom from passions. (This is not the same meaning as our word *apathy*, although *apathy* does come from *apatheia*.) Gregory believed that at the Second Coming, when believers are received into glory, they will be in a state of perfect *apatheia*.

594. John Chrysostom (c. 344–407)

This amazing preacher was bishop of Constantinople, capital of the Byzantine Empire. He dared to preach sermons against worldliness and luxury, and he often found himself in trouble with the emperor for daring to preach true Christianity. While many Christian laymen and clergy of his day doubted whether hell was eternal, Chrysostom took both heaven and hell seriously: "A man cannot enter into the kingdom of heaven unless he is born again of water and the Spirit. How without them will it be possible for a man either to escape hell-fire or to reach the crowns which are laid up for us?" (Chrysostom, by the way, was not his name but a nickname, from the Greek *chrysostoma*, meaning "golden-mouthed.")

595. Ambrose (c. 339-397)

The bishop of Milan in Italy, Ambrose was one of the great men of the Middle Ages, a profound influence on Augustine, one of Christianity's greatest theologians. Ambrose based his beliefs firmly on the Bible, yet he had some curious ideas of his own about angels and the afterlife. The world was, he believed, filled with evil spirits out to do men harm, and to aid man there were ninety-nine angels per person. He believed there were seven heavens (a belief shared by many in the Middle Ages), while hell was divided into three regions, the lowest being the worst. Hades was the place where people awaited the Last Judgment, and purgatory was the place of "second baptism" or the "furnace of fire," where the human soul was refined.

596. Augustine (354–430)

Born in northern Africa, Augustine led a wild youth but throughout his life was a restless seeker of the truth. Eventually the prayers of his Christian mother were answered and he found the truth, and peace, in Christianity. He became the bishop of the city of Hippo and throughout his long life wrote theological works that touched on practically every subject. His *Confessions* are still widely read, and for centuries his theology dominated Catholic thought.

Writing in Latin, Augustine was a formidable opponent of the various Christian heresies of the day (and there were *lots* of heresies). Some Christian teachers were toying with the idea of universalism—the belief that all people would eventually be saved. But Augustine was a firm predestinarian—that is, he believed that it was eternally decreed that some people would be saved and some would not. To those who taught, or hoped, that there was really not a hell, Augustine argued that, yes, there really was a material hell, a lake of fire and brimstone, the place of torment for both sinful men and the demons. Since we are all sinners, Augustine argued, all of us really deserve hell, but through trusting in Christ some people will escape hell and enter heaven. But he made it clear that hell would be more densely populated than heaven.

If this all sounds harsh, it helps to remember that Augustine was in fact a kind and charitable man, one who had more to say about the joy of heaven than about hell. But he did use his influence to steer the church away from any idea of universal salvation.

597. Gregory I (c. 540–604)

Known to history as Gregory the Great, he was elected pope at the age of fifty. He encouraged the evangelization of England and gave his blessing to what became known as the Gregorian chant. Gregory was also a theologian, and he used his influence to spread the doctrine of purgatory. Like a number of Christian thinkers, Gregory believed that Christians would, after death, be purged of their sins before entering heaven. Gregory took the belief a little further and suggested that the pains of those in purgatory could be shortened and softened by the prayers of their friends still on earth. This idea of praying for one's departed Christian friends was not harmful in itself, but in time it led to abuses, as people became less and less concerned about the sins they committed in this life, since their friends (or priests they had hired) would pray for them after their death.

Gregory also helped spread the idea that Satan was originally Lucifer, an angel who became proud, rebelled against God, and was thrown out of heaven, along with his followers. Envious of God's love for man, Satan and his crew (who became demons after their fall from heaven) tempt man into sin. Gregory coined the term "Apostate Angel" for Satan.

THINKERS: THE MIDDLE AGES

598. the nine orders of Pseudo-Dionysius

Christians get (or *should* get) their beliefs about angels from the Bible, but one of the most powerful influences on belief about angels was the medieval author known as Dionysius the Areopagite. Acts 17:34 mentions that the apostle Paul converted a man named Dionysius in the city of Athens. (Paul spoke at a place called the Areopagus, so this convert came to be called the Areopagite.) But the man who wrote theological works under the name Dionysius probably lived around the year 500, and is known to history (since we don't know his real name) as Pseudo-Dionysius. This author (whatever his real name, or names, may have been) had an extremely orderly mind, the type that enjoys sorting things into neat categories. In the widely read book *The Celestial Hierarchy*, Pseudo-Dionysius explained that there are nine types of angels. Moving from highest to lowest, they are these: seraphim, cherubim, thrones, dominions (or dominations), virtues (or authorities), powers, principalities, archangels, and angels. The author did not pull all these names out of thin air, for they are all mentioned in the Bible, though never in one place. Colossians 1:16 mentions thrones, dominions, principalities, and powers all together, but it is doubtful that Paul himself had any belief in the "nine orders" that Pseudo-Dionysius described.

Being of a categorical mind, Dionysius not only categorized the angels but also described their work, and he emphasized the importance of rank—that is, the top category (seraphim) was most important, being closest to God, while the regular angels were the least important, but still vital, since they were the "foot soldiers" who dealt with most human beings.

Pseudo-Dionysius was widely read in the Middle Ages, even though most theologians were aware that he was not the real Dionysius of Acts 17. Probably no book (other than the Bible) has had more influence on beliefs about angels than *The Celestial Hierarchy*.

599. thrones

This is a particular type of angel—or so Christian tradition says. They are mentioned in the Bible only once, in Paul's letter to the Colossians: "thrones or dominions or principalities or powers" (1:16). It is clear from the context that Paul was talking about the angels, who, he made clear, are much less important than Christ. While Paul said nothing else about thrones, the Christian imagination supplied more details. The author known as Pseudo-Dionysius (see 598) wrote that, true to their name, the thrones "carry God"—that is, they support the divine will. Pseudo-Dionysius claimed that "God brings His justice to bear upon us" through the thrones. They resemble fiery wheels covered with eyes.

600. dominions, also called dominations

Like the thrones, these are mentioned (only briefly) in Paul's letter to the Colossians. Again, Paul supplied no further information about this order of angel. But the author known as Pseudo-Dionysius did, claiming that they are the angels of freedom, influencing earthly governments to uphold God. He ranked them fourth in his influential book *The Celestial Hierarchy*. He also claimed that "they regulate angels' duties . . . and through them the majesty of God is manifested."

601. virtues

This order of angels is, according to Jewish folklore, assigned by God to work miracles on earth. They bestow grace and valor upon mankind. Legend has it that the two angels who spoke to Jesus' disciples after the Ascension (Acts 1) were angels in the order of virtues.

602. authorities

This order of angels is mentioned in 1 Peter 3:22. Their name seems to indicate that they possessed power, perhaps over other angels.

603. powers

This was believed to be a high order of angels. Jewish tradition, and later Christian folklore, assigned them the role of halting the efforts to overthrow the world. In the New Testament, Paul mentioned them (only in passing) in Romans 8:38, Ephesians 3:10, and Colossians 1:16.

604. principalities

This is considered an order of angels, mentioned by Paul in Romans 8:38, Ephesians 3:10, and Colossians 1:16. Christian tradition says that these are the protectors of religion. Pseudo-Dionysius's *Celestial Hierarchy* ranks them seventh in the orders of angels and says they help watch over the leaders of the peoples.

605. archangels

These are higher in rank than mere angels. (The Greek prefix *arch-* means "ruling.") The Bible specifically mentions archangels only twice. In 1 Thessalonians 4:16, Paul referred to the archangel blowing the trumpet at the end of time, but this archangel was not named. Jude 9 speaks of Michael the archangel—the only time in the Bible that a particular angel is assigned a "rank." However, Christian imagination filled in what the Bible left out. One tradition says that the seven angels who stand before God (Rev.

8:2) are the archangels. The author of Revelation may have had in mind the Jewish tradition of there being seven archangels. According to the influential *Celestial Hierarchy* by Pseudo-Dionysius, the archangels rank eighth (second from the bottom, that is), which seems strange, since we know that Michael is an archangel and people often assume that Michael is the top-ranking angel. Pseudo-Dionysius wrote that archangels are the messengers bearing divine decrees.

606. Thomas Aquinas (c. 1225–1274)

What would you think of an intellectual who had written volume after huge volume of theology—then claimed at the end of his life that it was all useless and should be burned? Thomas Aquinas, the most famous theologian of the Middle Ages, did just that. But his colleagues valued his theology more than he did and preserved it, and for centuries he was *the* theologian of the Roman Catholic Church. His *Summa Theologica*, even though unfinished, was considered the most comprehensive work of Catholic theology, and in it he touched on every subject imaginable—including, naturally, angels, demons, and the afterlife.

Thomas affirmed the belief that each believer has a guardian angel assigned to him. Thomas must have been fascinated by the angels, for he wrote almost a hundred pages on them—their hierarchy, habits, knowledge, movements, and so on. Angels, he said, are the highest grade of creation, and they are incorruptible and immortal. He believed that the stars and planets are moved and guided by them. In his belief in angels he was deeply influenced by the writings of Pseudo-Dionysius (see 598). Catholic tradition refers to Thomas as the "Angelic Doctor," with *Doctor* meaning "Teacher."

He did not neglect demons, either. Demons, he said, are capable of all kinds of harm, even causing impotence in men. They may appear audibly or visibly to men, or they can speak through the human imagination. Thomas took witchcraft seriously (as did most people of the Middle Ages) and believed that women and men who consorted with demons could do all kinds of harm.

Curiously, for someone who opposed the occult and satanism, Thomas did believe in astrology—at least, he believed that some people might allow themselves to be influenced by the movements of the stars and planets, though it was not inevitable.

Hell, Thomas said, was a real material place, located somewhere in the lowest part of the earth. To those who thought that perhaps everyone might find salvation, Thomas gave a definite no.

But he also had much to say about heaven. The chief happiness of the saved person will consist in seeing God. The human soul, restless on earth, finds rest when it rejoins its Source.

THINKERS: REFORMATION TO TODAY

607. Martin Luther (1483–1546)

Luther's claim to fame is that he launched the Protestant Reformation. That whole movement was a "back to the

Bible" movement, because Luther and other Protestants believed the Catholic church had strayed a long way from the Christianity taught in the Bible. Luther, a German, was excommunicated from the Roman Catholic Church, and there were threats on his life, but he pursued his vision of Christian beliefs and morals based on the Bible. In his busy life he managed to write dozens of theological works and commentaries on much of the Bible.

Just how did Luther differ from the Catholic church in regard to angels, demons, and the afterlife? Regarding angels and demons, he hardly differed at all. He definitely believed in Satan. While hiding out in Wartburg Castle, he claimed to have been afflicted by Satan, so much so that he threw a pot of ink at him. (The castle still preserves the ink stain on the wall.) Luther claimed that the devil's main trait was pride. He advised Christians to "laugh that proud spirit to scorn, for he cannot endure to be mocked."

In regard to the afterlife, Luther had serious differences with the Catholic church. When he posted his Ninety-Five Theses in 1517 (the act that began the Reformation), one of his main points was the church's sale of indulgences. Luther disagreed with the whole doctrine of purgatory (which underlay the trade in indulgences). Throwing out purgatory, he also threw out the role of the Virgin Mary as intercessor for people in purgatory. With no purgatory, praying for the dead was useless also. Luther cast aside years and years of medieval sludge and went back to the Bible (and a few key theologians, such as Augustine) for his beliefs.

608. John Calvin (1509–1564)

Raised as a Catholic, Calvin got caught up in the Protestant Reformation and became one of its leaders, and probably its most noted theologian. Like all Reformation leaders, he emphasized the necessity of each Christian (not just ministers) to know and follow the Bible in daily life. He believed that Christian doctrine should be based strictly on the Bible. The Catholic church had, he thought, neglected the Bible and placed too much reliance on ritual and meaningless theological debates. He produced a theological classic, *The Institutes of the Christian Religion*, which he claimed was based solely on the Bible.

Like Martin Luther, Calvin threw out the doctrine of purgatory and all the abuses that went with it. Also like Luther, Calvin believed strongly in predestination: God has chosen some people from the beginning of time to be saved. (Why this belief has come to be known as "Calvinism" when Luther and other leaders held the same views, has always been a mystery.) Calvin, Luther, and several other Protestant leaders did believe there might be a Limbo for unbaptized infants.

Calvin believed in demons and resisted any rationalizing of them (that is, believing that demons are not real but merely an explanation for inner disturbances).

609. Francis de Sales (1567–1622)

Will people in heaven spend eternity in nothing but worship, or is there more to it? Francis, an Italian bishop, liked to preach on heaven, and he was certain that there was more to do than worship. The saints will meet Jesus Himself, and He will explain to each the meaning of suffering (His own and theirs) on earth. They will meet the great saints and martyrs, the angels, and the Virgin Mary. Friendships and family relations that were happy on earth will continue and grow richer. His focus on the human side of heaven made it sound quite appealing.

610. *A History of Angels*

Henry Lawrence (1600–1664) was a good friend of poet John Milton (see 721) and a noted Puritan author and political leader. His *History of Angels* states that "our communion is very great with the angels, good and bad." Both angels and demons may "write on our fancies" and "represent objects to our understandings and our wills which often take and move us." In order to give the good angels material to work with, we should stock our minds with good images. Lawrence, like many Christians, believed that good ideas don't necessarily just "pop into our heads," but may be there because of the influence of angels, just as bad ideas may result from the sinister power of the devils.

611. *De Doctrina Christiana*

The poet John Milton (see 721) was well versed in the Bible and Christian theology, and he wrote a summary of

Christian beliefs titled *De Doctrina Christiana*. In it Milton has much to say about angels, demons, heaven, and hell (things that he said much more poetically in his *Paradise Lost*). Like many Christians in centuries past, Milton firmly believed that whenever Christians gathered together, angels were also present, so that every Christian worship service has an "unseen congregation," the angels.

612. Richard Baxter (1615–1691)

Baxter was a noted Puritan preacher in England. In the religious wars of the 1600s he was sometimes on the winning side, sometimes not, and he spent some time in prison, as many Puritans did. Having reason to look for happiness in the next world, Baxter wrote a classic about heaven, *The Saints' Everlasting Rest*. While it is seldom read today, it deserves more attention, with its touching descriptions of heaven and even a manual on "heavenly meditation." It captures the Christian idea that earth is a prelude to the real life in heaven.

613. John Locke (1632–1704)

In the Age of Reason, the English philosopher John Locke never denied any of the beliefs of Christianity, but he emphasized that belief and morals are based as much on logic as on the Bible. Put another way, Christianity "makes sense"—in fact, Christian behavior is a series of "deals" we make. So we reject the short-term pleasures of vice and immorality and invest in the long-term pleasure of eternity. Unlike some people of his skeptical age, Locke said heaven and hell are real and should be taught, for otherwise people have no long-term reason to behave well. But if they believe in heaven and hell, sensible men will choose heaven, even if it means forgoing a few earthly pleasures.

614. Jonathan Edwards (1703–1758)

Edwards was the greatest theologian in colonial America, and a noted preacher in the revival movement known as the Great Awakening. Edwards wrote many volumes of theology, but is probably best known for one vivid "hell-fire sermon," "Sinners in the Hands of an Angry God." He did not base his sermon on any of the Bible's references to hell, but on a short passage in Deuteronomy 32:35: "Their foot shall slide in due time: for the day of their calamity is at hand" (KJV). Considering what an eloquent and sensitive writer Edwards was, and considering how often he spoke of the joy of heaven, it is unfortunate and unfair that he is typecast as a "hellfire preacher" because of this one sermon. For what it's worth, the sermon was highly effective: The congregation reacted with obvious emotion, including such signs as writhing, moaning, and trembling.

615. John Wesley (1703–1791)

He and his brother Charles founded the worldwide movement known as Methodism, and while he won the hearts of many, John Wesley faced serious persecution while doing the Lord's work. On his evangelistic travels he survived violence and numerous accidents, and he never hesitated to attribute his well-being to guardian angels. Wesley also had a firm belief in Satan, whom he believed incited the crowds of hooligans who tried to do him physical harm or shout him down while he preached. Like many persecuted Christians through the ages, Wesley had reason to believe in God's protective angels *and* in the wiles of Satan.

616. Søren Kierkegaard (1813-1855)

The Danish philosopher Kierkegaard was painfully aware of one thing: The state church of Denmark did not even remotely resemble the church of the New Testament. In many of his writings he attacked the emotionless, complacent, "respectable" religion that some people foolishly thought was Christianity. He noted that the urgency of the New Testament preaching was totally absent, and his fellow Danes seemed to assume that everyone would be saved. Kierkegaard took the New Testament seriously and wrote that "Christ, who is certainly best informed, said that only a few will be saved."

617. Pope Leo XIII (1810–1903)

The Catholic church, like the Protestant churches, faced the challenge of liberalism beginning in the 1800s. Pope Leo XIII, hoping to stem the liberal tide, issued a decree in 1879, affirming that hell is eternal, the devil is real, and Catholics should accept these beliefs. This was directed more at intellectuals than at the average Catholic, who most likely did believe in hell and Satan.

618. General William Booth (1829–1912)

Booth was the founder and first "general" of the Salvation Army, which reached out to the urban poor in England and later spread to America. The Army in its early days emphasized social service *and* evangelism, and the Army had its share of tough but compassionate evangelists who preached the love of God *and* the horrible reality of hell. Booth stated that people were more likely to convert if they heard hell preached: "Nothing moves like the terrifying. They must have hellfire flashed before their faces or they will not move." (A tidbit: American poet Vachel Lindsay wrote a stirring dramatic poem titled "General William Booth Enters into Heaven.")

619. D. L. Moody (1837–1899)

Moody is one of the most important and most fascinating figures in America's religious history. A successful businessman in Chicago, he was never ordained to the ministry but became one of the best-known evangelists on both sides of the Atlantic. Moody was conservative and definitely believed in the reality of heaven and hell. He even explained his mission by saying that God had given him a lifeboat and said, "Moody, save all you can." Yet Moody preferred to accentuate the positive (heaven, that is), so he was hardly the stereotypical hellfire preacher. On one occasion he noted that "terror has never won a man yet." Emphasizing the good news rather than the bad news, Moody published *Heaven: Where It Is, Its Inhabitants, and How to Get There.* Like his sermons, it is a straightforward, plain-language piece of work, full of comfort.

620. Karl Barth (1886–1968)

One of the best-known theologians of the twentieth century, Barth wrote a huge multivolume theology titled *Church Dogmatics.* Yet Barth, in the tradition of John Calvin (see 608), claimed that Christian belief should be based on the Bible and kept as simple as possible. Regarding angels, Barth believed that the basic Protestant attitude was right: Stick with the Bible, and ignore all those long medieval writings about the angels, for they are mostly just speculation. Barth wrote, "Holy Scripture gives us quite enough to think about angels." Barth departed from the Bible in one significant area: He toyed with universalism, the belief that everyone will eventually be saved.

621. Fulton J. Sheen (1895–1979)

For years this Catholic bishop was a fixture of television with his *Life Is Worth Living* series in the 1950s and 1960s. In this popular program the highly intellectual scholar managed to talk theology so that everyone could understand. Sheen spoke often about heaven, speaking of it in traditional Catholic terms as an eternal enjoyment of the Divine Presence.

622. Billy Graham (b. 1918)

America's great evangelist is also a noted author, writing with the same appealing directness and warmth he uses in his preaching. In 1975 his *Angels: God's Secret Agents* became a best-seller and was issued in a new edition in 1994. It is still one of the best books on the subject of angels and on the activity of Satan and his demons (who are fallen angels) as well. In his book Graham declared that he is an optimist, not a pessimist, because "I've read the last page of the Bible" with its vision of heaven.

623. Hal Lindsey

In 1972, the year before the movie *The Exorcist* had the whole country talking about demons, Lindsey published a best-seller, *Satan Is Alive and Well and Living on Planet Earth*. While he has drawn some snickers for miscalculating the date of the end times, Lindsey did the Christian world a service with this book, nudging Christians to look at a topic (Satan and demons) that had been too long ignored. Lindsey looked at the frightening rise of satanism, the occult, and the vast movement that was soon to be called the New Age.

624. Peter Kreeft

By a curious coincidence, John F. Kennedy, C. S. Lewis, and Aldous Huxley all died on the same day. Professor Peter Kreeft used this fact as the basis of his *Between Heaven and Hell,* subtitled "Dialogue Somewhere Beyond Death." Lewis the Christian, Kennedy the humanist, and Huxley the pantheist engage in an imaginary dialogue on the afterlife, miracles, the nature of God, and such. Kreeft is clearly on the side of Lewis and Christianity.

12

Church Life: Music, Worship, and More

625. the Annunciation

The word simply means "announcing." It refers to the angel Gabriel's visit to the Virgin Mary to tell her she was to bear the child Jesus. It was a popular subject with artists, and art museums are filled with *Annunciation* paintings. The Catholic and Orthodox churches celebrate the Feast of the Annunciation on March 25 (exactly nine months before Christmas, if you see the connection).

626. the Visitation

Two amazing pregnancies are recorded in Luke 1: the Virgin Mary and her previously barren relative, the elderly Elizabeth, wife of the priest Zechariah. Elizabeth gave birth to John the Baptist, and Mary gave birth to Jesus. Both the pregnancies and births were foretold by the angel Gabriel. The Catholic church celebrates the visit of Mary to Elizabeth as the Feast of the Visitation on July 2.

627. Lent

Some churches observe the forty days before Easter as Lent, a time of soul-searching and penitence. The practice dates from around A.D. 300 and was based on Jesus' forty days of fasting during the time He was tempted by Satan (Matt. 4:2; Luke 4:2). In earlier times, Christians did fast during Lent, but later the idea developed of some alternative form of self-denial—"giving up something for Lent," as many people phrase it.

628. angel feast days

The Catholic and Eastern Orthodox churches have numerous feast days to celebrate the various saints whom the churches honor. (The one the secular world is most familiar with is March 17, Saint Patrick's Day.) The Catholic church celebrates September 29 as the Feast of Michael, Gabriel, and Raphael, the three archangels. In times past this was a major church holiday and was generally called Michaelmas. The Orthodox churches celebrate November 8 as the Feast of Michael the Archangel and the Angelic Hosts.

629. All Saints' Day

Originally, *Halloween* meant "eve of All Hallows," and All Hallows' Day was another name for All Saints' Day, November 1. While the various saints recognized by the Catholic church all have separate feast days (for example, Saint Patrick is commemorated on March 17), November 1 is a kind of "group celebration," honoring all the saints of the church, those who are in heaven.

630. All Souls' Day

A saint, in official Catholic usage, is someone whom the church acknowledges as being in heaven. Presumably all Christians will be there eventually, and those who are not there (yet) are in purgatory, being prepared for heaven. All Souls' Day, celebrated every November 2, is the day of commemorating the dead who died in the faith. You might say it is a celebration of all Christians, those already in heaven and those on their way.

631. Advent

Many churches refer to the weeks before Christmas as Advent, a time of spiritual preparation for the coming of Christ at Christmas. (The "seasonal color" used in some churches during Advent is purple, traditionally the color of repentance.) Advent had another significance: not only preparing for Christ's first coming (as a baby in Bethlehem) but also for His second coming in glory at the end of time. Some churches today still emphasize spiritually preparing oneself during Advent for the Second Coming.

632. the Assumption of Mary

Catholics believe that Jesus' mother was taken directly to heaven at the end of her earthly life. A legion of angels transported her to paradise, and every year the Feast of the Assumption is celebrated on August 15. Many great artists have painted the Assumption. The Bible says nothing whatsoever about Mary's death or the Assumption, but many centuries of devotion to Mary led Catholics to believe that a woman they thought to be sinless, would not die as an ordinary human.

WORSHIP LIFE

633. *gloria in excelsis Deo*

This Latin phrase means "glory to God in the highest." It was part of the angels' song to the shepherds as they announced the birth of Jesus (Luke 2:14): "Glory to God in the highest, and on earth peace, good will toward men!" The "gloria" has been set to music hundreds of times, notably as the chorus of the Christmas song "Angels We Have Heard on High."

634. *Ave Maria*

It is Latin for "Hail, Mary," and is a common Catholic prayer to her. It is based on the words of the angel Gabriel in Luke 1:28 "Hail, thou that art highly favoured, the Lord is with thee"(KJV) and the words of Mary's relative Elizabeth in Luke 1:42: "Blessed art thou among women, and blessed is the fruit of thy womb" (KJV). The popularity of Mary as an object of Catholic devotion is one of the reasons that the angel Gabriel became popular as well.

The *Ave Maria* has been set to music countless times and is extremely popular at weddings. Franz Schubert's version may be the most loved.

635. heavenly smells

In a world a lot less sanitized than ours, anything fragrant was highly valued. Small wonder that most world religions, including ancient Israel's, used incense in worship. Israel's law had guidelines for making the special incense used in worship (Ex. 30:34–38). Israel's high priest burned incense daily in the tabernacle. It was burned on an altar of pure gold.

Incense is not mentioned much in the New Testament, although one of the gifts of the Magi to the baby Jesus was a form of incense (Matt. 2:11). The book of Revelation speaks of incense in heaven, using it as a symbol: The elders in heaven hold "golden bowls full of incense, which are the prayers of the saints" (5:8). Since the smoke of incense drifts heavenward, it is easy to see how it symbolizes prayer. Some churches still use incense in worship.

636. Holy, Holy, Holy

A much-loved Christian hymn has this title (see 666), and the Catholic mass uses it. In the Bible this phrase is found in Isaiah's vision in the temple, where he sees seraphs (angels) calling to one another: "Holy, holy, holy is the LORD of hosts; the whole earth is full of His glory!" (Isa. 6:3). A similar vision is found in Revelation 4:8: "Holy, holy, holy, Lord God Almighty, who was and is and is to come!"

637. the sign of the cross

The familiar gesture used by Catholics, the Orthodox, and some Protestants was more than mere ritual in times past. In a more superstitious age, believers thought that the sign of the cross had real power over demons. Little wonder that it made its way into the official rituals for exorcism.

638. the Angelus

This is the Roman Catholic prayer for heavenly protection, a prayer beginning "Angel of the Lord who announced to Mary . . ." In times past this was a sort of morning devotional, later done at evening, with the time of the prayer being announced by ringing the church bell. You may have seen the famous painting by Millet, *The Angelus*, showing a farm couple pausing for prayer in the field.

639. nude baptism?

In the earlier centuries of Christianity, baptized persons were sometimes required to be nude. Odd, you say? Perhaps. But the nudity served a purpose. It reminded the congregation—and the person being baptized—that all persons are naked before God, whether a king or a beggar. But there was another motive for nude baptisms. Early Christians took demons seriously, and some people believed that demons were skillful at hiding. They could even hide in a fold of clothing. Since driving away demons was a part of most baptismal services, it was thought to be a good idea to have the person naked, just in case a demon might hide itself in the garments.

THE CREEDS

640. Jesus' descent into hell

The Apostles' Creed, a classic summary of Christian belief, states that between Jesus' burial and resurrection "He descended into hell." This puzzles many people—why would the sinless Jesus be in hell, even if it was only temporary? The problem is one of translation: The Creed, written in Greek, says Christ descended into *Hades*, the Greek word for the region of the dead, not a place of eternal punishment. Paul, in Ephesians 4:9, said that before He ascended into heaven, Christ "also first descended into the lower parts of the earth." So, "descended into hell" is more accurately translated "descended into Hades" or "descended into the realm of death." Many churches solve the difficulty by simply omitting "descended into hell" from the Creed. But "descended into the realm of death" is important, reminding us that Christ did, indeed, die a normal human death before God raised Him.

641. the universal creeds

People like creeds for their nice, neat summaries of beliefs. Happily, most of the universally used creeds of the church have been brief. Almost all of them refer to belief in an afterlife, though what they say is minimal.

Consider the old favorite known as the Apostles' Creed (even though it dates from a time much later than Jesus' first apostles). It includes an affirmation that the risen Jesus "shall come to judge the quick and the dead," and ends with a statement of belief in "the communion of saints, the forgiveness of sins, the resurrection of the body, and the life everlasting." Nothing here about hell (although Jesus' judgment implies it), and no details about heaven or hell.

The longer (but still brief) Nicene Creed dates from the 300s. It speaks of Jesus who "shall come again with glory, to judge both the quick and the dead; whose kingdom shall have no end." It ends with "I look for the resurrection of the dead, and the life of the world to come."

Now consider the much longer, much more detailed statement known as the Athanasian Creed. According to it, at Jesus' second coming "all men shall rise again with their bodies and shall give account for their own works. And they that have done good shall go into life everlasting, and they that have done evil into everlasting fire. This is the catholic [that is, universal] faith, which except a man believe faithfully, he cannot be saved." This is certainly more direct, and more detailed, than the other two creeds, isn't it? We can assume in our tolerant, "nonjudgmental" world that such a creed has fallen out of use for the most obvious reason: It mentions hell.

642. the *Book of Concord*

Published in 1580, this was and is a guide to the basic beliefs of the Lutheran churches. Martin Luther, like the other Protestant leaders, wanted to sweep from the church many of the superstitions it had accumulated over the centuries. This included praying to saints and angels, which was and still is practiced by many Catholics. The Book of Concord holds the basic position of most Protestants: Angels guide and protect us, but we are not to pray to them or hold services in their honor, or believe that angels have particular functions in our daily lives. We are to worship God only and pray only to Him.

643. *The Churching of America*

In 1992 Roger Finke and Rodney Stark published *The Churching of America, 1776-1990: Winners and Losers in Our Religious Economy.* The book looks at a phenomenon that has existed for years: Liberal churches are losing members, while conservative churches are growing. Why? The authors did extensive research to find out. One authority they quote is Methodist bishop Richard B. Wilke, who observed that "the churches that are drawing people to them believe in sin, hell, and death. Jesus, who knew what he was talking about, explained them, experienced them, and conquered them. If there is no sin, we do not need a Savior. If we do not need a Savior, we do not need preachers." In other words, hell may be a touchy subject, but the simple fact is that churches that ignore it tend to lose members, not gain them. Wilke also asked another painful question: "When hell is gone, can heaven's departure be far behind?"

BURIAL AND ETERNAL HOPE

644. Handel's *Messiah*

Though it's most often performed around Christmas, George Frideric Handel's 1742 oratorio is more about resurrection and eternal life than about Jesus' birth. It does contain a "Christmas section," which includes the angels' song ("Glory to God in the Highest"). But the entire third section of *Messiah* is a collection of Bible verses (most of them covered elsewhere in this book) dealing with Jesus' triumph over death and the glorious resurrection of the righteous.

645. "ashes to ashes"

The familiar words of a burial service are from the Episcopalians' *Book of Common Prayer*: "earth to earth, ashes to ashes, dust to dust, in sure and certain hope of the resurrection to eternal life, through our Lord Jesus Christ." The words are not taken precisely from the Bible, but they reflect such passages as Genesis 18:27 and Job 30:19.

646. cemetery

We forget that before this word meant "graveyard," it referred to a "sleeping place," which is what the Latin *cemeterium* means. The word was widely used by the early Christians because they saw death as temporary, only a "sleep" from which the faithful would awaken when Christ returned and took them home to heaven. So a cemetery was only "temporary lodging," heaven being the permanent home.

647. joyous funerals?

Hard as it is to believe, burial services among the early Christians were occasions of joy, not mourning. While the deceased person's family and friends regretted his parting, they were so convinced of his entering a better life that the usual color for Christian funerals was white, not black. The Christian's death day was seen as a birthday into eternity. By about the eighth century a change had come about, with funerals being sad and solemn occasions again.

648. temple of the Holy Spirit

Paul, in 1 Corinthians 6:19, reminded Christians to treat their bodies well (and morally), for the believer's body is the "temple of the Holy Spirit." He and the other New Testament authors were certain that man is raised, body and soul, at the Last Judgment, even though we will have new "spiritual bodies" then. Because the body is important, not just something to be discarded at death, Christians have for centuries insisted on burial instead of cremation. This has changed in recent years (along with a general trend in society toward more cremations).

649. Holy Communion

People don't give much thought to what the "communion" part of Holy Communion means. From the very beginning it was a way for Christians to share a symbolic meal in genuine fellowship, not only with one another, but with the departed brothers and sisters. Just as the creeds referred to the "communion of saints," so the Communion service was a reminder that living Christians and dead Christians were bound together, some on earth, some already in heaven. To honor those who died as martyrs for the faith, Communion services were sometimes held at their tombs.

650. prayers for the dead

Because Catholics believe in purgatory (see 34), they believe in praying for souls there, since these are the souls of Christians who are being "purged" of their sins and made ready for heaven. Just as prayers for the living can benefit the living, so prayers for the dead in purgatory can benefit them, shortening their time there or lightening their burden. Masses for the dead are also celebrated.

MICHAEL AND THE CHURCHES

651. Prince of the Heavenly Hosts

This is the name (one of many, actually) that the Catholic church uses to refer to the archangel Michael. It is based on the Bible, which refers to him as leader of the heavenly armies of angels. This exalted figure is a popular figure of Catholic devotion, which is why so many cathedrals and smaller churches are dedicated to him. One of these is the magnificent Mont-Saint-Michel on the coast of Brittany, France, one of the most stunning Gothic churches in the world. The grand church was built on a site where the angel had supposedly appeared.

652. Michael and battle

As the leader of heaven's armies of angels, Michael the archangel is a favorite of soldiers. There is an old prayer to Saint Michael, begging his protection for Christians who are involved in battle.

653. "the Church Militant"

Jesus taught peace and forgiveness of enemies—but also declared open war on Satan and his demons. The term "the Church Militant" refers to the church in its battle against evil. The archangel Michael, because he is pictured as leader of heaven's armies in the book of Revelation, is often a symbol of the Church Militant.

A HANDFUL OF HYMNS

654. "herald angels" or "welkin"?

Charles Wesley (1703–1791) was one of the world's great hymn writers. The brother of the more famous John Wesley, founder of Methodism, Charles gave the Methodist movement (and the world) hundreds of spiritual songs based on the Bible and rich in emotion. Perhaps Charles Wesley's most famous composition is the much-loved Christmas song "Hark! the Herald Angels Sing"—which isn't the way Charles originally wrote it. The first version of the song's first lines went "Hark, how all the welkin rings / Glory to the King of Kings." So just what is a "welkin"? It's an old English word meaning "skies" or "the heavens." Evangelist George Whitefield, a friend of the Wesleys, altered the lines to the familiar form: "Hark! the herald angels sing, / Glory to the newborn King." Whitefield's revision has had a lot of staying power.

655. "Angels from the Realms of Glory"

What is Christmas without angels, and what are Christmas carols without references to angels? James Montgomery (1771–1854), an evangelical newspaper editor in England, penned more than four hundred hymns, some of which have become classics. One of these is the familiar "Angels from the Realms of Glory." Montgomery first published it in his own newspaper in 1816, giving it the title "Nativity." In the first lines of the song the author refers to the angels as "ye who sang creation's story," reflecting the ancient belief that angels were present (and full of praise) when God created the universe.

656. angels in Latin, French, and English

One of the most familiar of Christmas songs is "Angels We Have Heard on High," with its refrain in Latin: *Gloria in excelsis Deo*—the angels' words to the shepherds, "Glory to God in the highest." The song "Les Anges

Dans Nos Campagnes," first appeared in a French song-book around 1855, and by 1862 it appeared in English in an American hymnal, with the chorus still in Latin.

657. Noel and angels

Noel is the French word for Christmas, and it appears in many English hymns. Probably the best known is the anonymous carol "The First Noel," which "the angel did say" to "certain poor shepherds."

658. angels bending with harps

The accounts in the Gospels of Jesus' birth mention angels, though they do not mention angelic musical instruments. But imagination has a field day with angels, as in the Christmas carol "It Came upon the Midnight Clear," which speaks of "angels bending near the earth / To touch their harps of gold." One of the oddities of this hymn is that its author was not, strictly speaking, a Christian. Edmund H. Sears (1810–1876) was a Unitarian minister in Massachusetts, and as a Unitarian he did not believe that Jesus was the Son of God. So although his popular song speaks of angels and describes God as "heaven's all-gracious King," and though it is obviously concerned with the birth of Jesus, it never speaks of Jesus as God's Son, or as the Christ or Messiah.

659. "A Mighty Fortress Is Our God"

Martin Luther (see 607) believed in the reality of Satan and demons. Nowhere is this seen more clearly than in his great hymn "A Mighty Fortress Is Our God." Consider the words from the hymn's first stanza: "For still our ancient foe [Satan, that is] / Doth seek to work us woe— / His craft and pow'r are great, /And, armed with cruel hate, / On earth is not His equal." And consider a later stanza: "And though this world, with devils filled, / Should threaten to undo us . . . The prince of darkness grim, / We tremble not for him— / His rage we can endure, / For lo! his doom is sure." As a man who felt he had literally confronted Satan himself, Luther could not help but pour his experience into poetic song.

660. Isaac Watts (1674–1748)

In a time when Christian hymns were limited to the Psalms, Watts injected some new life. He versified psalms himself, but also wrote hundreds of hymns, many of them still in use throughout the world. Among his many classics are several hymns on heaven, such as this one: "There is a land of pure delight / Where the saints immortal reign; / Infinite day holds back the night / Where pleasure replaces pain."

661. "Amazing Grace"

A former slave trader, John Newton became a pastor and close friend of poet William Cowper. They both wrote excellent hymns, and Newton wrote one of the church's favorites, "Amazing Grace." Newton included heaven in the hymn, of course: "When we've been there ten thousand years, / Bright shining as the sun, / We've no less days to sing God's praise / Than when we'd first begun."

662. "On Jordan's Stormy Banks I Stand"

"Jordan" and "Canaan" are more than just place-names in a Bible atlas. They are, in Christian thought, names for "dying" and "heaven." (See 951 and 952.) Samuel Stennett combined the two nicely in his 1787 hymn. Consider its first verse: "On Jordan's stormy banks I stand, / And cast a wishful eye / To Canaan's fair and happy land / Where my possessions lie. / O the transporting rapturous scene / That rises to my sight! / Sweet fields arrayed in living green / And rivers of delight."

663. "When We All Get to Heaven"

Hymns are usually cataloged by their first lines, but here is one that is best known by its famous chorus. Eliza Hewitt's hymn, written in 1898, begins "Sing the wondrous love of Jesus," but the chorus is much better known: "When we all get to heaven / What a day of rejoicing that will be! / When we all see Jesus, / We'll sing and shout the victory!" It was a favorite hymn of tent revivals.

664. "Lo! He Comes, with Clouds Descending"

Charles Wesley, brother of Methodism's founder, John Wesley, wrote so many hymns that he covered practically every Christian doctrine. Naturally he did not neglect Jesus' second coming. This is the theme here: "Lo! He comes, with clouds descending, / Once for favored sinners slain; / Thousand, thousand saints attending / Swell the triumph of His train; / Hallelujah! Hallelujah! Hallelujah! / God appears on earth to reign." The original Methodists, as is true of most vibrant Christian groups, had a serious and life-changing interest in heaven.

665. "Ye Watchers and Ye Holy Ones"

This hymn, with words by J. A. L. Riley, is a song of praise to God, and one of the few hymns in existence that use most of the Bible names of the orders of angels. Consider the first verse: "Ye watchers and ye holy ones, / Bright seraphs, cherubim, and thrones . . . / Cry out, dominions, princedoms, powers, / Virtues, archangels, angels' choirs." In one stanza of the hymn, Riley enlisted all the angels of heaven in a vigorous "Alleluia!" By the way, if you're unfamiliar with the "watchers" and "holy ones," see 90.

Of the 121 words in this hymn's text, 30 are Hebrew, so it is a very "biblical" hymn.

666. "Holy, Holy, Holy"

This much-loved hymn by Reginald Heber takes its title from the song of the seraphim in Isaiah 6. Appropriately, in one stanza of the hymn Heber mentions "cherubim and seraphim" falling down before the throne of God. Written in 1827, this was reputed to be the favorite hymn of the great English poet Tennyson.

667. "Michael, Row the Boat Ashore"

This old black spiritual is addressed to the angel Michael. According to tradition (though not the Bible itself), the angel Michael is the guide of departed souls to heaven. Thus in the song, Michael guides the person's soul across the river Jordan (representing death) to the shore (heaven). One verse of the song is "Jordan's river is chilly and wide, / Milk and honey on the other side." Of course, this song sung by slaves might have had another meaning: a plea to be taken across the river (the Ohio, that is) into the nonslaveholding states.

668. "Swing Low, Sweet Chariot"

American slaves had a less-than-perfect life in this world, so naturally many of them sought consolation in religion. Small wonder, then, that many of the best-known spiritual songs came anonymously from the slaves. One of the most popular was and is "Swing Low, Sweet Chariot," clearly based on the story of the prophet Elijah, who did not die but was taken to heaven in a fiery chariot (2 Kings 2:11). Like many black spirituals, this one may have had a double meaning: The slave may have been yearning to be taken to heaven, but also might have been yearning to escape into the parts of the United States where slavery was illegal—not necessarily via fiery chariot but by regular chariot, or whatever form of transportation would get him there.

669. "Jerusalem the Golden"

One of the oldest and best-loved hymns about heaven is "Jerusalem the Golden," with its original words (in Latin) written by the great medieval saint Bernard of Cluny. Bernard wanted to contrast the corruption of medieval society with the glories of heaven. The subject so moved him that his poem ran to 2,966 lines. Happily, the whole poem does not appear in any modern hymnals.

The "Jerusalem" of the hymn is not the city in Israel, of course, but the "New Jerusalem" of the book of Revelation, heaven. In the translation by John Mason

Neale, the last stanza runs as follows: "O sweet and blessed country, / The home of God's elect! / O sweet and blessed country / That eager hearts expect! / Jesus, in mercy bring us / To that dear land of rest."

670. "Ten Thousand Times Ten Thousand"

The tiny epistle of Jude, found just before the book of Revelation, was the inspiration for this wonderful hymn by Henry Alford. "Behold, the Lord cometh with ten thousands of his saints" (Jude 14 KJV). The triumphant hymn tells of "Ten thousand times ten thousand / In sparkling raiment bright, / The armies of the ransomed saints / Throng up the steeps of light; / 'Tis finished, all is finished, / Their fight with death and sin; / Fling open wide the golden gates, / And let the victors in." Alford wrote the hymn in 1866, and it was sung at his funeral in 1871.

671. "I'm Just a Poor Wayfaring Stranger"

This American folk hymn from the 1800s has a haunting melody to match its haunting words: "I'm just a poor wayfaring stranger, / A-traveling through this world of woe; / But there's no sickness, no toil or danger / In that bright world to which I go." The song echoes the theme, found throughout the New Testament, that we are strangers and pilgrims in this world, and that our true home is in heaven.

13

Art and Artists: Picturing the Unseen

THE "LOOK"

672. halo

Why do works of art often depict saints and angels with rings of light around their heads? A halo (also called a nimbus) is an old symbol of divinity, glory, or holiness. The halo is a way of saying, "This person [or being] is special in a sacred way." Halos are never mentioned in the Bible, however.

673. art's earliest angels

Not much art exists from the earliest days of Christianity. This is not surprising, since most Christians expected the world to end soon, with Christ coming to take His people home to heaven. With such expectations, why bother with painting and sculpting? But in time (for people are creative and decorative by nature), Christian art began to emerge. The earliest paintings (such as those in the catacombs under Rome) are illustrations of Bible stories, some of which include angels. However, these generally don't show angels with wings, and if you were not familiar with the particular Bible story being illustrated, you might not know the figures were angels. It took some time before the tradition of angels with wings took hold. For what it's worth, Jesus in some of the early pictures did not look like the bearded Jesus we know so well. He was often shown clean-shaven.

674. Eros and erotes

Eros was the ancient Greek god of love, corresponding to the Roman god Cupid. Often (though not always) he was depicted as a young man with wings. Besides his role as love god, Eros was also believed to play a role in guiding a person's soul to the afterlife. So it was common for a stone tomb to have a carving of the winged Eros. Sometimes there were two on a tomb (*erotes*, in the plural). The ancient practice no doubt had some influence on the very old Christian custom of having a statue of a winged angel on a tomb.

675. Nike with wings

Most people are familiar with the magnificent (although headless) statue called *Winged Victory*. It is now in the famous Louvre museum in Paris, and was probably carved around 190 B.C. The statue is a woman's body in flowing robes, with widespread wings instead of arms. It presents Nike, the Greek goddess of victory, whom the Romans called Victoria. Just as the Greeks sometimes carved winged images of Eros on tombstones, so the Romans had winged statues of Victoria on tombs. For the Romans in the early church, it was appropriate to have a Victoria statue on the tomb, because the statue represented the final victory (over death, that is).

676. why so smooth-faced?

Angels are usually male, but with a definite genderless look and always clean-shaven. Why? Hard to say. Since the important men of the Old and New Testaments were bearded (as Jewish men always were in those times), perhaps the beardless look was a way of looking otherworldly. Before wings became a standard feature in pictures of angels, the beardless look was a visual clue that the figure was an angel, not a man.

677. "Fear not!"

Angels in artwork often appear sweet-faced and mild, but more than once in the Bible their appearance is so startling that they have to say "Fear not!" to the humans they approach (Gen. 21:17; Judg. 6:23; Dan. 10:12; Matt. 28:3–5; Luke 1:13; 2:10).

678. why white?

Angels are most often depicted wearing white. Why so? The Bible gives good reason for it, particularly in the New Testament, which many times states that the angels were in white apparel. White, of course, symbolizes purity, innocence, and holiness. Presumably the angels' garments are not only white but spotless, with no earthly stain on them. You might say that white is the color of heaven.

679. the face of an angel

Stephen is an appealing character in the book of Acts, an eloquent speaker and the first Christian to die for his faith. Dragged before the Jewish council and charged with blasphemy, he was at no loss for words or nerve. "All who sat in the council, looking steadfastly at him, saw his face as the face of an angel" (Acts 6:15). This doesn't mean "pretty," of course. It also doesn't mean that mild, milk-soppish look on the faces of angels in so many works of art. This hostile council, if indeed they thought Stephen had the face of an angel, must have perceived something else: a kind of inspired, "heavenly" look that artists have never adequately captured on canvas (perhaps because artists have never seen an angel).

680. lilies

We associate lilies with Easter. In Christian art they usually symbolize purity and innocence. Because the Catholic church taught that the Virgin Mary remained a virgin throughout her life, the lily is one of her symbols. By association with Mary, the angel Gabriel is also shown in art with lilies, and lilies are found in many pictures of the angels.

681. the peach

For some reason, many ancient cultures saw the peach as a symbol of immortality. It made its way as a symbol into the art of Europe, where the Virgin Mary is often depicted beneath a peach tree or holding the fruit in her hand.

682. the pearl

Pearly gates (see 282) are a feature of heaven, based on Revelation 21. The pearl has also been a symbol of the redeemed sinner. A real pearl results from a grain of sand inside an oyster causing irritation and being enveloped in something beautiful. So Christians used the pearl as a symbol of the sinful soul being wrapped up in God's grace, a thing of beauty fit to be in heaven.

683. flaming swords

Genesis 3:24 speaks of the angels and the flaming sword that barred man's access to Eden. Based on this, many angels are shown with flaming swords.

684. a staff

In the earliest Christian art, angels had no wings, nor any part of the "look" we associate with angels. But in pictures they might be shown carrying a staff, the traditional symbol of a herald bearing a message (and appropriate, since *angelos* means "messenger").

685. open books

In some works of art, angels are holding open books. Are angels avid readers? Of course not. The open book symbolizes the angel's knowledge.

686. standing on wheels

Ezekiel's unusual visions of heavenly visitors gave rise to the tradition of painting angels standing on wheels. When a picture shows an angel on a wheel, this indicates that the artist intended to paint cherubim, the type of angel that Ezekiel described as "wheeled."

687. scales

What would angels use scales for? Why, to weigh the good and bad deeds of human beings, of course. Thus angels are frequently shown in art bearing scales in their hands.

688. red roses

Artists like to paint roses because, well, they're just pretty. But in Christian symbolism, red roses also represent Christ's suffering on the cross. For this reason angels are often depicted holding red roses, or they wear robes with rose designs.

689. demons in chains

Revelation tells us that Michael and the angels will triumph over Satan and his demons. For this reason angels in art are sometimes shown leading away demons in chains. Normally the angels in such pictures are also wearing armor and carrying swords.

690. feathers

Wings on angels are discussed elsewhere in this book (see 3). The idea of flight led to the tradition of some artists painting angels wearing robes made of feathers.

691. David and Goliath

The early Christians loved the Old Testament, and they read symbolism into its many stories. On one level, the story of David and Goliath is the story of a spunky shepherd boy defeating an armored giant. But the Christians saw something more in it: a symbol of Christ's vanquishing. This is the reason early Christian art (such as in the catacombs of Rome) often showed David defeating Goliath.

692. Lazarus in the catacombs

The Roman catacombs contain the earliest Christian art, so they tell us much about what the Christians believed in the early years. Images that we assume would be common—Jesus' crucifixion, the Nativity in Bethlehem—are not shown. One of the most common images is (not surprisingly) of Jesus raising Lazarus from the dead—an appropriate image for a Christian burial place. The Lazarus story reminded Christians that their deceased Christian friends—and they themselves, in time—would be raised to a new life with Christ.

693. the upright serpent

Is a serpent just a snake . . . or was the serpent in the Garden of Eden different? Genesis 3 tells us that God cursed the serpent for causing Adam and Eve to sin, and part of the curse was forcing it to move about on its belly on the ground. So we can assume that at the time it tempted Eve it was more upright. And since it could speak, perhaps it had more human features? Artists have had great fun illustrating the temptation story, often showing the serpent as human-looking from the waist up, with its body ending in a snakelike tail. (This is how Milton describes the character Sin in his *Paradise Lost*.) Jewish and Christian traditions state that the serpent/Satan was quite beautiful before God's curse upon it.

694. Noah's ark

What does Noah's ark have to do with heaven and hell? A lot, if you believe the many theologians and Bible commentators who read a great deal of symbolism into the Noah story. Noah, the righteous man, was saved while all the sinful world was exterminated. Some commentators say that this is a "preview" of God's plan for humankind, with the righteous remnant being saved for heaven, while the unrighteous face destruction. This is why Noah's ark was a favorite subject for the earliest Christian artists.

695. "Behold, I stand at the door"

A favorite Bible verse—and one that has inspired many artists—is Revelation 3:20: "Behold, I stand at the door and knock. If anyone hears My voice and opens the door, I will come in to him and dine with him, and he with Me." Jesus spoke those words, and there are many paintings of Him standing outside a door with His hand raised, preparing to knock. The verse seems to suggest both heaven (if we invite Jesus in) and hell (if we ignore Him). Free will is the factor here, for Jesus gives us an eternally important "if"—"if anyone opens the door . . ."

696. *putti*

The word is Italian for "boys," but it refers to the chubby, naked, and usually winged figures in artwork that many people take to be angels. Were they? These cute, charming figures seem nothing like the awesome and very adult angels found in the Bible. (*Cute* is the last word anyone would use to describe the angels of the Bible.) Nonetheless, *putti* became commonplace in religious art in the baroque period, and many baroque churches feature them. If they do not inspire awe (and they don't), perhaps they make the congregation feel warm and relaxed. Sometimes putti are also called *amoretti*. (See 84 [cherubim].)

697. *The Golden Legend*

How did the artists of the past know how angels looked? The Bible doesn't provide many details, but artists had a book, *The Golden Legend*, to aid them. Written in the 1200s by Jacobus de Voragine, its teachings on the angels are based on the writings of Pseudo-Dionysius (see 598). At the root of these writings are the various attendants at the Byzantine court. Their official "uniforms" are the basis of many centuries of angel costume in art.

THE ARTISTS

698. Michelangelo (1475–1564)

He excelled at painting, sculpture, architecture, and poetry—a true Renaissance man, and one whose art was deeply influenced by the Bible. Michelangelo was fascinated by the human body, and his driving ambition was to re-create it in stone. He succeeded, and his statue of the biblical *David* is familiar to everyone, as is his *Moses*. But Michelangelo is also famous for his biblical paintings in the Vatican in Rome. People who know nothing about art are familiar with the image of the gray-bearded God, surrounded by angels, reaching out His finger to the newly created, naked Adam. This, along with other scenes from the book of Genesis, appears on the ceiling of the Vatican's Sistine Chapel, unveiled in 1512. On a wall of that same chapel, Michelangelo painted *The Last Judgment*, showing the rising of the dead from their graves, the ascent of the righteous to heaven, and sinners getting their just deserts in hell. Wingless angels blow the trumpets announcing the judgment. Unlike earlier artists, who had portrayed demons in the shapes of real or mythical beasts, Michelangelo showed them in human form, although hideously bald, and with horns and donkeys' ears, or ears in the form of bats' wings. The story goes that the pope began to tremble when he first saw these frightening images. In an age when most people took hell seriously, Michelangelo's images weren't just artworks, they were stern warnings to get right with God. In his old age, Michelangelo became obsessed with fears of hell. Perhaps he was thinking back to his younger days, when he was deeply moved by the preaching of Savonarola (see 380) on divine judgment. (Cuban dictator Fidel Castro visited the Sistine Chapel in 1996 and posed in front of *The Last Judgment*. Columnist George Will noted this, and also noted that the Last Judgment is "an event Castro will find instructive.")

By the way, the artist's name means "the angel Michael," so one of the world's greatest artists is named for an angel.

699. Sandro Botticelli (1444–1510)

The Birth of Venus is a familiar artwork, showing the naked goddess rising from the sea. This Italian master painted many scenes from mythology, but later in life he experienced a religious conversion that led him to paint more spiritual subjects. Living in the worldly city of Florence, Botticelli got caught up in the city's religious revival under Savonarola (see 380). With his mind on eternity, Botticelli created masterpieces like the *Mystic Nativity*, showing the familiar Christmas scene of the newborn Jesus but also showing airy angels dancing in a golden heaven, while Satan is being trodden down and his demons flee in terror. Botticelli was one of many artists who illustrated the great Italian poem *The Divine Comedy* by Dante (see 726), visualizing Dante's striking descriptions of heaven, hell, and purgatory.

700. Giacomo Cimabue (c. 1251–1302)

By Cimabue's time, angels in art had the distinctive look they would have for the next six centuries: halos, feathered wings, beardless faces, and a generally sexless look. The great Italian painter was a master of frescoes, including some based on the book of Revelation.

701. Albrecht Dürer (1471–1528)

The famous "Praying Hands" picture is Dürer's, and the actual title is *Hands of an Apostle*. Dürer was a superb painter, but was most noted for woodcuts and engravings of Bible scenes. He illustrated most key events in the life of Jesus, but his most ambitious—and most disturbing—work was his set of illustrations from the book of Revelation, his *Apocalypse*. The book with its images of angels, dragons, devils, plagues, and the "four horsemen" comes to vivid life in Dürer's pictures. He excelled in creating hideous faces and bodies for his demons. (His images are still studied by Hollywood designers who work on horror movies and science-fiction epics.) In the picture *The Temptation of St. Anthony*, Dürer depicted the calm hermit Anthony surrounded by demons more hideous than anyone's worst nightmares.

702. Mr. Blake and the angels

William Blake (1757–1827) deserves a place in this book because of his writings *and* his art. One of England's most-read (and possibly least-understood) poets was also a painter and an engraver who illustrated most of his own books of poetry. He also produced some famous illustrations for the book of Job and the great epic poem *The Divine Comedy* by Dante. These naturally gave him opportunities to produce pictures of both angels and demons. Of course, Blake believed himself to be in communication with angels. (When his portrait was being painted by another artist, he coaxed Blake into a pleasant smile by getting Blake to think of how he felt while the angel Gabriel spoke to him.) The brilliant man was religious in an odd way, but hardly a conventional Christian. He knew the Bible well, but stated that he had to create his own system of thought and could not be enslaved by anyone else's. Thus in his later years he wrote incomprehensible works with titles such as *The Marriage of Heaven and Hell*.

703. Rembrandt (1606–1669)

The great Dutch master painter apparently never read any book but the Bible, so many of his masterworks have biblical subjects. Rembrandt was an "earthy" painter, with little interest in portraying heaven, hell, or demons. However, he did include angels in some of his biblical paintings. A famous one is *The Angel and the Prophet Balaam*, and another is *Jacob Wrestling with the Angel*. In the painting *Matthew the Evangelist*, the author of the gospel is depicted with an angel whispering at his shoulder, a sign of the divine inspiration of what he wrote.

704. Pieter Brueghel (c. 1525–1569)

One of the greatest of Flemish painters, Brueghel is probably best known for his happy scenes of peasant life. (His *Wedding Dance* has been so often reproduced that it is almost as familiar an image as Grant Wood's *American*

Gothic.) But like most artists of his time, Brueghel did numerous religious paintings. He had a vivid imagination and could capture on canvas things no one had ever seen, so his *Fall of the Rebel Angels* is amazing to behold. In this unforgettable scene the rebel angels, thrown out of heaven for rebelling against God, change to beasts and goblins while still in midair. Like many painters of the demonic, he showed the evil forms as beasts (both real and mythical), or as ghastly combinations of human and animal forms. His sons also became noted painters, and one of them, excelling at painting the horrors of hell, actually became known as "Hell Brueghel."

705. Hieronymus Bosch (c. 1450–1516)

This great Dutch painter is famous for his bizarre allegorical paintings, such as *The Garden of Earthly Delights.* Yet he painted many, many religious pictures, and his original style came into play when depicting such unseen wonders as angels and demons. Like many painters, he enjoyed portraying *The Temptation of St. Anthony,* with the desert saint surrounded by all manner of fearsome-looking and grotesque demons. Bosch's images were so bizarre and otherworldly (as demons would look, we assume) that many people accused him of belonging to some secret anti-Christian sect. Bosch also painted many depictions of heaven and hell. In the tradition of his age, many churches had altar paintings, with one side depicting heaven and (for balance, and as a warning) the other side depicting hell.

706. Fra Angelico (1387–1455)

A monk whose real name was Giovanni da Fiesole, he was so well liked by his fellow monks that they called him Fra Angelico ("Angelic Brother"). He became one of the best-known painters of his day. Like most of the great religious painters of the period, he made a dramatic painting of *The Last Judgment*. He also painted a striking archangel in his *St. Michael*. Art historians believe he was probably the first painter to depict angels in female form. Earlier they had always been male, or painted in such a way that their gender was unknown.

707. Giotto (c. 1266–1337)

He was probably the greatest painter of the Middle Ages. Like most artists of his day, he painted mostly religious subjects, and he gave them a more realistic quality than had been seen before. Medieval art looks very "stiff" to modern eyes, with its people and angels so unlike real human beings. Giotto's saints and Bible characters and angels are softer, more human. His scenes of demons and tormented souls in hell are still terribly frightening.

708. Raphael (1483–1520)

Born the same year as Martin Luther, Raffaelo Sanzio was named for the angel Raphael (found in the book of Tobit in the Apocrypha). He, along with Michelangelo and Leonardo da Vinci, is considered the best of Italy's Renaissance painters. (Note that of the three, Raphael and Michelangelo were named for angels.) Raphael's paintings have a softness and serenity that were his trademark. He became known for his striking Madonnas (pictures of the Virgin Mary) and scenes from the life of Christ. He also painted numerous angels, including those in *Virgin and Child with St. Raphael and St. Michael.*

709. Edward Hicks (1780–1849)

Hicks was a Quaker preacher but is remembered as a self-taught painter, famous for his many versions of *The Peaceable Kingdom*, an image from Isaiah 11 about a new world where the wolf and the lamb lie down together in peace. The image frequently appears on Christmas cards in one form or another.

710. Coventry cathedral

Every cathedral in the world has some painting or sculpture of angels, but perhaps the most famous is the metal sculpture on the front of Coventry cathedral in England. The cathedral and the entire town suffered horribly from German bombs during World War II. After the war a part of the cathedral was rebuilt in modern architecture, with a striking image of a very muscular archangel Michael holding a spear and standing triumphant over a bound (and horned) Satan. Known as *St. Michael Triumphing over the Devil*, the sculpture not only calls to mind Revelation 12, but also the defeat of the Nazis.

711. *The Bark of Dante*

French painter Eugène Delacroix (1798–1863) painted very few religious pictures, but he did produce *The Bark of Dante*, illustrating a scene from Dante's *Divine Comedy*. In the painting, Dante and his guide through hell (the Roman poet Vergil) are in a boat on a river in hell, with the water alive with the anguished souls of the damned. Like Dante's poem, it is enough to put a real fear of hell into anyone who sees it.

712. Matthias Grunewald (c. 1460-1528)

"Make the punishment fit the crime" is a guiding principle when authors and artists try to show what hell is like. The great German painter Grunewald used this principle in his *Damnation of Lovers*, which shows a man and a woman who, while alive, lived only to satisfy their carnal desires. In hell their bodies are old, wrinkled, hideous with oozing wounds and maggots. They are as unsexy as could be imagined, reminding them eternally of how they wasted their lives on earth.

713. El Greco (c. 1541-1614)

This Greek painter who made his reputation in Spain was hardly religious, yet most of his great paintings were done for the church and thus have Christian themes. In his *Burial of Count Orgaz*, he portrayed a saintly nobleman's burial. The man's soul is joyfully taken into heaven by Saint Augustine and Saint Stephen, and angels and other saints join in the celebration. The joy in heaven contrasts with the count's mourners, who are joyless and draped in black. The picture reminds us that the death of a saint is, from heaven's viewpoint, a wonderful thing.

714. Gustave Doré (1832–1883)

One of the best-known artists of heaven and hell images was this popular illustrator of books. He did many superb illustrations for the Bible, but also depicted both heaven and hell in his woodcuts for Dante's *Divine Comedy* and Milton's *Paradise Lost*. Working without color (since woodcuts are in black and white), he conveyed the hopelessness of hell and the wonders of paradise to many generations of readers.

715. Auguste Rodin (1840–1917)

Rodin's *The Thinker* is probably one of the best-known sculptures in the world. Few people realize it was actually part of an enormous work called *The Gate of Hell*, which occupied him during the last twenty years of his life, and which he never finished. Rodin picked images of hell from Dante's *Divine Comedy* but also drew inspiration from artworks such as Michelangelo's *Last Judgment*. We think of *The Thinker* as a philosopher type, but Rodin originally meant him to be a condemned soul reflecting on his wasted life on earth.

716. Luca Signorelli (1441–1523)

Michelangelo's painting of *The Last Judgment* is probably the most famous, but many other painters tackled the same subject, including Signorelli. In his stunning *Last Judgment* in the Orvieto cathedral, people stand naked before God (as in Michelangelo's version), though the angels wear flowing robes. Like most Renaissance painters, Signorelli was fascinated by anatomy and enjoyed painting nudes. The idea that we are all naked before God (spiritually speaking, anyway) gave a good excuse for artists to incorporate nude bodies into a religious painting. Signorelli also painted *The Coronation of the Elect*, showing the saved in heaven receiving their crowns, as the Bible promised (1 Cor. 9:25; James 1:12; 1 Peter 5:4; Rev. 2:10).

717. The Vision of Hell

Modern painter Salvador Dalí (1904–1989) was hardly religious in the normal sense, but he accepted a commission to do a painting showing the torments of hell. An anonymous donor believed hell had ceased to be a reality in the modern world, and he had Dalí paint a picture that would make it seem real. The picture was given to a Catholic organization. It pictures a soul being tormented with sharp forks in a bleak, hellish desert.

14

Literature, Notable and Otherwise

718. C. S. Lewis (1898–1963)

A quick quiz: What famous author died on the same day as John F. Kennedy? Why, C. S. Lewis, a professor of literature in England, author of children's books and science-fiction novels, and, coincidentally, some of the most widely read books of theology written in the twentieth century. Lewis, who became a convert fairly late in life, was an orthodox Christian, but one with a rare knack for writing well. He enjoyed presenting beliefs via imaginative stories, and even his children's stories and science fiction are veiled theology.

Lewis accepted heaven and hell as realities, which he affirmed in his *Mere Christianity*, a highly readable account of basic Christian belief. He took a more imaginative approach to heaven and hell in *The Great Divorce* (see 720).

In his role as literary scholar, Lewis wrote *Preface to Paradise Lost*, an introduction to John Milton's classic poem about Satan and the temptation of Adam and Eve.

Though writing as a literary analyst, Lewis admitted he was a Christian and that, like Milton, he accepted Adam, Eve, God, Satan, and the angels as realities, not as fictional characters. For more about Lewis's view of demons, see 719 *(The Screwtape Letters)*.

719. *The Screwtape Letters*

People who would never dream of reading a theological book about demons have read and enjoyed this book by English author C. S. Lewis. Lewis was a layman, not a theologian, and he wrote excellent "street-level" theology. *The Screwtape Letters* takes the form of letters from the demon Screwtape to his nephew (and less experienced demon) Wormwood. The devil's eye view of how to prey on human weakness and how to thwart God (or try to) is sometimes humorous, sometimes touching. Lewis clearly understood the human soul in all its frailty. First published in 1941, it was the book that introduced Lewis to the world as a talented layman writer of sound theology. Popular as the book was, Lewis was asked to write a sequel in which one good angel advises another, but he admitted that human beings can probably understand demons better than angels.

720. *The Great Divorce*

What is hell like? C. S. Lewis (see 718) depicted it as a dreary, rainy English town, populated by petty, selfish people. They take a bus ride to the edges of heaven, a beautiful land of green mountains and ever-blue skies. The people of hell discover that the residents of heaven are much more real and solid than themselves. Some of the people like heaven and wish to stay, but most prefer returning to their drab life in hell. One of Lewis's key messages is that people *choose* hell or heaven.

721. *Paradise Lost*

John Milton (1608–1674), England's great Christian poet, not only knew the Bible from cover to cover, but he also knew it in the original Hebrew and Greek. Milton's masterpiece was the long poem *Paradise Lost*, the story of the temptation of Adam and Eve and God's promise of deliverance. Milton was able to make a book-length poem out of the third chapter of Genesis. He accomplished this by focusing on the serpent who tempted Adam and Eve. Milton (like most everyone else) identified the serpent with Satan, and *Paradise Lost* has a lot to say about Satan. Many of the pagan gods of the Old Testament (such as Moloch) appear in the poem as demons. Milton stated that the false religions had "Devils to adore for Deities."

722. *Paradise Regained*

This was John Milton's sequel to *Paradise Lost*. While Milton's earlier poem told the sad tale of mankind's succumbing to Satan's temptation, *Paradise Regained* (as the name implies) reverses this. That is, Christ, the "new Adam," is tempted by Satan but does not give in. In the poem the main characters are, of course, Christ and Satan. Milton drew on the gospels of Luke and Matthew for his story of the Temptation, but he added a lot of detail of his own invention. The Gospels say nothing of how Satan looked while tempting Christ, but Milton described the tempter not as some horned fiend with a pitchfork but as a simple rustic in a plain cloak.

723. Satan as hero

Literary critics have been analyzing John Milton's *Paradise Lost* for three centuries, and though they know that Milton was a Christian, some of them have concluded that Milton intended his Satan to be a hero, not the villain, in the poem. Where did they get such an idea? Admittedly, Milton's Satan is a fascinating character—more fascinating than God, Adam, Eve, or the angels in the poem. Clearly Milton expected readers to sympathize in some ways with the selfish being who hates any authority over him, and who sneers at those who submit meekly to God. But Milton just as clearly saw Satan as not only a fool (he can't really thwart God, much as he tries) but also as genuinely evil, a destructive force that will corrupt not only Adam and Eve, but all of humankind. "Better to reign in hell than serve in heaven" is Satan's creed, but Milton proved that this is wrong.

Milton reminded us that Satan, before he rebelled against God, had been a glorious angel. Even after his fall from heaven he retains some magnificence, but by the end of the poem he and his fellow demons have been transformed into a mass of hissing snakes. Satan as hero? Hardly.

724. Robert Burns (1759-1796)

Scotland's most famous poet was a notorious womanizer who despised Christianity. He wisely chose not to publish his most anti-Christian poems during his lifetime, but people who knew him were aware that he believed all Christians to be hypocrites more or less. In his younger days Burns read John Milton's *Paradise Lost*, and (like many other readers with a rebellious nature) took Satan to be the real hero of the poem. Burns wrote, "Give me a spirit like my favorite hero, Milton's Satan." He had the spirit.

725. *Memnoch the Devil*

Anne Rice has made a fortune with her vampire novels. In this one her favorite character, the vampire Lestat, is taken on a tour of heaven and hell by the devil himself (called Memnoch). In Rice's heaven, there are warmth and fellowship and also an "observation deck" from which one can see what happens on earth, past and present. The devil tells Lestat that he himself is kinder than God, for it is he, not God, who brings human souls to paradise. Lestat is unwilling to believe the devil, who presents God as indifferent to human beings.

726. Dante (1265–1321)

The Divine Comedy is one of the world's masterpieces. In it, the great Italian poet Dante Alighieri journeys through hell, purgatory, and finally heaven. Along the way he encounters people from the Bible, history, and even mythology, who speak about their lives on earth, the punishment they endure for their sins, and the ecstasy of eternal life with God. He also encounters various angels and demons.

More than any other author (outside the Bible, that is), Dante's word images have inspired numerous artists. Sandro Botticelli, William Blake, and Gustave Doré are only a few of the gifted artists who have illustrated Dante's timeless descriptions of the hereafter.

By the way: Dante gave his poem the simple title *Commedia*—a "comedy" because it ends with the supreme joy, heaven. Centuries later the comedy began to be called *divine*, for obvious reasons.

727. Dante's *Inferno*

Inferno is the Italian word for hell, which is Dante's destination in the first section of his *Divine Comedy*. His guide is the Roman poet Vergil, who himself is a resident of hell, but in the Limbo section, reserved for the "good" pagans who never knew Christ. Dante's famous inscription over the entry to hell is "All hope abandon, ye who enter here." Hell is the realm of hopelessness because people are punished eternally for their sins in life. They experience what Dante calls "a hopeless life of unfulfilled desire." Hell is a sort of funnel, arranged in nine concentric circles. Dante is guided through the first and least-horrible circles, which hold those guilty of carnal sins. Further down are the heretics, then the violent, suicides, blasphemers, hypocrites, and evil counselors, then traitors, all the way down to the lowest level. There, at the very center of earth, is a gruesome three-headed Satan. In one of his mouths he gnaws eternally on Judas Iscariot.

Though he was a good Catholic, and though his poem paints a vivid word-picture of Catholic belief, Dante had the nerve to put some of the popes in hell. Dante was a Christian but a human being as well: He pictured many of his personal enemies in hell.

No other author has had such a powerful influence on people's views of hell. Where the Bible says little about the appearance or location of hell, Dante's striking descriptions stirred the imaginations of artists the world over.

728. Dante's *Purgatorio*

A journey through purgatory forms the second section of Dante's *Divine Comedy*. The people in purgatory are

Christians being made ready for heaven by being purged of their sins. While his Inferno (hell) was arranged in nine concentric circles, the Purgatorio is a terraced seven-story mountain. As Dante meets the various people in purgatory, he realizes they are being cleansed from the Seven Deadly Sins that the church had defined. An angel takes a sword and carves seven Ps on Dante's forehead, and as he ascends up each of the seven levels of "purging," one of the Ps is erased. The sinners are being punished appropriately for these sins—for example, those who committed the sin of pride have to bear heavy stones on their backs (to humble them, of course). As Dante ascends the mountain, he meets people of less and less grievous sins.

729. Dante's *Paradiso*

Heaven, like hell and purgatory, is arranged in sections—nine hollow crystal spheres revolving about the earth. It is clear to Dante that not everyone in heaven is on equal footing. The more saintly a person was in his earthly life, the closer he is to God in heaven. But there is no envy or discontent, for every soul in heaven is pleased with his position. ("God's will is our peace" is the theme of the *Paradiso*.) At the center of heaven is God's court, which Dante pictures as a white rose, with the petals formed of angels and saints. Dante's final image in the poem is the radiance of God: "My will and my desire were both revolved, / As in a wheel in even motion driven / By Love, which moves the sun and all the stars."

730. Fyodor Dostoyevsky (1821–1881)

The great Russian novelist wrote many classics, including *The Possessed* (1871), a novel about political radicals. According to the author, he took the title from the gospel account of Jesus healing a demon-possessed man (Mark 5:9).

731. *The Brothers Karamazov*

The renowned Russian author Fyodor Dostoyevsky gave us this 1880 masterpiece in which four brothers are forever struggling with the problem of good versus evil. The author, a Christian, seemed to believe in a real hell and a real Satan, but he also believed that *hell* could be defined as "the suffering of being unable to love."

732. *Hannibal*

In 1999, novelist Thomas Harris published this long-awaited sequel to *The Silence of the Lambs*. It continues the story of the vile (yet intelligent and quotable) Hannibal Lecter, whom Harris paints as a kind of human Satan. Harris's chilling story is full of Bible quotes and allusions. At one point, the horrible Hannibal is described as "going to and fro in the earth, and walking up and down in it"—the words used to describe Satan in Job 1:7.

733. John Bunyan (1628-1688)

For many years Bunyan's *Pilgrim's Progress* was one of the best-selling books in the world. In England and America, if a poor family owned just one book other than the Bible, it was probably *Pilgrim's Progress*. This allegory of the Christian soul facing the hazards of this life and finally entering the Celestial City has enchanted millions of readers. But Bunyan wrote several other books, including one on heaven (*The Holy City, or the New Jerusalem*) and a brief one on hell (*A Few Sighs from Hell*), which describes in detail the horrors of hell. Bunyan's allegorical book *The Holy War* is concerned with a city named Mansoul (get it?). Mansoul is besieged by Diabolus (the devil) and his army but rescued by Emmanuel (Christ, of course).

734. Shakespeare and purgatory

The great poet-dramatist William Shakespeare (1564–1616) made all of the human experience the subject of his plays and poems, so naturally he did not omit religion. His plays contain numerous references to angels, demons, God, Christ, Satan, heaven, and hell. His works are not by a professional theologian but by an author very much in touch with public tastes, so in Shakespeare's plays we see all manner of religious beliefs—some of them being orthodox Christian beliefs, some of them mere superstitions.

Recall his most famous play, *Hamlet*. When Shakespeare wrote it, England was (in theory) a Protestant country, and its church had cast aside the belief in purgatory. Yet many people still believed in purgatory, perhaps even Shakespeare himself. At any rate, *Hamlet* begins with the ghost of Hamlet's murdered father visiting his castle. In the play the ghost tells his son, Hamlet, that his walking upon the earth is his form of purgatory, since he died without having atoned for some of his sins. In this state he is in a "prison house," suffering "till the foul crimes done in my days of nature / Are burnt and purged away." This was perfectly acceptable to Catholic thought (that is, even though the Catholic church had no official teaching on the subject of ghosts; ghosts could easily fit with the belief in purgatory). The ghost tells Hamlet that he cannot even tell about the things he has witnessed in the afterlife, but if he could,

> I could a tale unfold whose lightest word
> Would harrow up thy soul, freeze thy young
> blood, Make thy two eyes,
> like stars start from their spheres,
> Thy knotted and combined locks to part,
> And each particular hair to stand on end
> Like quills upon the fretful porcupine.

Put another way: Hamlet, son, the things I've witnessed beyond the grave would make your hair stand on end, so don't even ask me.

735. Shakespeare and angels

Writing in the late 1500s and early 1600s, Shakespeare in his plays referred many times to angels and demons. When Hamlet dies, his friend Horatio utters the words, "Good night, sweet prince, / And flights of angels sing thee to thy rest." In the same play is the line "Angels and ministers of grace, defend us!" Echoing the Bible's teaching that Satan can masquerade as an angel of light, Hamlet states that "the Devil hath power to assume a pleasing shape." Near the end of *Othello,* the title character sees the villain Iago and says "I look down at his feet," for he expects Iago to have goatlike feet as Satan did. Lady Macbeth calls upon the powers of evil, those "murdering ministers" that "wait on nature's mischief." These are only a few examples. All in all, Shakespeare's world is one overflowing with good and evil angels.

736. *Something Wicked This Way Comes*

Ray Bradbury (b. 1920) is one of the deans of American science fiction, but sometimes he ventured into fantasy and religion as well. This 1962 novel centers around a sinister carnival, run by Mr. Dark (Satan, of course), who grants wishes to the frustrated people in a New England town. As happens in all stories where the devil gives people what they want, there is a dire price to pay. The tale has an age-old moral: Satan can enter in through our selfish longings.

737. Don Juan, in various forms

If you saw the movie *Amadeus*, you might recall that Mozart's famous opera *Don Giovanni* ends with its hero, the wicked Don of the title, being dragged into hell by demons. Mozart's opera is based on the old legend of Don Juan, an immoral Spanish nobleman who seduces women right and left, but who finally meets his doom. In the usual version of his story, Don Juan kills the father of one of the women he has seduced. Later, seeing a statue of the man he has killed, he jestingly invites the statue to dinner. To his surprise, the statue agrees. The statue shows up and commands Don Juan to repent or be damned. The wicked man refuses, and the statue grasps Don Juan's hand, giving him into the custody of demons. Don Juan and his final reward comprise one of the most commonly told sinner-goes-to-hell stories of all time.

738. hell on stage

In Shakespeare's day, and long before, most theaters featured a kind of trapdoor somewhere in the stage floor. This served various purposes, one being to represent an opening into hell, the place where Satan or demons might enter and exit, and also the place where demons would drag the sinner to his doom. In the Middle Ages, when most drama was under the direction of the Catholic church, plays often proved a moral point, and it was not unusual for the trapdoor to be decorated as a literal mouth, a kind of fanged and ghastly "hell-mouth" that would devour the wicked. Workmen would use wood, fabric, or whatever to create a beast head to set over the trapdoor. Jaws could be hinged and fixed with cables and winches so as to open and close. In one case, the actual jawbone of a beached whale was used. Artisans applied their cleverness so that smoke and flames (as well as screams, of course) would issue from the hell-mouth.

739. Marlowe's Faustus and Mephistopheles

Literature is full of tales of men who made bargains with devils, but none are more famous than the Faust legend. The real Faust was probably a German magician who lived in the late 1400s. According to legend, he was a brilliant scholar who also dabbled in the occult arts. Not satisfied with the knowledge he had attained, he wanted more, and to fulfill this desire to be godlike, a devil named Mephistopheles offered him knowledge and power . . . but in exchange for his soul.

Shakespeare's contemporary Christopher Marlowe wrote a tragedy, *Dr. Faustus*, about the legend. Marlowe, who was anything but an orthodox Christian, clearly sympathized with this selfish seeker of power and knowledge, but he ended the play in the expected way, with the devils making good on their bargain and dragging Faustus away to hell. Faustus stubbornly refused to accept divine mercy and forgiveness, so in a sense he brought about his own destruction. The play also includes two characters, the Good Angel and the Bad Angel, who battle over the soul of Faust.

For another famous version of the story, see 740 (Goethe's *Faust*).

740. Goethe's *Faust*

The great German poet Johann Wolfgang von Goethe (1749–1832) wrote a long poetic play, *Faust*. Selling his soul to the demon Mephistopheles (who is portrayed as worldly wise and suave), the old scholar Faust is given all sorts of worldly powers. He is made young again, and he selfishly seduces a young girl, who bears his child. But the Faust of Goethe's play isn't totally selfish, and later on he uses his powers to better society. At the end of the play, instead of being dragged to hell as the story usually ended, Faust is saved, with a choir of angels singing that one who exerts himself in constant striving can find salvation.

The Faust legend has been a rich mine for authors and composers, serving as the basis for several operas, including Charles Gounod's *Faust* and Arrigo Boito's *Mefistofele*. As a result of such exposure, Mephistopheles is probably one of the best-known demons in the world. His name, by the way, means "not loving the light."

741. Dorothy Sayers (1893–1957)

Famous for her mystery novels and her association with C. S. Lewis (see 718) and his circle, Sayers wrote several plays on Christian themes. One of them was *The Devil to*

Pay, her version of the old Faust legend (see 739) of the man who sells his soul to the devil.

742. demons into deities

One of the great theological writers of the 1500s was Richard Hooker, whose *Laws of Ecclesiastical Polity* was widely read. Hooker has been largely forgotten, though in his famous book he set forth the common belief that the gods of the pagans were actually demons, the rebel angels God had cast out of heaven. "The fall of the angels was pride. Since their fall, they have by all means labored to effect a universal rebellion against God's laws. These wicked spirits the heathens honored instead of gods, some in oracles, some in idols, some as household gods." Hooker believed that child sacrifice, ritual orgies, and other horrors of pagan worship could only be the result of worshiping the demonic. This common view was also held by John Milton, which is why several of the demons in his *Paradise Lost* bear the names of pagan gods.

743. *Christ and Satan*

Written in Anglo-Saxon (also called Old English) this long poem from about the year 800 concerns itself with Satan's envy of the Son of God. In Part I, "The Lament of the Fallen Angels," Satan and his demons bewail their fate in hell and also the rumor that God's Son is fated to rule over mankind. Part III is concerned with Satan's tempting of Jesus. Satan actually lifts Christ upon his shoulders to show Him the world and its riches. He even offers Christ heaven itself (not that it is his to give away). Christ mocks the tempter and orders him back to hell, demanding that he measure it with his own hands. Satan finds that it measures 100,000 miles in every direction.

744. Tobias Swinden, scientist

Some call the 1700s the "Age of Reason." Certainly it was a time when many educated people became very skeptical about the Bible and Christian belief and began to believe that human reason might be the answer to man's problems. But not everyone gave up on traditional beliefs. In 1714 Tobias Swinden published his *Enquiry into the Nature and Place of Hell*. Swinden calculated that after so many centuries, the inside of the earth could not possibly be big enough to contain all the sinners condemned to hell. (Plus, he said—being of a scientific mind—there was not enough oxygen inside the earth to keep the fires of hell burning.) So where was hell? The sun, of course, since it was large enough and hot enough for the purpose. While these ideas seem laughable to us, consider the author's purpose: He was a scientist but also a Christian, striving to make a basic Christian belief seem intellectually respectable.

745. William Whiston, scientist

A fellow scientist and an admirer of the scientists Isaac Newton and Edmund Halley, Whiston published in 1740 his book _The Eternity of Hell Torments Considered_. Whiston claimed that all dead souls were contained (though not actually punished) in a huge Hades inside the earth. There, awaiting the Last Judgment, they would have a chance to repent. At the Judgment, the righteous would rise in spiritual bodies and enjoy heaven, while the unrepentant would keep the bodies they had at their death. At the world's end they would be consumed along with the rest of creation.

746. John Donne (1573-1631)

You might say there were two John Donnes: the poet of erotic love poems ("lust poems" might be more accurate) and the poet of deep Christian faith. Donne apparently led a wild youth, but he became a much-loved preacher in London, and his tomb is still there in St. Paul's cathedral. Donne lived in an age when people were beginning to be skeptical about the reality of hell— or, at least, the traditional view of hell with fire, sulfur, and various tortures. In one of Donne's sermons he wrote that there was no physical torment imaginable that might compare with the most horrid fate of all: to be excluded eternally from the presence of God. You might say that this is a "modern" view—that Donne did not believe in a "literal" hell. But, as he emphasizes in his sermon, the "psychological" torment of separation from God is far worse than any "literal" torment. Donne was not making hell seem less horrible but, if anything, more horrible.

747. *Religio Medici*

One of the most fascinating books written in the 1600s is this delightful work by Thomas Browne, an English physician. Browne was a Christian, but a worldly one. (Not that he was immoral, but rather that, like many people of his times, he was somewhat skeptical of Christian beliefs.) Browne never actually denied a belief in hell, but he firmly denied that anyone had ever been frightened into belief by the fear of hell. "I can hardly think there was ever anyone scared into Heaven." But there were plenty of preachers in his day who would have disagreed, confident that it was necessary to scare some (perhaps not all) people into faith.

Browne believed that angels were a benevolent influence on people, and in his book he wrote that "many mysteries ascribed to our own inventions have been the courteous revelations of Spirits [angels, that is]; for those noble essences in heaven bear a friendly regard" for people on earth. He believed demons were real, and that disbelieving in them is almost the same as atheism.

748. hell on the inside

Robert Burton (1577–1640) was an English scholar who poured his years of wide reading into his one great book, *The Anatomy of Melancholy*. Essentially this is a long, exhaustive look at mental health, as the people of the 1600s defined it. One quotable from Burton: "If there is a hell on earth, it is to be found in a melancholy man's heart." Burton did believe in a hell after death also, but he was correct in his statement that sadness of the soul is a horrible thing.

749. *The Devil and Daniel Webster*

This popular story by Stephen Vincent Benét concerns Jabez Stone, a New England farmer who sells his soul to the devil in return for prosperity. Naturally the devil returns to claim the man's soul, but Jabez is saved from damnation by the eloquence of the great statesman Daniel Webster. The orator has the challenge of his life, for it is not a human jury that he has to sway but a jury of demons. Naturally he wins the case. The story has been made into an opera and the movie *All That Money Can Buy*.

750. Thomas Heywood (1570–1641)

He was a contemporary of Shakespeare and also a noted playwright and poet. One of his works was *The Hierarchie of the Blessed Angels*, which gives us insights into what people in the 1600s believed about angels.

751. *Le Morte d'Arthur*

King Arthur has been a favorite subject of poets and storytellers, and Sir Thomas Malory's *Le Morte d'Arthur*, written in the 1500s, is a classic collection of Arthur stories. Malory pictures guardian angels standing watch over the virtuous knight Sir Galahad, while fallen angels (disguised as fair ladies, priests, and religious hermits) tempt the various knights of the Round Table. A multitude of angels convey the soul of Galahad to heaven.

752. the Brownings

They were England's great literary couple of the 1800s, Robert Browning and Elizabeth Barrett Browning. Both were intimate with the Bible and had much to say about angels and demons. Elizabeth's "The Seraphim" is a dialogue of two angels at the time of Jesus' crucifixion. In "A Dream of Exile," she wrote about Adam and Eve's banishment from the Garden of Eden. In "The Seraph and the Poet," she wrote that angels and poets both sing— angels sing of God's glory, poets sing of man's sorrows. Robert featured angels in several of his poems, including Gabriel in "The Boy and the Angel."

753. *Pearl*

This long poem was written sometime in the late 1300s, in what we now call Middle English (the same form of English used in Chaucer's *Canterbury Tales*). *Pearl* is a kind of dream vision of heaven, depicting it as a place of light and jewels, separated from earth by a great river. The poem bases its images on the vivid description of the New Jerusalem in Revelation 21–22.

754. Daniel Defoe (1660–1731)

The great English author who gave the world *Robinson Crusoe* and other classics also wrote *The Political History of the Devil*. Defoe definitely believed in a real Satan, but in his book the stories he tells about diabolical encounters seem to be geared toward telling a colorful story, not making people more religious.

755. Nathaniel Hawthorne (1804–1864)

The author of such American classics as *The Scarlet Letter* and *The House of the Seven Gables*, Hawthorne also wrote *The Celestial Railroad*, a story in which he travels to heaven. Instead of a difficult journey (as in Bunyan's *Pilgrim's Progress*), he makes his way there via a comfortable train. Hawthorne was poking fun of liberal Christianity and trendy philosophies and their assurances that hell was not real and that the way to heaven was easy.

756. Charles Williams (1886–1945)

Williams, an English author, is often read by fans of C. S. Lewis, who was a friend of Williams. Like Lewis, Williams wrote "secular" books that have Christian themes, as well as books that were openly Christian. Williams's novel *Descent into Hell* has one character who is taken over by a demon lover, and another who barely escapes possession herself.

757. George Macdonald (1824–1906)

Scottish author Macdonald was greatly admired by C. S. Lewis (see 718), who claimed he owed much to him ("I regarded him as my master"). Macdonald, a former minister, wrote juvenile fiction and a number of fantasy novels. One of his novels, *Lilith*, is concerned with demon possession (see 425 [Lilith]).

758. G. K. Chesterton (1874–1936)

Chesterton, a Catholic, is still widely read by Christians of all persuasions. Like C. S. Lewis (see 718), he was a layman, and so could talk theology to a large audience. His books *Orthodoxy* and *The Everlasting Man* are excellent summations of Christian belief. Regarding heaven, Chesterton wrote that "we need to be happy in this wonderland without once being merely comfortable." (In other words, enjoy earth, but realize there is something better and more enduring.) Chesterton also wrote that the question "Why does God allow suffering?" is answered by heaven—everlasting joy is the answer to temporary pain.

759. *The Day of Doom*

This long poem, based on the Bible's images of the Last Judgment, was published in 1662 by New England poet Michael Wigglesworth. The poem tells of Christ's return at midnight to judge the sinful world. He separates the sheep from the goats, following Jesus' parable of the Last Judgment (Matt. 25).

This was America's first best-seller.

760. George Herbert (1593–1633)

Herbert was a devoted minister in the Church of England and author of *The Country Parson*, a guide for pastors. But he is best remembered for *The Temple*, his collection of devotional poems on every aspect of Christian belief. In his poem "To All Angels and Saints," he addresses the angels as those who "See the smooth face of God, without a frown." His "Antiphon" has men and angels praising God together.

761. Edward Taylor (c. 1642–1729)

Born in England, Taylor became a Puritan pastor in Massachusetts. Many years after his death it was discovered that he wrote poetry, some of the best American poetry of the early 1700s, all of it Christian in theme. Taylor was an orthodox believer, but he played down the role of angels in human life and insisted that the angels were merely messengers, deserving our respect but certainly not deserving the devotion that many Christians gave them. In Taylor's view, a redeemed sinner is of much more value in God's eyes than is an angel.

762. *Ambrosio, the monk*

The temptation and fall of a saint has always fascinated people. In this Gothic novel by Matthew Lewis, the saintly monk Ambrosio falls under the evil spell of a woman demon sent to him by Satan. Together the two commit horrible crimes, including rape and murder. Ambrosio tries to repent, but too late, and Satan bears him away to hell. Horrid as it sounds, this 1796 tale was a runaway best-seller.

763. Clive Barker (b. 1952)

Fewer and fewer people claim to believe in hell, but you would not guess it from the flood of books and movies dealing with hell. English author and filmmaker Barker is a kind of hell expert, best known for the popular movie *Hellraiser* and its sequel. Many of his other novels and short stories deal with demons from the underworld, and his vision of the afterlife is anything but comforting.

764. *Damn Yankees*

The most popular American musical dealing with Satan and hell is this romp about Joe, a baseball fan who wants his team to win so badly he makes a deal with the devil (Mr. Applegate). Joe is willing to sell his soul for his team, but whenever he inquires about the afterlife in hell, Mr. Applegate always changes the subject. Joe manages to escape hell through the devotion of his loving wife.

765. Aldous Huxley (1894–1963)

Christians who work in delivering people from demonic influence know that there is a connection between drugs and the demonic. British author Huxley (best known for his novel *Brave New World*) experimented with drugs, writing about his hellish drug-induced visions in *The Doors of Perception* and *Heaven and Hell*. Drug use, as Huxley knew, does not always lead to bliss.

766. Hans Christian Andersen (1805–1875)

Andersen is loved worldwide for his fairy tales, such as "The Ugly Duckling" and "The Little Mermaid." As in many tales, there is a dark and frightening side. In his tale "The Girl Who Trod on a Loaf," a selfish child stumbles into a horrible hell that is icy cold. She is eventually released because her loving mother continually prays for her. Andersen's tale is one of many that warn children, "Be good—or else!" On the other hand, in "The Little Match Girl" a pitiful girl is taken to heaven to escape her cruel father.

767. *The Devil and Billy Markham*

Author Shel Silverstein, known for his children's book *The Giving Tree* and for his pop songs (he wrote "A Boy Named Sue" for Johnny Cash), also wrote this odd play about Satan and hell. Billy Markham is a failed musician, an unloving and selfish character who finds that hell is populated with people like himself. Instead of hell being a place of fire and brimstone or other physical torments, hell is a place of supreme selfishness and pettiness.

768. *The End of Satan*

French novelist Victor Hugo was famous for his *Les Misérables* and *The Hunchback of Notre Dame*, but he was also a noted poet. His poem *La Fin de Satan* ("*The End of Satan"*) looks at Satan, the rebel angel, as he falls from hell and realizes at last that his rebellion has led to eternal separation from God. Even when God speaks and reminds Satan that repentance is always possible, Satan is too proud to return to God.

769. *The Haunting of Hill House*

People sometimes joke about hell, saying that it will be a place with amusing companions. This novel takes the more Christian position that hell will not be pleasant at all and that one will be totally alone there. Shirley Jackson, author of the famous short story "The Lottery," wrote about a bizarre haunted house, which attracts an unhappy spinster. She finds her earthly life so dreary that she hopes the house and its demons will give her some sort of joy. When the house finally "takes" her, she finds she is alone for all eternity.

770. *The Afterlife Diet*

Christianity teaches that heaven's standards are quite different from those of earth. People considered unattractive on earth may be precious in the eyes of God. Author Daniel Pinkwater, in this goofy 1995 novel, spoofs our current obsession with diet and thinness by presenting a heaven where the overweight are second-rate citizens. God tells fat jokes, and the chubby play a game of chance in which they try to win reincarnation on earth in a new (and slender) body. While the novel is a spoof, it does bring an interesting fact to mind: Artists have rarely ever depicted chubby saints in heaven.

771. The Gates Ajar

In the late 1800s this was a popular novel by Elizabeth Stuart Phelps about the afterlife. Quite different from the usual picture of saints and angels always worshiping God, the heaven in this novel is like a pleasant American town, only with all the sin and selfishness gone. Cranky and irreverent Mark Twain (see 789) found her description of heaven extremely boring and spoofed the book in some of his essays.

772. Carousel

This popular Rodgers and Hammerstein musical tells of Billy, an unemployed carnival barker who is killed while committing a burglary. He begs the Almighty for a chance to redeem himself, and God allows him to visit his daughter, who has had a rough life, stuck with the stigma of being the daughter of a criminal. Billy manages to steal her a star from heaven, and God sees that Billy truly loves his daughter, so he is allowed into heaven.

773. The Littlest Angel

Here is a true Christmas classic. Written by Charles Tazewell in 1946, it is the story of a little boy who dies, enters heaven, but is bored, missing the fun he had on earth. All the angels are busy preparing for the birth of Jesus in Bethlehem. The Littlest Angel has no grand gift to offer, but he gives his prized treasure box, with its collection of stones, bird eggs, feathers, and other little boy things. The older angels mock this, yet the Christ child selects this as His favorite gift. The box now shines so brightly that it turns into the star of Bethlehem, shining over the place where Jesus is born.

774. Four Saints in Three Acts

This highly unusual twentieth-century opera has music by Virgil Thomson and a libretto by author Gertrude Stein. It actually features more than four saints, some of them quite famous, all of them assembling at the end to share the joy of their reward in heaven.

775. Green Pastures

Is heaven like an eternal fish fry? This Pulitzer Prize-winning play by Marc Connelly, also made into a movie, suggests that it is. With an all-black cast, the play retells some favorite Bible stories with "de Lawd" (God, that is) and

His angels watching events on earth from their happy land of the fish fry. Seeing that things on earth are in bad shape, He leaves the angel Gabriel in temporary charge of heaven and goes to earth to help people. The play actually makes heaven look like a very pleasant place to spend eternity.

776. Hannele's Ascent into Heaven

Most of the plays of German author Gerhardt Hauptmann are rather gloomy, but this one is different. Written in 1893, it concerns a lovable child, living in poverty and finally succumbing to illness. While dying she sees Jesus, who welcomes her to heaven and tells her that her sufferings are over. Hauptmann was always sympathetic to the poor, and his play showed that he understood the need that the poor have for a hope of heaven.

777. Our Town

Thornton Wilder wrote this ever-popular play, which won a Pulitzer prize in 1938. It concerns the lives and loves of the people in a small New England town. In the last act, Emily, the female lead, dies in childbirth and finds herself in the cemetery, conversing with people she has known. They give her no assurance of a heaven (though they don't rule it out), but remind her that every day on earth is important, something to be treasured. Emily is allowed to relive a day of her life and learns how beautiful life was.

Wilder's play insists that "something's eternal," but isn't clear about just what that involves.

778. *Piers Plowman*

This is a classic of English literature, an allegorical poem about creation, the fall of man, and the joys of heaven. Written sometime in the 1300s by William Langland, the poem describes virtues and vices, as well as conversations with Satan and with the angels Michael and Gabriel.

779. Gil Vicente (1470–1536)

He was a playwright and poet in Portugal, and he wrote a trilogy about the afterlife: *The Ships of Hell, Purgatory,* and *Glory.* Like Dante's *Divine Comedy*, it looks at the three states of the afterlife in traditional Catholic terms.

780. Friedrich Klopstock (1724–1803)

A noted religious poet in Germany, Klopstock was inspired by reading John Milton's *Paradise Lost* to write his own Christian epic. In 1773 he completed it, calling it *The Messiah.* Like Milton, he had read widely in Christian folklore about angels and demons, so while the poem is (naturally) the story of Christ, angels and demons play a large role. Klopstock included a rebel angel named Abbadona, who starts out on the side of Satan but then repents.

781. *The Faerie Queene*

Shakespeare was one of many great poets in the reign of England's Elizabeth I. Another was Edmund Spenser (1552–1599), whose masterpiece was *The Faerie Queene*, a long, allegorical poem in which characters represent various vices and virtues. Numerous angels and demons appear also. In Book I of the poem, the Red Cross Knight (who represents holiness) fights various fiends, including the demon queen Lucifera (representing Pride, the sin of Lucifer). He meets Archimago (his name means "arch-magician," and he represents Satan as a deceiver, and also the Antichrist). Eventually the knight slays the Dragon (also Satan). Book I also contains a poetic description of the New Jerusalem (heaven), based on Revelation 21–22. In Book II, the knight Sir Guyon comes to the den of Mammon (representing greed for worldly goods, as in the New Testament).

A key theme of the poem: Satan is seldom ugly or evil on the outside; in whatever form he takes in the poem, he is unusually attractive, and can even take the form of a religious person. As the New Testament has it, Satan the Great Deceiver transforms himself into an angel of light (2 Cor. 11:14).

782. *Everyman*

In the Middle Ages, morality plays were allegorical dramas, with characters representing such qualities as Faith, Worldly Goods, and so on. *Everyman*, which is still staged occasionally, was a morality play dealing with Everyman (whose name is self-explanatory) facing eternity and finding that his friends Beauty, Companionship, and Worldly Goods cannot help him now. The play is a warning that those who live for worldly pleasure must eventually face a day of reckoning.

783. *Beowulf*

This epic poem was written in Anglo-Saxon (Old English) and relates the adventures of the warrior Beowulf, who fights and slays a man-eating monster named Grendel. After Grendel is slain, Beowulf finds in the monster's cave an ancient sword, which is inscribed with an account of giants long ago, destroyed in a universal flood and punished for their sins. The poem is referring to the "giants on the earth" mentioned in Genesis 6:4 (see 7).

784. Anne Bradstreet (c. 1612–1672)

America's first notable woman poet was a devout Christian, and almost all her poems reflect her faith. In the poem "The Flesh and the Spirit," she gives a lovely poetic description of the New Jerusalem (heaven) based on the images found in the book of Revelation (21:2–22:5).

785. *contemptus mundi*

This Latin phrase means "contempt for the world," and it is used to describe a type of Christian literature of the Middle Ages. In *contemptus mundi* writings, this earth is pictured as a place of suffering and selfishness, a place of only fleeting pleasures, a place the true Christian is glad to leave so as to move on to his real home, the eternal home, heaven. Such writings include descriptions of heaven and hell in much more detail than the Bible provides.

786. *The Kingdom of Heaven Is Like*

Here's a book for children about heaven, based on nothing other than what Jesus Himself said about heaven in his parables. This 1993 book by Merula Salaman was beautifully illustrated and is probably as appealing to adults as it is to children.

787. *Elucidation*

Sometime around the year 1100, this description of paradise was circulated throughout Europe. It described heaven as a restored Garden of Eden, re-created after the Last Judgment. The garden is lush with meadows and flowers and, as in Eden, people are naked but not ashamed. All will be equal, with no class distinctions.

788. *The Life of Samuel Johnson*

Samuel Johnson (1709–1784) was a renowned English author and critic, but he is remembered today because he is the subject of a wonderful biography by James Boswell. Living in an age of skepticism about Christianity, Johnson was adamant about holding on to belief in heaven and hell. Johnson was unsure of his own eternal destiny and admitted he feared his own death, refusing to discuss the subject even with close friends.

THE SKEPTICS

789. Mark Twain (1835–1910)

He was born Samuel Langhorne Clemens, but as Mark Twain he became one of America's most-read authors and humorists. He gave the world such classics as *Huckleberry Finn, Tom Sawyer, The Innocents Abroad, The Prince and the Pauper*, and many others. Twain was extremely skeptical about Christianity and about religion in general. One of his lesser-known works is *Captain Stormfield's Visit to Heaven*. In it he takes a few jabs at Christians and their beliefs about the afterlife. The bluff sea captain learns after his death that people can do whatever they like in heaven. While many of them start out playing the expected role of wearing white robes and halos and playing golden harps, they give up on this pretty quickly and find other ways to pass the time.

Twain's *The Mysterious Stranger* is an extremely bitter book. The devil, its main character, announces at the end that there is no God, no heaven, and no hell—it is all a grotesque and foolish dream.

His *Letters from the Earth* is based on the book of Genesis, but with a twist: The temptation of Adam and Eve is told from the viewpoint of Satan.

790. Lord Byron (1788–1824)

One of the greatest poets in the English language, Byron led a scandalously immoral life and took delight in shocking people more moral than himself (which included the majority of the population). Though he wrote such semi-religious poems as "The Destruction of Sennacherib," and though he knew the Bible well, he was too much of a rebel to ever be even remotely Christian. Among his many poems is the poetic drama *Cain*, in which the real hero is Lucifer (Satan). In the poem, Lucifer carries Cain to a sort of science fiction–type Hades far out in space. The rebellious Byron is clearly on the side of anti-God figures such as Lucifer and Cain. For Byron, a God who stands in the way of human impulses is the evil one, not Satan. In another poetic drama, *Manfred*, the rebellious hero will bow to neither God nor Satan. At the poem's end he stubbornly refuses to be dragged to hell, even though he will have none of heaven.

791. Percy Bysshe Shelley (1792–1822)

He was one of England's great poets, but his beliefs and morals were in deliberate conflict with Christianity. One of his books was *On the Devil and Devils*, expressing his view that neither God nor Satan is the proper object of man's devotion. Shelley differed from his friend and fellow poet, Lord Byron (see 790), who liked to make heroes of Satan and Satan-like characters.

792. the satanic school

Scorning Christianity is nothing new. In the early 1800s many noted authors heaped abuse on the morals and beliefs of Christianity. Though this was never an organized movement, it has loosely been called "the satanic school," and it included such major poets as Byron (see 790), Shelley (see 791), Victor Hugo, George Sand, and many others. In some cases, such as Byron's, their works defended Satan and other rebels against God, admiring them as independent and proud. Robert Southey, England's poet laureate at the time, coined the term "satanic school" and referred to the "immoral writers, men of diseased hearts and depraved imaginations."

793. "The Flowers of Evil"

Evil fascinates people, and though we may boo and hiss the villains in a movie, they intrigue us. As Christianity began to lose its hold on Europe, some authors began to be rather open about their fascination with evil. One of these was the French poet Charles Baudelaire (1821–1867), who died young and insane because of syphilis. Baudelaire's poetic masterpiece, if you can call it that, was his *Les Fleurs du Mal*—"Flowers of Evil." Practically every poem in it refers to Satan, hell, corpses, or some sort of vice. Guided by drugs and vice, he took a ramble through hell and seemed to enjoy it. He did not imply that it was pleasant, but he hinted that it was better than having to submit to God. Baudelaire was (and still is) widely read by intellectuals, and his poems are a textbook example of the modern rejection of the afterlife (even though, as the poems make clear, this rejection does not bring peace or happiness).

794. Alexander Pope (1688–1744)

This noted English poet was fairly skeptical about Christianity, like so many authors and intellectuals of his time. He observed, correctly, that the Church of England spoke rarely of heaven and even more rarely of hell. He claimed that he had heard a minister preach, telling the congregation to "give their lives a new turn, or they must certainly go to a place which he did not think it fit to name in that courtly audience." The Church of England still believed (officially) in heaven and hell, but as Pope observed, its ministers were almost embarrassed at having to speak of the subjects.

795. *The Sorrows of Satan*

This book was published in 1895 by novelist Marie Corelli. It was part of a trend in the late 1800s for "sympathy for the devil," with authors trying to shock people by claiming sympathy for Satan, whom they admired as an independent type, a rebel against a too-strict God.

796. *Man and Superman*

George Bernard Shaw (1856–1950) wrote numerous plays that still please audiences. A religious skeptic, Shaw wrote *Man and Superman*, with a section called *Don Juan in Hell* that is sometimes performed separately. In the play, heaven is dull and boring, while hell is a jolly place full of good companions. In fact, the people in heaven wish to go to hell.

797. *No Exit*

French philosopher Jean-Paul Sartre (1905–1980) was an atheist, but one of his most popular writings was a play about hell. In *No Exit*, no God, devil, or angel appears.

Rather, a small group of deceased people is shown to a shabby hotel parlor, where they quarrel and behave pettily and spitefully (and eternally). The play's most often quoted line is "Hell is other people." With the type of people Sartre presents, this is definitely true.

798. William Beckford (c. 1760–1844)

Beckford was a textbook example of the "eccentric author." He was obsessed with the occult, and he lived in a weird Gothic mansion, surrounded by physically deformed servants, with fires burning throughout the house even in summer. Apparently he wished to make the creepy place look like hell. His famous book was *Vathek*, a weird tale of a man who sells his soul to the devil and at the end grieves over his choice to spend eternity in torment.

799. Archibald MacLeish (1892–1982)

A noted poet and playwright, MacLeish wrote on biblical themes, but definitely not from the usual Christian viewpoint. His *Songs for Eve* takes the position that Adam and Eve's disobedience was a good thing—that is, the Fall was up, not down, for man became independent. His play *J.B.* is a modern retelling of the story of Job, while *Nobodaddy* retells the story of Adam, Eve, Cain, and Abel. In these two plays, God is indifferent or even cruel to mankind, and Satan is not by any means the villain.

15

Moving Images:
Movies, TV, Video

THE SCARY

800. *The Exorcist*

One of the best-selling novels of the 1970s was *The Exorcist* by William Peter Blatty. It became a phenomenally popular (and some would say phenomenally disgusting) movie, leading both believers and nonbelievers to discussions of demon possession and exorcism. On its most shallow level, the movie was simply a crude freak show, depicting a pitiful young girl, possessed by a demon, in horrible physical contortions, mouthing obscenities and blasphemies—almost (but not quite) triumphant over the Catholic priests trying to expel the demon. Three priests served as consultants on the film, and some people were surprised to learn that yes, in the modern world, the Catholic church does still have a ritual for exorcism.

The demon who possessed the girl had a name, by the way—Pazuzu. Early in the movie we see an image of this hideous Assyrian demon-god—a sort of winged gargoyle. This wasn't an invention of author Blatty, for the Assyrians really did believe in this ghastly being. Blatty was following the old Christian tradition of identifying the pagan gods as demons.

801. *What Dreams May Come*

This 1998 movie dared to show a real hell that people might actually end up in. (The visuals were based on classic paintings of heaven and hell, many of them mentioned in this book's chapter on art.) Robin Williams and Annabella Schiorra play a married couple who die and get an up close and horrifying look at hell. There's no doubt that the special effects in the movie are dazzling (and disgusting), but, typical of our times, the movie has a theological loophole: Hell isn't really eternal, for the movie hints that even a person in hell will be reincarnated eventually. On top of that, God is mentioned but never seen in heaven.

802. *Dante's Inferno*

Back when special effects were pretty low-tech, this Spencer Tracy movie (made in 1935) dazzled audiences with a nightmarish vision of hell. The movie is about a ruthless carnival owner who gets too big for his britches. He has a vision of hell (induced by one of his own carnival's attractions) and, of course, changes for the better.

803. *Highway to Hell*

Hell can be both funny and horrifying. In this 1992 movie, two teens get lost on their way to Vegas and end up in hell, which is like a parade of criminals fighting, beating, and raping. But the movie has some humor: The HellCops stop for a bite at Pluto's Donuts, and everyone in hell drives a Volkswagen Beetle.

804. *The Omen* trilogy

Three popular horror movies based their plots on the book of Revelation. Beginning with *The Omen* in 1976, they chart the life story of an adopted boy who, we learn, is the Antichrist. In spite of efforts to destroy this wicked one before he reaches adulthood, he lives on, bringing death and destruction to those who oppose him. The horror continued in *Damien*, but in *The Final Conflict* the adult Antichrist, posed on the brink of world domination, meets his end in a confrontation with Christ.

805. *Fear No Evil*

This weird 1980 item is basically a horror movie, but with an interesting idea: A teenager is the human embodiment of Lucifer, and he commits acts of murder and destruction. His opponent is an eighteen-year-old girl, who is the incarnation of the angel Gabriel.

806. *The Black Hole*

This 1979 Disney science-fiction movie focuses on a mad scientist on the edge of space, about to explore a black hole. The expedition sent to investigate him learns that the black hole is a gateway into hell, from which the mad scientist can never escape. The idea is interesting in light of how people in the past often debated about just where hell was located.

807. *The Wicker Man*

To get an idea of why the Jews and early Christians were so repulsed by pagan worship, rent this 1973 movie. But be warned: It's horrifying. It's the story of a Christian trapped on an island where the citizens practice a demonic religion capped with sexual rituals. A biblical theme comes through: The wild pleasures of the pagans are a thin veneer over their evil hearts.

808. *Needful Things*

Here's an idea in keeping with the Bible: The devil in the guise of a charming, soft-spoken shopkeeper who gives people their inmost desires, then watches them wreck their own lives and those of others. Based on a Stephen King novel, this often violent movie actually does come fairly close to the Christian concept of the devil.

809. *The Devil's Advocate*

A young Florida lawyer gets the job of his dreams at a prestigious New York law firm, only to learn that he has sold his soul—literally, for his boss is Satan in human form. As a kind of joke, the boss's name is John Milton, the name of the Christian poet who wrote *Paradise Lost,* with its cast of demons and angels. This 1997 movie features Al Pacino in the role of the sinister Satan.

810. *Rosemary's Baby*

Back in the 1960s, when satanism and the occult were new to movies, this movie really shocked audiences. Young Mia Farrow plays a sweet young wife who becomes pregnant but has some strange recollections about the night she conceived. It turns out that she is carrying the devil's child, and her seemingly lovable old neighbors are a gang of witches.

811. *Brainstorm*

Here's an interesting premise: a device that can record a person's emotions and thoughts, then play them back for another person. A scientist uses the device to record her heart attack, death, and journey to the next world. A colleague uses the machine to replay the experience himself. In the process of dying, memories good and bad are replayed, and finally there is a joyous journey toward light, with angels in white robes and silken wings.

812. *Amityville 3: The Demon*

Just what the world needed: the horrors of hell shown in 3-D. This appalling 1983 movie was a commercial flop, and deservedly so, but it holds the record as the first 3-D movie to show demons and other horrors of hell leaping out at the audience.

813. *Angel Heart*

Robert de Niro as Satan? Sounds like good casting. In this weird 1987 movie, de Niro plays Lou Cyphre (Lucifer—get it?), who has some mysterious claim on a pop singer. We learn that the singer sold his soul to Lucifer in exchange for fame, then disappeared in the hope that Lucifer wouldn't find him to claim his soul. The old Faust legend (selling one's soul to Satan) is still with us.

814. *The Devil's Rain*

This creepy 1975 movie is about Satan worshipers in America's Southwest. The filmmakers hired an "expert," Anton Lavey, founder of the Church of Satan, who was listed as a "technical adviser."

815. *The Beyond*

Are there gateways to hell? The ancient Greeks and Romans believed there were, and so did many Christians. Such an opening would be extremely dangerous (the demons might get out), and this serves as the background for many books and movies. In the 1981 movie *The Beyond*, a run-down Southern mansion is the "hellhole," and the mansion's owner has to find a way to get the fiends from hell back where they belong and seal off their exit.

816. *Black Roses*

Much of heavy metal music poses as "music from hell." This 1988 movie took that idea literally, giving us a metal band whose lead singer is the real Satan himself, working to open a gateway from hell to earth so that demons can kill parents. Eventually even the teen fans themselves are transformed into demons.

817. *Flatliners*

Many people who have clinically died report heavenly visions during their near-death experiences (see 382). This 1990 movie has an interesting premise: Four medical students research such experiences by using medical equipment to bring them about. The results aren't pleasant—quite the contrary. One of the students is tormented by a boy he had accidentally killed in his youth. Another of the students confronts her father, who had committed suicide. Another is hounded by women he had used as sexual playthings. The hell of *Flatliners* is a harsh confrontation with the sins of one's earthly life. As one of the students says in exasperation, "Everything we do matters."

THE HEARTWARMING

818. *It's a Wonderful Life*

This 1946 film is probably one of the most-watched movies in the world. It stars Jimmy Stewart as George Bailey, a sweet small-town guy whose life has taken several turns for the worse. He wants to commit suicide but is saved by the intervention of a wingless angel, Clarence. This angel is an A-S2—Angel Second Class—and he requires the aid of a supervisor, Joseph. Miraculously, Clarence shows George how terrible life in the town would have been had George not existed. George embraces life with a new appreciation, and Clarence, for his efforts, finally gets his wings.

819. *Clarence*

The angel Clarence was an important character in the 1940s classic movie *It's a Wonderful Life*. In 1991 the Family Channel aired *Clarence*, featuring the same angel character, and with some new revelations about guardian angels: As they do good deeds for the people they protect, they grow younger, so their "final stage of growth" is as baby angels, cherubs.

820. *All Dogs Go to Heaven*

Some don't, according to this popular animated movie. Charlie, a dog, dies and goes to heaven, but finds it boring and wants to go back to earth. He sneaks past heaven's gate, but while back on earth has a nightmarish vision of dog hell and is pursued by a Satan dog. He saves the life of an orphan girl and is rewarded with heaven again, this time glad to stay.

821. *The Bishop's Wife*

Suave, debonair Cary Grant as an angel? In this charming 1941 movie he played an angel named Dudley, who comes to the aid of a bishop (David Niven) who is having trouble getting a new cathedral built, and who is neglecting his wife and daughter to boot. Dudley, as the bishop's guardian angel, makes everything right, of course. Even better, when he leaves and everything is in good order, he works a spell so that no one remembers that he intervened. The movie was remade in the 1990s as *The Preacher's Wife*.

822. *Highway to Heaven*

The late Michael Landon played Jonathan Smith, an angel in disguise as a traveling odd-jobs man, in this TV series of the 1980s. Landon, who built a career playing nice guys, spent each episode helping people in trouble and giving the audience a good dose of warmth.

823. *Touched By An Angel*

TV in the 1980s had Michael Landon as an angel, and the 1990s gave us Roma Downey, Della Reese, and John Dye as Monica, Tess, and Andrew, three angels who help people in trouble. In an era when people, especially parents, lament the sex and violence on TV, *Touched By An Angel* is a nice change of pace.

824. *Here Comes Mr. Jordan*

This Hollywood classic from 1941 starred Robert Montgomery as a boxer killed in an accident. An angel directs his soul to heaven, but the angel's supervisor, Mr.

Jordan, tells the angel he has made a mistake: The boxer didn't die in the accident, but, alas, by the time they realize their mistake and try to put the boxer's soul back in the body, it's already buried. So Mr. Jordan has the task of finding another body for the boxer to occupy. The plot was borrowed for a 1978 remake, *Heaven Can Wait*, which featured Warren Beatty as a football pro (instead of a boxer) and James Mason as Mr. Jordan.

825. *A Guy Named Joe*

The World War II years saw a number of angel movies come out of Hollywood. Perhaps in such times of stress it is comforting to believe that angels are watching over us. This 1944 movie tells of a pilot who is killed but comes back as an angel (or ghost, depending on your point of view) to oversee his girlfriend's new romance with another pilot, whom the angel also assists in battle. Spencer Tracy, always the reliable nice guy, played the angel.

826. *Always*

This 1985 movie was a remake of *A Guy Named Joe*. As in the original, a pilot (Richard Dreyfuss this time) is killed, and he becomes the guardian angel of a younger pilot who steals his girl's heart. Dreyfuss had a lovely angel supervisor, Audrey Hepburn.

827. Charley and the Angel

Since this 1973 movie was made by Disney, naturally it has a good dose of both humor and sentiment. Fred MacMurray, Cloris Leachman, and Harry Morgan star in a tale of a coldhearted man who changes his ways when an angel informs him that he hasn't long to live.

828. I Married an Angel

Nelson Eddy and Jeanette MacDonald were a popular singing duo in a number of movies. In this one, made in 1942, Eddy is a playboy whose life takes a turn for the better when he is struck by the beauty of an angel.

829. Heaven Only Knows

A comedy western with an angel? That's what this offbeat 1947 film is. Robert Cummings plays an angel sent out west to reform an evil man.

830. The Fighting Sullivans

People tend to be more religious in wartime, certainly more prone to believe in an afterlife, and this was clearly true of America in World War II. The 1944 movie *The Fighting Sullivans* told the true story of five brothers in the U.S. Navy, all killed in the Battle of Guadalcanal. The scene at the end showing their happy reunion in heaven was a boost to both patriotism and religion.

831. *Made in Heaven*

The story: A man dies while doing a good deed, goes to heaven, falls in love with a soul there, but loses her when she is born on earth as a new baby. He begs to be born as a baby himself, in the hope he can find his lost love. Naturally, since this is a Hollywood movie, he does. The heaven depicted in this 1987 movie is typical of heaven in most movies: angels and pleasant scenery, but no God.

832. *My Life*

Can you get to heaven on a roller coaster? Michael Keaton did in this 1993 movie. He plays a businessman dying of cancer, who seeks various cures, including a "spiritual cure" from an Asian. He learns he has led shallow life with no spirituality. At the end he has changed and is willing to let go of earthly life. As he dies, he sees himself giddy and happy on a roller coaster, which takes him into a blue heaven.

833. *Stairway to Heaven*

Who will make it into heaven? In this 1946 movie about a British pilot who goes there, the answer is "people from every race and culture." All the people speak a common language and can understand one another perfectly. Such famous people as Socrates and Lincoln are there, along with great men of the Bible, of course. An enormous white escalator connects heaven with earth.

834. *The Three Lives of Thomasina*

Are our beloved pets in heaven? They are, according to this sentimental Walt Disney movie, made in 1964. Thomasina is a beloved cat who dies, leaving her little girl owner distraught. The cat loves heaven but misses her owner, and for a time she returns to earth.

835. *You Never Can Tell*

There are animals in heaven, according to this 1951 comedy, but they no longer prey on one another. Everything is harmonious, but a German shepherd named King doesn't want to be there yet, having some unfinished business on earth. He returns to earth in human form to correct everything.

836. *Hi, Honey, I'm Dead*

If we mess up our earthly lives, can we correct things afterward? Not according to the Bible, but pop culture has a different view. This 1991 comedy tells the familiar "second chance" story of a selfish man who dies and gets a "bad grade" from the heavenly review board, but has a chance to do some good deeds for the family he neglected.

837. *Wings of Desire*

This German film, released in the United States in 1988, was widely seen in America. Unlike typical American films featuring angels, this one isn't really a comedy. It's about angels observing human behavior in Berlin, with two angels longing to experience life as humans do. While it isn't exactly "according to the Scripture," it raises some interesting questions about the nature of angels and how they differ from humans.

THE GOOFY

838. *Michael*

The 1996 movie *Michael* features John Travolta in the unlikely role of an angel. But this Michael, quite unlike our normal vision of angels, has an appetite for tobacco, alcohol, women, and sugar. Interestingly enough, in the movie Michael claims to have written one of the Psalms. This wasn't an invention of the scriptwriters, for Jewish legend relates that the archangel Michael did indeed write Psalm 85.

839. *Beetlejuice*

Most modern movies dealing with the afterlife take the view of universalism—that is, everyone, good or bad, winds up in heaven. *Beetlejuice*, an offbeat fantasy, suggests the opposite: Everyone winds up in hell, a weird bureaucracy staffed by ghouls and freaks. This popular 1988 movie was certainly not intended to be taken seriously.

840. *Ghost*

This was the most popular movie of 1990, and the story was definitely fascinating: A murdered man (Patrick Swayze) plays guardian angel to his fiancée, contacting her through a storefront psychic (Whoopi Goldberg). Swayze protects the fiancée from the same hood who murdered him, and in a very chilling scene the gangster is dragged away to hell by devils. Swayze himself enters a brightly lit blue heaven.

841. *The Horn Blows at Midnight*

The end of the world is a serious thing, but it's treated humorously in this 1945 movie. Jack Benny plays a trumpeter who dreams he is the archangel who blows the trumpet announcing the end of the world. Since the whole thing is presented as a dream, it's not as offensive as it could have been.

842. *Forever Darling*

Lucille Ball and Desi Arnaz made a few movies together as well as their ever-popular sitcom. In this one Desi plays a chemist who neglects his poor wife. Lucy enlists the aid of her guardian angel (James Mason) to help rekindle the marriage.

843. *The Devil and Max Devlin*

This 1981 Disney movie has an interesting story line: The recently deceased Max enters a truly frightening and fiery hell, only to strike a bargain with the devil (played by Bill Cosby): Max will be released from hell if he can get three other people to sell their souls to Satan. Naturally, this being a Disney movie, he fails, and finds his own salvation in the process.

844. *Defending Your Life*

Jewish comic Albert Brooks wrote, directed, and starred in this offbeat 1991 comedy about the afterlife. Brooks dies and, like everyone else, goes to Judgment City, where one's life is reviewed. Those who are good enough go on to heaven, while those who are found lacking are sent back to earth, to be reincarnated for another go-around. It's a charming movie, but typically modern in accepting reincarnation instead of hell. (In the movie, one of the joys of heaven is eating whatever you like and never gaining weight.)

845. *Heart and Souls*

This cutesy comedy of 1993 has an interesting premise: Four people die in a bus accident, all four with unfinished business on earth. Each of them is reincarnated—temporarily—in a young man who was born the moment they died. It doesn't bear the slightest resemblance to the Christian view of the afterlife, but it's fun, especially the "heavenly bus" that pursues them.

846. *Stay Tuned*

Is hell a series of sadistic TV shows where one is punished by being "channel surfed" from one torturous program to another? It is in this off-the-wall 1992 comedy, with John Ritter as a couch potato who is sucked in by a satellite dish from hell (literally). The movie shows that people who neglect their real-life families for TV fantasies will be punished by losing their souls in some *very* unpleasant programs—forever. Some inside jokes: One of the demons is named

Crowley [see 535, Aleister Crowley], and some of the shows are *I Love Lucifer* and *Wayne's Underworld*.

847. *Time Bandits*

This wacky 1981 fantasy-comedy concerns a boy kidnapped by dwarfs traveling through various time periods. Curiously, two key characters are the Supreme Being (God, that is) and Satan. Satan is reminded by one of his aides that the Supreme Being created him, which Satan stoutly denies, though the audience sees that it is true. He does some horrible damage before being bested by the Supreme Being. When the boy asks the Supreme Being why He allows evil in the world, the Supreme Being replies, "Has something to do with free will, I believe." Who would have thought an off-the-wall comedy could state Christian theology so well?

848. *Bedazzled*

The story of Faust (see 739), the man who sells his soul to the devil in exchange for worldly pleasures, has been told and retold. This wacky 1968 British comedy tells the story of a lowly cook who sells his soul for popularity, money, and the woman of his dreams. Everything backfires, and he finds that greed and lust aren't very satisfying after all.

849. *The Phantom of the Paradise*

Would a man sell his soul to be famous? Of course. This unusual 1974 rock music fantasy looks at an aspiring composer who strikes a devilish deal with a sinister music entrepreneur (Satan, played by songwriter Paul Williams). Williams also wrote the songs for the movie, catching an important biblical theme in his lyrics: "Gain the world and you lose your soul, / And that's the hell of it."

850. *Gabriel over the White House*

Angels as do-gooders are a favorite movie theme. In this 1933 film, a corrupt politician manages to get elected president. While recovering from an accident, he is told by the angel Gabriel to mend his ways. He does, much to the chagrin of his corrupt political cronies, who believe he has gone insane.

851. *Heaven Can Wait*

Don Ameche was perfect in roles that required him to play a womanizing cad. He does so in this 1943 movie, in which, after death, he has to convince Satan that his philandering wasn't so bad after all. The movie's morals are questionable, for there's never any doubt that this roguish tomcat will end up in heaven, not hell.

852. *The Angel Levine*

This 1970 movie features Zero Mostel as an elderly Jewish tailor who complains to God about his bad luck. He is sent an angel, but, much to his shock, the angel is black. (It's Harry Belafonte.) The movie is offbeat, to say the least.

853. *Cabin in the Sky*

Eddie Anderson (best known as Jack Benny's butler, Rochester) plays an idle, gambling husband who reforms after God and Satan battle over his soul. Released in 1943, this warm, funny musical features such players as Ethel Waters, Lena Horne, and Cab Calloway.

854. *For Heaven's Sake*

Actor Clifton Webb often played snide, acid-tongued characters, but in this 1950 movie he plays an angel, paired with another angel (Edmund Gwenn) to repair the marriage of a Broadway producer.

855. *Oh, Heavenly Dog*

In this 1980 movie, God is the unseen "Boss," while heaven is administered by angel bureaucrats. The angels find that the people now coming to heaven are barely saints at all, so they send some back to earth for "remedial work," after which they return to heaven or go to hell. Chevy Chase plays one of these "marginal" cases, and he is returned to earth in the form of a dog. This is one of many "heaven as a second chance" movies.

856. *The Witches of Eastwick*

Sometimes disgusting, this 1987 comedy was based on a John Updike novel about three small-town women who find sexual fulfillment with Satan himself, played by Jack Nicholson. The three eventually turn on him and use black magic to banish him from their lives.

AND THE TRULY TASTELESS

857. *South Park*

Somehow a vulgar, tasteless animated TV series of the 1990s became extremely popular, spawning this vulgar, tasteless 1999 movie. In this painfully offensive (and blatantly anti-God) film the most sympathetic character is Satan, who is depicted in a homosexual relationship with Iraqi dictator Saddam Hussein. People who wail over cultural and moral decline wailed a bit louder.

16

A Wide, Wild World of Beliefs

858. *Time* and angels

In the 1980s, who would have predicted that angels would make the cover of major magazines? They did in the 1990s, proving that people are spiritually minded—or trendy. *Time* ran the feature "Angels Among Us" in its 27 December 1993 issue. The feature noted, with journalistic objectivity, that people are religion-hungry, but prefer one without a personal God to answer to. "Angels are the handy compromise, all fluff and meringue, kind, non-judgmental. They are available to everyone, like aspirin." *Time*'s sister publication, *Life*, referred to the "angelism" movement as "God Lite."

859. *A Book of Angels*

Author Sophy Burnham had a best-seller with this book (riding on the wave of interest in angels, and also helping to create that wave). Her book—which Christians might well see as a "feel-good" book with little basis in the Bible—gives readers angels that are (to use her words) "utterly compassionate." Burnham assumes that most people dislike the old concept of God as judgmental. She assures the reader that angels are never judgmental, nor do they punish. Her angels are "warm fuzzies" for people who want spirituality without morality. She seems to have no place for the Bible's teaching about angels' role in the Last Judgment, angels at war with the forces of Satan and demons, and so on.

860. *Ask Your Angel*

This popular 1992 book (by Alma Daniel, Timothy Wyllie, and Andrew Ramer) is a genuine "how-to" manual, with numerous "exercises" such as a "centering meditation." This is a long way from the Bible's view that angels are sent at God's pleasure, not at man's beck and call.

861. *The Case for Heaven*

Mally Cox-Chapman's 1995 book has the subtitle *Near-Death Experiences as Evidence of the Afterlife*. Like most of the spate of books about near-death experiences (see 382) published in the 1990s, this one is based on interviews with people who claim to have had NDEs. As is typical of such books, most of the interviewees report heavenly experiences, and even those who report hellish ones claim they were brief (meaning that hell, in NDE form, is nonjudgmental and noneternal). The author assures us that people of all creeds, even atheists and agnostics, go to heaven. It is a typical piece of fuzzy New Age spirituality—no judgment, no morality that matters in the long run, no God who is righteous and desires the same of human beings.

862. *Talking to Heaven*

Can we—or *should* we—try to contact the dead? Apparently many Americans think so, for they made James Von Praagh one of the most popular authors and talk show guests in recent years. Like most so-called psychic mediums, Von Praagh believes everyone goes to heaven, and practically everyone (but especially himself) is capable of contacting them in the hereafter. His book *Talking to Heaven* was popular enough to spawn a sequel, *Reaching to Heaven*.

863. Edgar Cayce (1877–1945)

An American psychic known as the "sleeping prophet," Cayce began reading the Bible as a child and claimed to be able to see nonphysical beings who were his companions.

An angel, feminine in appearance, asked him to make a wish, and he expressed a desire to help the sick. In his twenties he began his "readings," in which he went into a sleeplike state, awakened, and gave a diagnosis and cure for someone's illness. Many people claimed that he helped them. He taught reincarnation and believed his own past lives gave him a knowledge of medicine. He claimed that while he was in his trances the angel Michael appeared to him nineteen times, using a booming voice. He also claimed that another angel named Halaliel (not mentioned in the Bible) spoke to him.

Cayce considered himself a Christian, but many of his beliefs and practices were way out of touch with the Bible. His Association for Research and Enlightenment in Virginia Beach is today a noted New Age center offering everything from "transpersonal studies" to massage courses.

864. the Findhorn community

Way, way up in far northern Scotland is this "spiritual community" founded in the 1960s. It attracted a lot of attention in the early days because of the amazing size of the vegetables grown there, in soil and climate that are normally unproductive. The community was reported to be "tuned in" to nature spirits, which the community members sometimes called "angels." With all the fuss over the environment, Findhorn was held up as an example of earth-friendly spirituality, a New Ager's dream of ecology merged with a semireligion. One of its founders claimed there was an "Angel of Findhorn," and later an angelic presence named "Limitless Love and Truth."

865. Green Hope Farm

This family-owned garden in Meriden, New Hampshire, is similar to the Findhorn community in Scotland (see 864). Like Findhorn, its vegetation is under the care of beings that its founders call "angels" or "devas" or "a spectrum of energy." The founders believe the farm shows how humans can work in harmony with angelic forces. The various spirits who aid the plants are Raphael, Thela, Immanuel, Ascended Masters, and Pan (yes, the same name as the Greek god of the woods and fields).

866. the Theosophical Society

Aren't all religions basically the same? Some supposedly "enlightened" people have held this view, which sounds "tolerant" and "nonjudgmental." One of the "enlightened" was Helena Blavatsky (1831–1891), who helped establish the Theosophical Society. She taught that all religions are rooted in the same ancient wisdom, and their common ground is their belief in angels in some form. She believed these *devas*, as she called them, had been part of man's religion since ancient times. She spoke of nature devas, and New Age devotees, with their obsession with the environment, are fond of these.

867. Geoffrey Hodson (1886–1983)

Hodson, an Englishman, dabbled in the occult, but his turning point came when a "heavenly being" named Bethelda explained how the angels are organized and how they relate to mankind. Hodson published *The Brotherhood of Angels and Men* in 1927, which included teachings about Angels of Power, Angels of Healing, Angels of Nature, and so on. The book contains prayers for contacting the various orders of angels and encourages people to set up angel shrines in their homes. His book is never blatantly anti-Christian but does take the view that all world religions have similar aims and are all valid.

868. Steiner and Anthroposophy

Theosophy (see 866) takes its name from the Greek words meaning "god" and "wisdom." Anthroposophy is from the words for "human" and "wisdom." Anthroposophy's founder, Rudolf Steiner (1861–1925) was involved with theosophy, but believed (correctly) that it was overly influenced by Eastern religions. He wanted to develop a more Christian alternative (not that anthroposophy would qualify as fully Christian, for it is not). Steiner said much about Christ, God, and the angels, but his writings were based much more on his own speculations than on the Bible. He taught that the archangel Michael had triumphed over the Dragon in 1879 (fulfilling the prophecy of Rev. 20), meaning that now mankind could become more spiritual.

Angels, Steiner said, help guide mankind toward universal brotherhood and teach us to gain spiritual insights. Anthroposophy still exists, and Steiner's many writings are very much a part of New Age spirituality.

869. Summerland

New Agers sometimes refer to the afterlife as "heaven," but for a time the term "Summerland" was popular. The name comes from the writings of Swedish author Emanuel Swedenborg (see 393).

870. life reviews

Some people who have had near-death experiences (see 382) report hellish experiences, not heavenly ones. In some cases they face a judge or judges, in what becomes a "life review," who look at the good and bad in the person's life and hold him accountable for it. (The judge may be someone they've known personally, such as a parent, or even a biblical-looking figure in a long robe.) The people reporting such experiences say that their "life review" wasn't intended to lead to reward or punishment, but was only to increase their self-knowledge. Assuming people are honest about these experiences, we have to ask an obvious question: If the person is held accountable for his errors, why no punishment? In effect such experiences say, "You were bad in your life—but it doesn't matter at all."

871. the UFO theory

Several years ago Erich von Daniken had a best-seller with his book *Chariots of the Gods*. It is still in print, for people are still intrigued by the notion that aliens visited earth centuries ago, leading earth people to believe in gods, angels, and demons. (By the way, in the Bible, "the chariots of God" refers to angels [Ps. 68:17].) Subscribers to the "UFO theory" claim that certain supernatural encounters in the Bible—notably the prophet Ezekiel's vision of the "living creatures" that were so bizarre in appearance—were actually encounters with aliens. What Christian tradition believes were angels were, some say, visitors from other galaxies. Possible? Most likely the fascination with alien life-forms is a symptom of a religious yearning in society. People want to believe that something, or someone, is "out there"—but they don't want the moral, righteous (and judging) God of the Bible.

872. the Gnostics

The word comes from the Greek *gnosis*, meaning "knowledge." They were a diverse group, with their beliefs developing before, and later alongside, Christianity. The first Christians were aware that they constituted a threat to Christian beliefs and morals. While there was never a single Gnostic creed that they all subscribed to, there were a few common beliefs. Generally, they considered matter as evil, and most believed the world was not created by the good

God but by some lesser (and evil) being. They placed a lot of emphasis on the "in-group" (themselves, naturally), "enlightened" ones who knew and understood secret "knowledge" that most people could not grasp. (Thus it had an elitist quality that Christianity opposed, since Christ was for everybody.) The Gnostics, or many of them, found various roles for angels, and even when Gnostics incorporated Christ into their beliefs, Christ had to compete with angels and various other cosmic beings. Gnostic writings have gained a new life as New Agers have rediscovered them.

873. archons

The Gnostics (see 872) were a serious rival to the early Christians. They were particularly troublesome because they incorporated many Christian beliefs into their own system, confusing many people who could not distinguish between the Christian gospel and the bizarre Gnostic system. Gnostics spoke of *archons* as the ruling angels of the heavens and the underworld. They are more like demons than angels, being called "Rulers of Darkness" and "Rulers of Unrighteousness."

874. Carl Gustav Jung (1875–1961)

Jung was one of the most influential psychiatrists of the twentieth century. Jung appeals to many religious people because, unlike so many psychiatrists and psychologists,

Jung believed in God. His beliefs never fit in with any one particular religion, however, and he merged his wide readings from mythology, mysticism, and his own near-death experience after a heart attack. Jung believed in angels, not in the usual sense, but as messengers from a "higher consciousness" to our own. He also believed in reincarnation, saying that our lives moved us on to higher consciousness.

ISLAM

875. Gabriel in Islam

Mentioned in both the Old Testament and the New, the angel Gabriel is also an important figure in Islam. Here he has the Arabic name Djibril. On what the Muslims call the "night of power," Djibril appeared to Muhammad and commanded him to recite from the book he was carrying. Muhammad resisted, so Djibril tried to smother Muhammad, and Muhammad finally gave in. Afterward Muhammad saw the angel in the air, proclaiming to him, "O Muhammad, you are the messenger of Allah, and I am Djibril."

The book was, of course, the Muslims' holy book, the Koran. It was Djibril who dictated the Koran, in bits and pieces, to Muhammad. The angel later took Muhammad on a winged horse on the famous "night ride" to Jerusalem, then to the seven heavens, where he met such prophets as Moses and Jesus. Only Muhammad could see or hear the angel.

Muhammad, an Arab, had come into contact with both Jews and Christians, so it is no wonder that he knew about Gabriel/Djibril.

By the way, the Koran itself does not give all the details about the angelic visitor. Muslim legend has supplied the name of Djibril and the story of the smothering.

876. Adam and the Muslim angels

Genesis tells us that man was created in the image of God. What exactly does that mean? People interpret it in different ways, but we can probably agree that creativity is a human trait that reflects the image of God. (Only God can create *out of nothing*, of course.) Muslim tradition states that when Allah (the Muslim name for God) created Adam, He ordered the angels to submit to Him. Some refused, regarding Adam as inferior to them. Allah then invited the angels to name things—animals, plants, and so on—and they couldn't, for they lacked creativity. But Adam could name things. When the angels saw that Adam had this creative power, they were impressed and submitted to him—all except one angel, named Iblis (which means "despair").

877. Iblis

In Islam, Iblis (sometimes spelled Eblis) is the equivalent of Satan. Islamic folklore relates that Iblis was the most exalted of the angels, but when Allah (God) created Adam and commanded the angels to worship Him, Iblis refused and was cast out of heaven, along with his followers. Obviously this is almost the same as the Christian tradition that the angel Lucifer defied God and was cast out of heaven with his followers.

878. genies and angels

We get our word *genie* from the Arabic *jinn*, which refers to angel-like spirits that can be either evil or good. The most famous *jinn* in the world is, of course, the one that inhabited a lamp and was so generous to Aladdin. The leader of the evil *jinn* is Iblis, mankind's implacable enemy.

879. Muslim heaven

Muslims believe that righteous men, those who fear and honor God, will spend eternity in heaven. But the Muslim heaven is a far more carnal place than the Christian heaven. The Koran, the Muslims' holy book, states that heaven will have "young women with swelling breasts" as a reward for righteous men. Muslim tradition refers to these maidens as *houris.* They sing, play music, and provide sexual pleasure in a setting of beautiful gardens. Each man in heaven will have seventy-two of them, their virginity is continually renewed, and they will never age. (Muslim women are in a separate heaven from the men, so they do not compete with the *houris.*) Heaven is a vast garden, with pleasant rivers and spreading trees. While Muslims on earth are forbidden to drink wine, there is wine aplenty in heaven. One compassionate note in the Muslim heaven: The poor will enter there five hundred years before the rich.

880. *jihad*

Thanks to the news media, most of us are aware of this word, which is applied to a Muslim "holy war"—war or terrorism done in the name of Allah (God). While the prophet Muhammad taught that converting people by winning their hearts and minds was best, he approved of a *jihad* using the sword. Many extreme Muslims believe that the "defense of Allah" justifies any sort of violence. Those Muslims who lose their lives in a *jihad* will be welcomed as heroes in the Muslim heaven.

881. the tears of Michael

According to the Koran, the Muslims' holy book, the archangel Michael (*Mikail* in Arabic) sheds tears over the sins of the faithful, and these tears form the angels known as cherubim. While Christians probably will not accept this bit of fancy, it is a touching reminder of angels' interest in our earthly deeds.

882. animals in Muslim heaven

Animals in heaven (see 2) is a disputed topic in Christianity. The Muslims affirm that a few select biblical animals will definitely be in paradise: the ram Abraham sacrificed to God, the whale that swallowed Jonah, and the dove that brought Noah an olive branch.

HINDUISM, BUDDHISM, TAOISM

883. karma

Technically, one can be a Hindu or a Buddhist and not believe in any god at all. This is partly why these religions appeal to many non-Asians: no personal God watching one's actions. The impersonal law of karma operates with perfect justice—you reap what you sow; you live your next life based on what you did in this one. Unfortunately, this means these religions are literally merciless—no God or Christ as Judge, but also no God or Christ as merciful Savior.

884. Nirvana

Many people believe that Nirvana is the Buddhist name for heaven. While Nirvana is the state that Buddhists hope to achieve, it is not much like the Christian heaven. While Christians in heaven will still be distinct individuals, and will know God as a personal Being, Nirvana is an annihilation of individuality altogether. The spirits of people merge with the universal force, leaving behind their mortal bodies and all attachments. Before this can be achieved, people must be reincarnated many, many times.

885. the Pure Land

Most Buddhists believe that the highest and best state is Nirvana (see 884), where individuality is snuffed out, and the person's soul merges with a universal being. This impersonal immortality does not appeal to everyone, and many Buddhists of Japan and elsewhere believe in the Pure Land, something closer to the Christian view of heaven. Worth noting: Philosophies and religions that teach an impersonal afterlife are never very popular with the mass of people.

886. hell in Buddhism

Buddhism in the strictest sense has no god, no final judge of people's lives, which probably explains why Buddhism is popular today in America. People who only dabble in Buddhism overlook something: It has hell—lots of hells, in fact. While Buddhism teaches that people's souls are reincarnated many times (so nothing is really *final*), souls also spend time in hell for their transgressions. Various Buddhist writings describe in grisly detail the horrors of the many hells. The punishments may be "temporary," but that might involve centuries, not hours.

887. the Jade Empire

A blissful heaven with a ruling god who keeps account of man's deeds—sounds familiar, doesn't it? In this particular version (Chinese Taoism), the Jade Emperor is lord of paradise, who can admit people into his Jade Empire or force them to be reincarnated on earth. The immortals live in a beautiful palace surrounded by fragrant gardens with enchanted plants, including a Tree of Immortality. Its fruits grant eternal life to those who eat them.

THE GREEKS AND ROMANS

888. Elysian fields

The ancient Greeks, like the ancient Hebrews, saw the afterlife as a kind of cheerless, half-conscious state in the underworld—not really a place of punishment, but definitely less desirable than life on earth (see 891 [Hades]). However, it was widely believed that certain special people—the great heroes such as Achilles and Odysseus—would reside eternally in a heavenly place, the Elysian fields. Some Greeks even believed that all good people might go there. The terms "Elysian fields" and "Elysium" passed into the Christian vocabulary as alternate names for heaven. (A trivia tidbit: The name of the famous street Champs Elysées in Paris is French for "Elysian fields.")

889. the river Styx

Here is an image from Greek mythology that made its way into Christian art and literature. The Greeks believed that the Styx was the chief river of Hades, the land of the dead. The dead were ferried across it by a ferryman named Charon, and once crossed, there was no coming back. It was often called the "river of hate," and its waters were said to be loathsome. Whenever one of the Greek gods or heroes swore an oath, he would swear by the river Styx.

Christian authors and artists made Styx their own, claiming it was the river of hell, which the damned had to cross before entering the infernal regions. The adjective *Stygian* comes from the name Styx and is sometimes used to mean "infernal," as in the phrase "Stygian darkness."

890. the Greek god Pan

Not all the many gods of the Greeks were represented in beautiful human form. One notable exception was the god of the wide-open spaces, Pan. This wild god of the hills and woodlands is usually represented as having a man's head and torso, but with the shaggy legs and hooves of a goat, and often with a goat's ears, horns, and beard to boot. His appearance was similar to that of satyrs, minor gods of the wild places, always shown as lecherous and uncivilized. As Christianity spread, and as the old religious beliefs of Greece began to wane, Christians associated the pagan gods with demons. This was easy to do in

Pan's case, given his ugly appearance. It is possible that the shape of Pan contributed in some way to the old image of Satan with horns, beard, and hooves.

By the way, the word *panic* is derived from his name.

891. Hades

Not so long ago the word *hell* was hardly spoken in polite company, and "Hades" was used as a substitute. The word is from the Greek, and it referred to the god of the underworld (also known as Pluto) and to the underworld itself. As the ruler of the land of the dead, Hades was a grim god, although a fair one, and he did not correspond in any way to the devil of Christian belief. Nor did his realm correspond to hell, although truly horrible sinners might suffer punishments in Hades, tortured for eternity because of their crimes on earth. But the average Greek did not expect to suffer in Hades—only to be there, conscious, but not having the pleasures he had while on earth.

Greeks thought of Hades as being underground, or perhaps on some distant point on the earth. Obviously the idea of its being underground developed out of the fact that dead bodies were there. This old idea was an obvious influence on the traditional belief of hell as being "down there." (See 892 [Tartarus].)

892. Tartarus

The ancient Greeks believed that the dead, both good and bad, went to Hades, a shadowy, dreary place, but not really a place of torment. But many Greeks also believed in a worse place, Tartarus, which was the lowest part of Hades. Fenced in by a bronze wall with iron gates, Tartarus was the place of confinement for various beings—such as the giants known as the Titans—who had rebelled against the gods.

A form of the name Tartarus occurs in the New Testament. The original Greek text of 2 Peter 2:4 speaks of the angels who rebelled against God and were *tartarosas*—"cast into hell," as it is often translated. Obviously Peter assumed his readers were familiar with Tartarus as the place of confinement for those who rebelled against the divine. Peter would not have believed in the Greek gods or the Titans who rebelled against them, but he would have noticed the similarity between that story and the Christian account of the angels rebelling against God and being cast out of heaven.

893. Pythagoras (c. 500 B.C.)

We remember him today as the mathematician who conceived the Pythagorean theorem. But he was also a philosopher, who taught that the human soul must undergo many reincarnations before breaking free and reaching heaven. As belief in reincarnation has spread, Pythagoras is pointed out as one of the brilliant Greek thinkers who believed in it.

894. Plato and the soul

The idea of a "spiritual body" is difficult to grasp or to explain. Even so, this is the clear teaching of the New Testament: The believer will be raised a whole person, in a glorified body similar to (yet different from) the earthly body. Most people, even most Christians, see it differently: The body dies, and the soul (the spiritual part) goes to heaven or hell. This was the belief of the ancient Greeks, and the philosopher Plato explained that after death the "naked soul" entered the spiritual realm, with the body cast aside as useless.

895. the Furies

In Greek mythology, the Erinyes, or Furies, were goddesses of retribution, sent to torment criminals who had managed to escape human justice. They were hideous creatures with snakes for hair, harassing the offender and eventually driving him mad. Awful as the Furies were, they were just. Their appearance and their role as punishers probably had some effect on how some Christians thought of demons and the torments of hell.

896. the land of Dis

One reason Christianity spread in the Roman Empire was that the old Roman religion offered little hope of a happy afterlife. Many Roman tombs have been found with such hopeless inscriptions as "I was not, I was, I am not, I care not." The ancient Roman religion taught that the dead went to Dis, a cheerless place of shadows, like the Greeks' Hades or the Hebrews' Sheol.

897. Cicero (106–43 B.C.)

Most of the ancient Romans had no clear concept of an afterlife. But the great Roman author and statesman Cicero believed that after death there would be a joyous reunion of loved ones, with no fear of their fellowship being interrupted by death again. Cicero was widely read by many Christian scholars, and some of them believed he was a "pre-Christian Christian" (that is, an enlightened pagan whose beliefs were fairly close to Christianity).

THE SECTS

898. Jehovah's Witnesses and eternity

Jehovah's Witnesses are annihilationists—that is, they believe the wicked person's body dies, and that is all, with no eternal punishment. The good are resurrected, the evil are annihilated.

Since the group was founded, they have been expecting Armageddon and setting up the kingdom of God on earth. This kingdom will be governed by Christ through 144,000 people in heaven, and governed on earth through an indefinite number of "Jonadabs." (In the early days, the Witnesses said that only 144,000 persons would be saved, but as their membership passed that number [over three million now], they allowed for the salvation of "other sheep," also known as "Jonadabs." The number 144,000 was based on the reference of the people "sealed" by God in Rev. 7.)

899. Jehovah's Witnesses and the angel Michael

Noted for their door-to-door evangelism, the Witnesses depart from Christian teaching in stating that Jesus is inferior to God Himself. Jesus Christ was, they say, the angel Michael, existing in heaven before He took the human form of Jesus. While an angel, He was not guaranteed immortality but had to earn it by taking human form and being crucified as a sacrifice for mankind. Just as Michael/Jesus was not originally immortal, any angel can die. Evil angels such as Satan will definitely die.

900. the Adventists

The various Adventist groups began in America in the 1840s, originally centered around expectation of the return of Christ. Today the main groups are the Seventh-day Adventists (known for worshiping on Saturday, of course), and the much smaller Advent Christian Church. Adventists are annihilationists, believing that the wicked are annihilated, not punished by eternity in hell. They also believe in "soul sleep" (see 21).

901. Mother Ann and the Shakers

The movement began as a spin-off of the Quakers. (Notice the similarity in names.) "Mother" Ann Lee of England led several followers to settle in New York State in 1774. The group's actual name was the United Society of Believers in Christ's Second Appearing. Members got the name Shakers from their ecstatic dance in worship. The Shakers encouraged speaking in tongues and believed in divine healing. They were also celibate, which naturally limited their membership. Mother Ann based their belief in celibacy on Jesus' words about the angels and human residents of heaven not marrying nor mating. She believed (as have many Christians who insist on celibacy) that humans in this life ought to act like angels, which includes being celibate.

902. disembodied and re-embodied angels

Mormonism's teachings about angels differ radically from traditional Christian belief. There are, the Mormons say, disembodied and re-embodied angels. The re-embodied angels are those who were once human beings; they were humans who died, became disembodied souls, then acquired bodies again in order to appear on earth. The disembodied angels, on the other hand, were never humans. These existed in heaven with God before the creation of the world. Some were divine and good, but some (Satan and his followers) were infernal, having rejected the rule of God.

903. Christian Science angels

The religion founded by Mary Baker Eddy in the 1860s claims that God is infinite Mind, and human beings are reflections of that Mind. Matter doesn't truly exist, and neither does evil. So what role might angels play in such a religion? Mrs. Eddy claimed that angels are nothing more than the thoughts of God that reach human beings.

COMMON GROUND WITH CHRISTIANITY

904. war in heaven: the universal story

Elsewhere in this book you will read about the Christian (and Jewish) tradition of Lucifer and his angels rebelling against God, making war, and being cast from heaven, after which they become Satan and his horde of demons. This "war in heaven" occurs in other religions and in mythology. Some Christians might reply, "So what? The Christian story is unique, and it also happens to be true." True, but perhaps this true story made its way to other lands, peoples, and belief systems. Consider the Greek myths: The gods of Olympus had to battle and vanquish the hideous Titans, who were kept locked safely underground. Consider Hindu legend, with its ancient epic of the savior Rama against the forces of the demon king Ravana. Consider the Norse myths, with the good gods battling the frost giants at the end of time (although in the Norse myths the bad guys actually win!). In the Zoroastrian religion of Persia, the forces of the good god Ahura-Mazda war with, and eventually conquer, the evil forces of Ahriman. Just as the story of Noah and the Flood are found in various forms worldwide, so we find the familiar gods-versus-demons war.

905. hells elsewhere

Christianity has taken a lot of flak in recent years, especially for its belief in hell. Critics overlook an obvious fact: There are hells in most of the world's religions. Consider a trendy religion of today, Tibetan Buddhism. Its ages-old *Bardo Thodol* (or Book of the Dead) contains horrifying descriptions of the torments that await evil people in the underworld. The tortures endure endlessly, for an immortal soul can never be destroyed. Trendiness in religion involves leaving out the parts one does not like.

906. picturing the Last Judgment

Hell has become unpopular in Christian circles, but in ages past it was a favorite subject for Christian artists. Scenes of the Last Judgment always showed both sides: the good entering paradise, the bad consigned to hell. Other religions have depicted their own versions of the Last Judgment. The ancient Egyptians, for example, showed the god Osiris judging the dead in his Hall of Justice. Some Asian religions show Yama, stern lord of the dead, judging their souls. And there are many Muslim pictures of Allah separating the wicked from the good. A logical question: With this belief in a final judgment so widespread, isn't it likely to be true?

907. the ladder image

Genesis 28 presents us with the famous story of Jacob's dream of a ladder (or stairway) reaching from earth to heaven. The image of the heavenly ladder crops up in many other world religions, including some of the native African religions. It seems to be a universal longing: a desire to see some connection between our world and the world of the divine.

908. the Dead Sea Scrolls

These ancient scrolls, discovered in a cave in 1947, have amazed scholars with their wealth of information about the Jewish group known as the Essenes. The scrolls say much about the angels (more than the Old Testament tells us). According to the scrolls, the flapping of the angels' wings creates its own joyous music in heaven. In the future there will be a great battle between the "Sons of Light" and the "Sons of Darkness." The good will triumph, and all enemies, including the devil, will be vanquished.

909. Tantalus

We get our word *tantalize* from the character Tantalus of Greek mythology. While on earth, Tantalus had committed an atrocity against the gods. His punishment in the underworld was to have food and drink just within his reach, but snatched away every time he reached for them. The idea of being eternally deprived of what one desires found its way into Christian beliefs about hell.

910. Hercules

In the early days of Christianity, many Christians tried to relate the Greek myths to Christian truths. In Greek myth, Hercules, the semidivine strongman, accomplished what some thought impossible: He triumphed over Cerberus, the monster dog who guarded the gateway to Hades to keep people from escaping. Some Christians said the Hercules myth was a "preview" of Christ, who rescued the people in hell by conquering sin.

911. guardians at hell's gate

Presumably no one would want to remain in hell, so in popular religion and mythology, hell always has some sort of monster guarding the gate. For the Greeks it was Cerberus, a hulking three-headed dog, and for the Norsemen it was Garm. Christianity has no official teaching about such a beast, but Christian authors and painters have often shown the gate of hell in the form of a beast itself, a gaping mouth with fangs that keeps people from escaping.

912. Yama

Many Asians believe in Yama, a green demon king with red eyes and fangs, who is accompanied by two monster dogs. Sometimes he is described as wearing a necklace of human skulls. He is judge of the dead, whom he may send to one of his hells, or back to earth for another life. Aside from the reincarnation factor, he bears a striking resemblance to Christian conceptions of Satan.

913. Cernunnous

There are various reasons why Satan is depicted with horns, one influence being that Cernunnous, the Celtic god of the underworld, was shown that way. (His name means "the horned one.") As Christianity spread to the Celtic regions such as Britain, the missionaries naturally identified this horrid deity with Satan. Cernunnous is by no means the only Satan-like character depicted with horns.

914. Ghede

The troubled land of Haiti contains an odd mix of Catholic practice and voodoo. In the voodoo legends,

Ghede is a kind of Satan, and with a distinctive look: dark glasses, top hat, long black coat. He can take people to hell but also resurrect the dead, turning them into zombies. Ghede is one of thousands of Satans in the world's folk religions, reminding us that Satan (under whatever name) is a fixture in human consciousness.

915. Hahgwehdaetgah

When the Europeans first came to North America, they discovered that most of the natives already believed in some form of Satan. The Iroquois, for example, believed in this evil figure with the long and unpronounceable name. He ruled over the dead in a horrible underworld and worked to thwart his twin brother, the good god. Sound familiar?

916. Cupay and other Satans

As Christian missionaries evangelized the globe, one part of their mission was fairly easy: to convince people that the devil exists. Most cultures, wherever they are, have some concept of a devil (or several), a hideous fiend that torments human beings, leads them to harm one another, and eventually lands them in hell. The Inca people of South America believed in such a fiend, Cupay, the god of death. The Catholic missionaries readily identified this Cupay with Satan.

917. happy hunting ground

The American Indians generally believed in an afterlife, at least for the good (and *good* might mean "courageous in battle" instead of "moral"). The afterlife would be an idealized version of an American landscape with no enemies to battle but plenty of wild game to hunt eternally. "Happy hunting ground" passed into the world's vocabulary as another name for heaven.

SOME CHRISTIAN SKEPTICS

918. John Scotus Erigena (c. 810–c. 877)

This controversial theologian was born in Ireland (which is what *Erigena* means) but made his reputation in the empire of Charlemagne. He was a skeptic who seemed to respect logic more than the revelation of the Bible. In the Middle Ages, when people who did not believe in hell rarely said so (for fear of being punished for heresy), he wrote that there was no eternal hell, and that when it is mentioned in the Bible it is referring only to the remorse felt by a guilty conscience. Heaven is not a place but is the joy of the divine vision. But like many people who don't believe in hell themselves, he thought that belief in hell was "useful" to the church, for without it many people might simply toss faith aside, and their morals to boot.

919. Henry More (1614–1687)

More was a member of an intellectual group known as the Cambridge Platonists. Most of them claimed to be Christian, but they were fascinated by the Greek philosophers and felt that philosophy and Christianity could be merged into a perfect "rational" religion. In his book *Immortality of the Soul,* More rejected the Bible's concept of a resurrected and glorified body and insisted that heaven is a purely spiritual state (a view the Greeks might have approved). Like most philosophers, he thought of heaven as a place that philosophers might enjoy.

920. God breaking His word

In the 1700s, the age of the so-called Enlightenment, skepticism about Christianity had a hold on intellectuals, and it even affected clergymen. Notably in the Church of England, belief about heaven and especially about hell was on the wane. One noted preacher told Queen Anne that though the Bible taught that hell was eternal, this was probably just the Bible authors' way of driving home the importance of repentance. While it was God's right to punish men eternally, God was free to break His word and make hell only a temporary punishment.

921. John A. T. Robinson

Bishop Robinson of the Church of England was "Mr. Liberal" after the publication of his 1963 book *Honest to*

God. This popular book was widely loved and hated, and Robinson's attempt to "update" Christian beliefs met with both cheers and sneers. Robinson, as a liberal, might be expected to shun belief in hell. Sort of—but not quite. Robinson claimed that after death we all go to be with God—which for some will be heaven, but not so for others. For those who have spent their lives selfishly, being in the presence of God will be painful.

922. Rudolf Bultmann (1884-1976)

Demythologizing was the word Bultmann made famous. This influential German theologian said that the New Testament and its many miracles had to be "demythologized," restated in terms that modern man could accept. Put another way, Bultmann pretty much threw out the miraculous parts of the Bible, including any belief in an afterlife. He claimed not to believe in heaven, but replied to one interviewer, "You can always hope."

923. liberation theology

Why seek heaven when you could transform earth into a utopia? That question was the driving force behind liberation theology, a theological movement popular in the 1960s and 1970s. As everyone now admits, it was more influenced by Marxism than by the Bible. Liberation theologians played down the New Testament's teachings on mercy, kindness,

and forgiving one's enemies and, instead, focused on political liberation, freeing people from oppression as God did the
Israelites in Exodus. Critics of liberation theology pointed
out that Exodus shows God as the liberator but that the
Israelites themselves did not use violence for their liberation—while liberation theologians condoned violence. As
Marxism declined in popularity, so has liberation theology. Its
influence lingers among liberals who prefer utopia to heaven.

SECULARISM VS. RELIGION

924. the Enlightenment

In the 1700s many people, particularly intellectuals,
began to put more faith in human ability than in
Christianity and the Bible. Enlightenment philosophers
stressed mankind's rationality, which could serve as a better guide to life than the Bible and the church, which were
"superstitious." Many Enlightenment leaders called
themselves "Deists," believers in God, but a God that
pretty much left mankind to itself. Christ was seen as a
moral teacher, not the Savior of mankind. Sin, said the
intellectuals, was not man's problem—ignorance was.
Some of them believed in an afterlife, some did not. Of
those who did, most did not believe in hell, or if they did,
they believed it was only temporary. Such skeptics had no
belief at all in angels or demons. Authors like Voltaire
helped popularize Enlightenment thought. It was a powerful influence on America's Founding Fathers, particularly Benjamin Franklin and Thomas Jefferson.

925. deism

Many Enlightenment thinkers (including Thomas Jefferson and Benjamin Franklin) considered themselves *deists*, believing in a God who created the world and pretty much left it to itself. Many deists (certainly not all) believed that heaven and hell were real, but that one's eternal fate was based on one's deeds, not on one's religious beliefs. People of any creed could be saved, and there was no place for the unique saving message of the Bible. The poet Alexander Pope, a nominal Catholic but really a deist, took the typical deist view that all religions are pretty much alike. In his poem "The Universal Prayer," he prayed to the "Father of all! In every age / In every clime adored, / By saint, by savage, and by sage, /Jehovah, Jove, or Lord!" Pope seemed to have the same belief as Linus in the comic strip "Peanuts": It doesn't matter what you believe, as long as you're sincere.

926. the "opiate of the people"

Karl Marx, founder of Communism, was an atheist who called religion the "opiate of the people." He meant that religion, by giving people spiritual consolation and a belief in an afterlife, kept them from starting revolutions and changing the world around them. Marx overlooked a basic fact: People *need* a spiritual opiate, and the hope of heaven is about the best. Worth noting: People who put their faith in Communism have been extremely disappointed, and some have thought religion was a wiser choice.

927. Utopia

Sir Thomas More (1478–1535), the chancellor of England who was beheaded for defying King Henry VIII, wrote this popular book about an ideal society. The book's title passed into the language as meaning such a society, a "heaven on earth." More was a Christian, and it is appropriate that utopia means, in Greek, "no place," for More did not truly believe such a perfect society could ever exist on earth. Hundreds of authors and social planners have thought otherwise, but their plans for utopia always fail (the selfishness of human nature being the cause). Utopia-seekers generally despise Christians, believing them to be too concerned with the next world and not enough with this one. Christians can reply to the utopia-seekers with a painful truth: Utopias don't work—never have, never will. (For details, look at the utopia-minded people who gave us Communism, the French Revolution, and so on.)

928. immortality of influence

Do people spend eternity in heaven or hell—or do they simply die and decompose? Most human beings prefer some concept of immortality to none at all. One view common among intellectuals is that we live via our influence on later generations—an "immortality of influence." Looked at in this way, the "immortals" would include Jesus, and also Muhammad, Plato, Aristotle, Shakespeare,

Washington, Lincoln—but also Freud, Darwin, Marx, Stalin, Mao, and many others not worth mentioning. (Influence can be either good or bad, obviously.) Victorian author George Eliot, a religious skeptic, expressed this view in a poem: "O may I join the choir invisible / Of those immortal dead who live again / In minds made better by their presence." Sounds charming, doesn't it—but not much of a comfort in life or on one's deathbed. Christianity has much more to offer, while not ruling out an immortality of influence.

929. impersonal immortality

Some world religions—as well as some modern beliefs about the hereafter—teach that immortality is impersonal. A person dies (perhaps after several reincarnations) and is absorbed into the Absolute, the One (perhaps called God, but not the personal God of the Bible). Being absorbed, we lose our individuality as a raindrop in the ocean loses its uniqueness. In such an afterlife there is obviously no memory, no awareness of "me," no sense of individual purpose or destiny. In other words, it's close to being annihilated. Hinduism and Buddhism both tend in this direction, and it appeals to many contemporary people (maybe because individual destiny might involve being accountable for one's individual sins?).

17

Words and Phrases

930. pandemonium

We use the word to mean a wild, chaotic uproar. The word was invented by English poet John Milton. In *Paradise Lost*, his epic poem about Satan and the temptation of Adam and Eve, Milton gave the name Pandemonium to the capital of hell, the dwelling place of demons. The word comes from the Greek *pan* ("all") and *daimon* ("demon")—so Pandemonium is the "place of all demons."

931. anathema

This refers to something horrible or accursed. It is an Aramaic word from the New Testament, a word Paul used to refer to the curse upon unbelievers when the Lord returns to earth. "If any man love not the Lord Jesus

Christ, let him be Anathema Maranatha" (1 Cor. 16:22 KJV). *Anathema Maranatha* means "accursed when the Lord comes." Over the course of time the Catholic church would "pronounce an anathema" upon a person excommunicated from the church—that is, outside the official church, a person was assumed to be bound for hell.

932. seventh heaven

Seven is one of the "sacred numbers" of the Bible, always a "good" number that suggests goodness, completeness. There are seven days in a week (with the seventh being the Sabbath, the holy day), and numerous other sevens. And seven is still, after all these centuries, a "lucky" number. Even someone who has never read the Bible probably knows that "seventh heaven" must mean "the best place to be." Does the Bible mention just how many heavens there are? No. But the apostle Paul did mention in 2 Corinthians 12:2 that he knew a man (he may have been referring to himself) who was "caught up to the third heaven." How many heavens did Paul believe in? We have no idea. But there was a Jewish tradition that there were seven, the seventh being the highest and best.

933. cloud nine

Seven is a "holy" number in the Bible, but nine isn't bad, either. In Dante's *Divine Comedy*, there are nine (not seven) heavens, the ninth being closest to God. Somehow "ninth heaven" passed into language as "cloud nine," meaning "a wonderful place to be."

934. "fool's paradise"

The phrase "fool's paradise" refers to someone in a bad state who believes that everything is fine. Centuries ago, many Christians believed there was a Paradise of Fools, a region where the feebleminded went after death. Since such people are not responsible for their acts on earth, they do not deserve hell, but do not deserve the full joy of heaven, either, so they reside eternally in a kind of "suburb" of heaven. Milton speaks of this region in his *Paradise Lost*. (See 935 [Limbo].)

935. Limbo

Before it was the name of a Caribbean dance craze, Limbo referred to a region where souls rested after death. The name comes from the Latin *limbus*, meaning "border-land." The early Christians puzzled over an obvious question: What became of the righteous people who lived before Christ? Since they had not put their faith in Christ (though this was no fault of their own), did that mean they went to hell? Some believers said, "Alas, yes." But some said there was a Limbo, a place for righteous pre-Christians who did not deserve hell, but who also could not be admitted to heaven, since they were not Christians. (Worth noting: Officially, the Roman Catholic Church only bestows the title "Saint" on Christians, but the Eastern Orthodox also bestows it on various Old Testament figures—so the Orthodox have a Saint Moses, Saint Elijah, and so on.) Some Christians believed that not only would the saints of the Old Testament be in Limbo, but also righteous people among the pagans, such as the philosopher Socrates. In his *Divine Comedy*, the poet Dante located the region of Limbo as near hell, but not actually part of hell. (See 934 [fool's paradise]; 11 [what about infants?].)

936. *heofen*

We get our word *heaven* from the Anglo-Saxon (Old English) word *heofen*, which meant nothing more than "the skies." The word itself has no theological meaning, but like most people across the globe, the Anglo-Saxons associated the skies with divinity.

937. Hel the goddess

We get our word *hell* from a very old Anglo-Saxon word, *helan*, meaning "to conceal." (Thus hell is a "hidden place.") But another related word was *Hel*, the name the Vikings gave to their goddess of death and the underworld. In time her name came to apply to the underworld itself (just as the name of the Greek god of the underworld, Hades, came to apply to his realm). In the area we now know as Germany, her name took the form *Hellia*. Interestingly, the Hel of the Vikings was cold, not hot. (Perhaps in their cold climate a hot hell might have sounded pleasant, not frightening.) The goddess Hel herself was, naturally, ugly—half flesh-colored, but half corpselike and rotting.

938. infernal

Infernus is the old Latin word for *hell*. Note the word for *hell* in these languages: Spanish, *infierno;* French, *enfer;* Italian, *inferno*.

939. empyrean

Empyrean is another word for "heavenly" or "celestial." Christians sometimes use "the empyrean" or "Empyrium" to refer to heaven, but it can also refer to the highest heaven, the "region of pure light." The high ceilings and windows of the great cathedrals were no doubt intended to remind worshipers of "the empyrean."

940. ". . . where angels fear to tread"

Probably one of the most-quoted lines in English literature is "Fools rush in where angels fear to tread," a poetic way of saying that people lacking wisdom or discretion will attempt things that the wise person (wise like the angels) would stay away from. The line sounds like Shakespeare, and most people attribute it to him, but the line is actually by Alexander Pope, found in his *Essay on Criticism*.

941. vale of tears

The Bible promises that God will eventually wipe away all tears of His faithful people (Isa. 25:8; Rev. 21:4). Heaven is tearless, but in the meantime this present world is a "vale of weeping" or a "vale of tears," a phrase that has passed into common usage. The phrase comes through a mistranslation of Psalm 84:6, which means the "Valley of Baca"; some older translations have "vale of tears," and this picturesque phrase came to mean "the world," the place where all people, even the saints, must endure their share of weeping.

942. doomsday

We use *doom* to mean "horrible end," but originally (in Old English) it meant simply "judgment," not necessarily bad. When the Anglo-Saxons spoke of "doomsday," it meant "judgment day," the Last Judgment, when people would give account for their deeds and be assigned to either heaven or hell.

943. devil's advocate

Used loosely, this term refers to one who argues the unpopular side of an issue. In fact, it refers to a person who plays a key role in the Roman Catholic Church's process of canonization (making a person an official saint). To prevent any unworthy person from being made a saint, the Catholic church appoints someone to search out defects (if any) in the life of the proposed saint. This person is generally called a "devil's advocate," based on the Bible's view of Satan as the "accuser of God's people." (Also, think back to Job: God was pleased with Job's saintliness, but Satan showed up to say, "Ah, he isn't as marvelous as You may think . . .")

944. "enough to make the angels weep"

Something supremely foolish is "enough to make the angels weep." The phrase is from Shakespeare's *Measure for Measure*: "Proud man . . . / Plays such fantastic tricks before high heaven / As make the angels weep."

945. "the devil looks after his own"

Good people aren't always successful (by worldly standards), and bad people often do succeed (temporarily). The old expression "The devil looks after his own" is true, but not eternally.

946. "all hell broke loose"

The phrase is from Book IV of John Milton's epic poem *Paradise Lost*, where Satan and his demons are important characters. It's possible the phrase was already in use when Milton found a place for it in his masterpiece.

947. "better the devil you know . . ."

In full, the familiar phrase is "Better the devil you know than the devil you don't." In other words, an evil we haven't experienced yet may be worse than one we're used to. The phrase may go back as far as the Middle Ages.

948. "the dickens you say"

In times past people took swearing more seriously, so no one would (in polite company, anyway) use "God" or "Jesus" in vain. Thus we get such expressions as "jeepers creepers" and "goldurn" and "gosh." People applied this same restraint to the devil and hell, so instead of "the devil you say," people substituted "the dickens you say" or "the deuce you say." Shakespeare used "the dickens" all the way back in the 1500s, so it has nothing to do with author Charles Dickens, who lived in the 1800s.

949. Beulah Land

An old gospel song about heaven is called "Dwelling in Beulah Land." Yes, Beulah is a woman's name, but the song takes the name Beulah from Isaiah, who prophesied that the land of Israel would someday be called Beulah, Hebrew for "married" (Isa. 62:4). How does a land "marry"? Again and again the Old Testament speaks of God as the "husband" of Israel. The early Christians liked this idea, and it also appears in the Bible's final book, Revelation, which speaks of the New Jerusalem (heaven) as a bride prepared for her husband (Rev. 21:2).

950. the promised land

Israel was the promised land, "promised" because when God called Abraham from the pagan land of Ur, He promised Canaan (later called Israel) to Abraham's descendants (Gen. 12:7). Their residency in the region ended when Jacob and his twelve sons moved to Egypt to escape a famine. Exodus relates that Jacob's descendants lived peacefully in Egypt until the Egyptians made them into slaves. Moses led them from Egypt back to Canaan— a journey that took forty years.

The early Christians read and loved the Old Testament, and they took the old promises regarding the promised land and spiritualized them—that is, it seemed obvious that the land of Israel itself wasn't the ultimate destination for God's people (since Christianity was spreading all over the world), so they took the promised land to be heaven.

951. Canaan

Many old hymns refer to "Canaan land." "Canaan" in the Old Testament referred to the general area occupied by the Israelites—roughly the same area occupied today by the nation Israel. As with "promised land," Christians adopted the name *Canaan* and gave it a new, spiritual meaning: heaven. Just as God in the Old Testament had designated Canaan as the home for His chosen people (the Israelites), so heaven is the "New Canaan" for His chosen people (Christians). When an old hymn speaks of being "on my way to Canaan land," it is referring to home in heaven.

952. crossing the Jordan

There was and is a real Jordan River in Israel, though many tourists claim it should be called "creek" instead of "river." It figures in several important Old Testament stories, such as the Israelites crossing it at flood stage (Josh. 3), a miracle similar to the parting of the Red Sea in the book of Exodus. The crossing was important to the Israelites because it meant that they had really entered Canaan, the land God had promised them. Because "crossing the Jordan" meant "entering Canaan," the early

Christians spiritualized the story in this way: Dying is the way we enter heaven (the "promised land"), so the phrase "crossing the Jordan" refers to dying.

Another remarkable story: Elijah the prophet, who struck the river with his mantle then crossed it on dry land just before he was taken to heaven in a fiery chariot (2 Kings 2). As with the story in the last paragraph, "crossing the Jordan" meant dying, entering heaven.

953. "gone west"

To "go west" is old slang for "to die," but more properly it means "to go to heaven." Many religions throughout the world associate the west with heaven, probably because the sun sets in the west. (Sunset equals death.) Some of the American Indians spoke of heaven as the Land of Sunset.

954. ghoul

This refers to a demon or ghost of hideous appearance. It comes from the Arabic *ghul*, a creature that robs graves and feeds on corpses. Ghouls, in various forms and called by different names, are a recurring part of religions around the world. They have no place in Christianity, but artwork showing hell often depicts people in hell as ghouls, hideous to behold.

955. "going to hell in a handbasket"

This common expression is actually the flip side of an older expression, "going to heaven in a handbasket." The original meant that one had life easy—that is, a person leading a "charmed life" appeared to be "going to heaven in a handbasket."

956. the road to hell

"The road to hell is paved with good intentions"—the proverb is used commonly, but who said it first? The English author and dictionary compiler Samuel Johnson said that "hell is paved with good intentions," and somehow "the road to" got added on later. It reflects a basic Christian idea: People can do much evil while thinking they are doing good.

957. angel visits

The British use this to refer to rare and/or brief social visits, as in "John hardly ever sees his poor mother, paying her just a few angel visits." The phrase is based on the idea that the visits of angels to humans (most humans, anyway) are brief and rare.

958. angelica

A vegetable from *Iceland*? That's angelica, though in most of the world it's an herb, not a vegetable. This aromatic herb is used as a flavoring and also in perfumes. The plant's "heavenly" aroma led to its being named for the angels. The lovely name was also used for a form of the musical instrument known as the lute, popular in the 1600s.

959. angel-hair

Artwork often show angels with normal human hair, but sometimes they are shown with hair of gold or some other metal, or hair of an extremely fine texture. Thus "angel hair" is applied to the very thinnest type of pasta, and also to a fine, weblike material sometimes draped over Christmas trees.

960. angel dust

There is nothing heavenly about the drug phencyclidine, which has been called angel dust since the late 1960s. It's true that the people using this drug have been known to see angels—as well as demons, pink elephants, floating houses, flying camels, and many other things.

961. angelfish

Artists sometimes show angels as human in general shape, but because angels are heavenly, artists could run wild with color and costumes. Because angels are often clad in bright, gemlike garb, the name angelfish has been applied to various species of fish. The brilliantly colored species common in coral reefs belong to the genus *Angelichthys* (Greek for "angelfish"). Curiously, the common angelfish of home aquariums, silvery with black stripes, is probably the least beautiful fish bearing the name.

962. angel slices

These cookies, made with pecans and coconut, have always been popular with children. One story is that Saint Peter at the gate of heaven gives them to children entering in to help them get over their homesickness for earth.

963. angels on horseback

These are a type of canapé, made with large oysters wrapped in bacon and served on small cocktail bread. It takes a serious stretch of imagination to see how they got their name.

964. devilfish

The octopus has been called this, but most commonly this name applies to several extremely large rays (fish, that is), whose broad, batlike wings and "horns" do, indeed, remind one of Satan.

965. devil theory

Do bad things just happen in the world, or is there a plot, a conspiracy? Long before "conspiracy theory" became a popular phrase, the term "devil theory" meant roughly the same thing: Crises in society are deliberately caused by evil or misguided leaders.

966. angelophant

The word *angelophany* means the appearing of an angel (from the Greek *angelos*, "messenger," and *phainein*, meaning "showing" or "manifestation"). The person to whom the angel appears is an *angelophant*. The Bible records several angelophanies, as do the traditions of the Jews and Muslims. After several centuries in which angelophanies have seemed quite rare, our own age has seen an increase in angelophanies (or, at least, more reports of them).

18

Odds and Ends,
Mostly Fascinating

967. hell in America

In terms of place names, there are more hells and devils on
the American map than there are angels and heavens. To
name a few: Hell's Canyon (on the border between Idaho
and Oregon), Devil's Den (Arkansas), Devil's Punch Bowl
(Oregon), Devil's Hole (New York), Devil's Postpile
(California), Hell's Gate (Idaho), the Devil's Playground
(California, naturally), Devil's Lake (two—North Dakota
and Wisconsin), Devil's Tower (Wyoming). On the more
pleasant side, Indiana has Angel Mounds.

968. the name bank

The Bible has always been a good source when people are
naming their children. Only two angels are named in the

Bible, and though Gabriel has never been all that common, Michael is one of the most common boys' names in the world. (And not just in the form Michael. Miguel is common among the Spanish-speaking, plus Michel in French, Michele in Italian, Mikhail in Russian, and so on.) And of course, the common girls' name Angela is just a feminine form of "angel," plus the male name Angelo is common in many countries.

969. Hell's Angels

This California-based group began around 1950 and established the trend for demonic images. The Angels, and the many bikers who imitate them, go for the color black, tattoos of Satan and demons, and a general look of the infernal. Why? First, it looks intimidating to outsiders, and second, it seems like the ultimate in rebellion. ("We're not nice guys, we're straight out of hell".)

970. angels of the four winds

Many old, old maps (the kind people like to collect and frame) show angels at the four corners. With their cheeks puffed out, they represent the winds from the four compass points. Oddly, this image is based on the Bible: Revelation 7:1 describes four angels at the four corners of the earth, holding back the four winds.

971. ape or angel?

Charles Darwin and his book *The Descent of Man* hit Christianity hard, and his teaching on evolution did and still does provoke controversy. For most people who are not Christians, the matter is settled: Darwin was right, the Bible is wrong, and man did descend from primates, end of discussion. But in Darwin's time the subject was still worth arguing about, even among intellectuals. Benjamin Disraeli, author and British prime minister, was a sophisticated and worldly man, yet he is also remembered for his quote on the subject of evolution: "Is man an ape or an angel? I, my Lord, am on the side of the angels."

972. police angels

In 1950, Pope Pius XII declared the archangel Michael to be the patron of policemen. Considering Michael's role as "captain of heaven's armies" that will defeat Satan at the end of time, he was a wise choice.

973. angelic post

The U.S. Postal Service is no longer a monopoly, for there are now many private carriers as competition (not to mention faxes and E-mail). Even so, people still make jokes about the slowness of the U.S. mail. Perhaps people hoping to have a letter or package delivered on time (and to the right address) might recall that the angel Gabriel has officially (for Catholics) been designated as the patron angel of postal workers. Since the Greek word *angelos* means "messenger," this is appropriate.

974. hell visions and horror movies

People of our time may snicker or feel disgust when told that people in the Middle Ages actually took pleasure in hearing sermons about hell, or viewing pictures showing the horrors of hell. Morbid, you say? Perhaps. But then, human beings seem to have a basic need for horror in some form. Horror movies—nowadays more graphic than ever before—are generally surefire hits at the box office. Morbid, you say? Or just human nature?

975. angelware

With angels becoming highly trendy in recent years, all manner of "angelware" has been marketed—T-shirts, stickers, key chains, jewelry, and whatnot. Among the more unusual items are animal figurines adorned with wings and halos. These are especially popular with animal lovers whose beloved pet has died.

976. HALOS

Angels are big business. Not only are books on angels popular, but so are all sorts of pictures, jewelry, cards, trinkets, and other items relating to angels. In 1993 Denny Dahlmann, owner of a store called the Angel Treasures Boutique, started an organization called HALOS—Helping Angel Lovers Own Stores.

977. more devils than angels in rock

In the titles of rock songs, the word *devil* outnumbers *angel*—two to one, in fact. (This is based on the databases of two major record store chains.) *Heaven* outnumbers *hell*, of course—but only because *hell* is still (just barely) considered profane.

978. the devil's missionary

This name has been applied to many people, most famously to the noted French author Voltaire (1694–1778), a widely read opponent of Christianity. Voltaire was no atheist, but there's no doubt that his writings helped lead many people away from faith.

979. Archangel

It's the name of a large port city in northern Russia. Built in the 1500s, its original name was Archangel Michael, named for the angel mentioned in the Bible. Surprisingly, in the long years of domination by a Communist government that was committed to atheism, this city with an angelic name never was pressured to rename itself.

980. Los Angeles

The name means, in Spanish, "the angels," but earlier it was known as "San Gabriel," named for the angel Gabriel. Later it was given a name we would translate as "Village of Our Lady of the Angels" (the Virgin Mary being the "Lady"). Eventually it was simply abbreviated to "Los Angeles," or, for those who are really lazy, "L.A."

981. the angel coin

Up until the 1700s, people in England would present themselves to the ruler to be cured of what was called the "King's Evil." (It was scrofula, a skin condition.) Standard procedure was for the king to touch the person, then to present him with an "angel." This was a coin, first minted in the 1400s, which on one side showed the archangel Michael slaying a dragon (Satan, that is).

982. choirs of angels

Music and worship go hand in hand in almost every religion. The prophet Isaiah pictured music in heaven, with the angelic seraphs saying "Holy, holy, holy" before the throne of God (Isa. 6:3). In his influential treatise *The Celestial Hierarchy*, the author known as Pseudo-Dionysius referred to the nine categories of angels as *choirs*.

983. the Jewish night prayer

A centuries-old Jewish prayer asks for the aid of four angels—two from the Bible, two from tradition: "May Michael be at my right hand, Gabriel at my left, before me Uriel, and behind me Raphael, and above my head the divine presence of God."

984. catacombs

These were the famous underground cemeteries of Rome, cut out of rock and used not only for burials but also as hiding places during persecution of Christians. The inscriptions on the Christian tombs tell us a great deal about how strongly the early Christians believed in the afterlife. Some examples: "Julia, in peace with the saints," "We know thou dwellest with Christ," "Aurelius, forever with the Savior and the angels." Heaven was a reality for these people.

985. burning the martyrs

Christians have been executed because of their faith by many means, but burning was a favorite in the early years. One reason was that persecutors knew that Christians placed a high value on the body and believed the whole person, body and soul, would be resurrected. Burning a Christian to ashes would (so the persecutors thought) prevent any resurrection, and also add an additional insult to the martyrdom.

986. Luther and Magdalena

Losing a child is never easy, even when both parent and child are assured of meeting together in heaven. The great Reformation leader Martin Luther lost his beloved daughter Magdalena when she was only fourteen. Just before she died, she told him that she would accept God's will—whether she would remain with her earthly father, or go to be with her Father in heaven. Luther held her when she died, grieving, "How strange it is to know that she is at peace and all is well, and yet to be so sorrowful!"

987. the knighthood ceremony

We're all familiar with the posture of the knighthood ceremony: The man being made a knight kneels before his lord, who touches him three times on each shoulder with the flat side of a sword. Curiously, the formula for making the knight includes mention of an angel: "In the name of God, Saint Michael, and Saint George, I make thee knight." Michael, whom the Bible and tradition portray as a heavenly warrior angel (see Rev. 12), was a favorite of knights, as was the soldiering Saint George, who (like Michael) was believed to be a dragon-slayer.

988. Kaiser Wilhelm

During World War I, the Allies used a recruiting poster showing Germany's leader, Kaiser Wilhelm, as Satan, horns and tail and all. The message: Join the army and conquer the German devil. This was not the first, and certainly not the last, time a nation involved in war whipped up patriotism by painting the enemy as satanic. Consider the countries that refer to the U.S. as "the Great Satan."

989. lawyer jokes

Hell is no laughing matter, but you would never guess that from the millions of jokes about the afterlife. A random survey of contemporary jokes suggests that of all the occupational groups associated with hell, lawyers receive the most mention.

990. comic books

Kids are fascinated by hell, as evidenced by comic books and their various Internet versions. Since the 1950s, horror comics centering around fiends from hell or demon-hunters who chase down the devils and return them there have been phenomenally popular. While liberals doubt if God would punish anyone eternally, there is a strong sense of justice in comic books, where villains get what they deserve.

991. "The Far Side"

Gary Larson "retired" his popular cartoon feature a few years ago, but its comical images are still marketed through books, calendars, and various other spin-offs. More so than any other contemporary cartoonist, Larson was fascinated by the comic potential of hell, always depicting it in the usual fire-and-brimstone fashion, but with humor thrown in (such as people being forced to do aerobics for all eternity).

992. computer games

Satan, hell, and demons are a fixed feature of the computer game industry, with such popular titles as *Virtual Hell; Doom II: Hell on Earth;* and *Quake*. Ironic, isn't it, that in a time when hell is hardly ever spoken of in churches, kids can see it, hear it, and play with it via the computer?

993. "The Devil Went Down to Georgia"

Charlie Daniels's popular country song was a variation on the old Faust theme: A man (Johnny, the champion fiddler) and Satan agree that if Johnny can outfiddle Satan, he gets a gold fiddle, but if Satan wins, he gets Johnny's soul. Johnny wins, of course. The song had a sequel years later, "The Devil Goes Back to Georgia," complete with a music video showing Satan in a molten, fiery hell.

994. "Tears in Heaven"

Eric Clapton wrote and recorded this song after the tragic death of his four-year-old son in 1991. The song must have touched a nerve, for it won several Grammy awards and sold extremely well. For a generation of New Agers, its vague message of "no more tears in heaven" seemed warm and comforting.

995. hell or cancer?

English author George Orwell (1903–1950) gave the world such classics as *1984* and *Animal Farm*. Orwell was a shrewd observer of humanity, a man who had no fear of pointing out hypocrisy and deception. Regarding the belief in hell, Orwell noted that "most Christians profess to believe in hell. Yet have you ever met a Christian who seemed as afraid of hell as he was of cancer?"

996. Boris the Bulgarian

The Bulgarians were a pagan tribe until Boris, their *khan* (chieftain), was converted via the preaching of the evangelist known as Methodius. Around the year 864 Boris was baptized, not only making himself a Christian but bringing his whole nation into unity with the Orthodox churches of eastern Europe. What brought about his conversion? Methodius preached the gospel of divine love and forgiveness, but fear played a part too. The story goes that Methodius painted a picture of hell on the wall of Boris's palace. Apparently the picture was vivid enough to send Boris running to the arms of the church.

997. *Mefistofele*

This popular opera is based on the old Faust legends (see 739). Composed by Arrigo Boito, it tells the Faust story mostly from the point of view of the tempter demon Mefistofele. He tempts Faust into selling him his soul, and Faust leads a wild life but finally repents and is taken to heaven. The opera has a notable "demon orgy" scene set in hell. It is one of many operas based on Faust stories, the most famous being the *Faust* by Charles Gounod (one of the most popular operas ever written).

998. *The Fiery Angel*

Igor Stravinsky believed this strange 1925 opera was his masterpiece. Dealing with demonic possession and the occult and including an exorcism in a convent, it is certainly an unusual subject for an opera.

999. angels on the head of a pin

To show how useless and pointless the theological debates of the Middle Ages were, people often cite the debate over "How many angels can dance on the head of a pin?" The first person to criticize such debates was Meister Eckehart, a German philosopher of the late Middle Ages. Eckehart, like many sensitive and thoughtful people, believed that Christians had better things to do than debate things that have no bearing on the Christian life.

1000. the stone of Scone

British rulers are crowned over the ancient rock known as the "stone of Scone" or "stone of destiny." For centuries it sat beneath the coronation chair in London's Westminster Abbey. A centuries-old legend says that it is the stone pillow that Jacob rested his head on while he had his dream of angels on a stairway to heaven (Gen. 28).

1001. Elisabeth Kubler-Ross

A Swiss psychiatrist noted for her work with terminally ill people, Dr. Kubler-Ross began publishing books based on her work. *On Death and Dying* was published in 1969, followed by *Death, the Final Stages of Growth*, and many others. While her books have been read by Christians and non-Christians alike, she is critical of traditional Christianity, for she claims her work with the dying has convinced her there is no hell, and she resents Christians who teach the reality of hell.

Index

Numbers refer to entry numbers, not to page numbers. The main entry for each topic is set in boldface. References to certain broad topics (such as angels, demons, heaven, hell, Satan, etc.) are so numerous that to list them all would be of little help to the reader.

About the Author

J. Stephen Lang is the author of twenty books, including *1,001 Things You Always Wanted to Know About the Bible But Never Thought to Ask*, *1,001 Thing You Always Wanted to Know About the Holy Spirit*, *The Complete Book of Bible Trivia* (which has sold more than 600,000 copies) and *The Complete book of Bible Promises*.

Lang has a B.A. in religion from Vanderbilt University and an M.A. in communications from Wheaton College. He is also a regular contributor to *Moody*, *Discipleship Journal*, *Christian History*, and other periodicals.

Also By J. Stephen Lang

- *1,001 Things You Always Wanted to Know About the Bible But Never Thought to Ask*

In this book you'll discover how the Bible has impacted language, U.S. history, worship, music, art, literature, movies, and theater; how the bible was passed down to us; plus every key person, place, event, and idea in the Bible. Best-selling Bible trivia author J. Stephen Lang's intriguing tidbits will leave you yearning to know more about the world's most fascinating book.

- *1,001 Things You Always Wanted to Know About the Holy Spirit*

What are the fruits and gifts of the Spirit? Why are the flame and the dove symbols of the Spirit? J. Stephen Lang answers these and hundreds of other questions about the Holy Spirit, a subject that has fascinated people throughout the centuries. Lang looks at key Bible passages dealing with the Spirit, great revivals and evangelists throughout history, the charismatic and Pentecostal movements, and the ways in which the Spirit moves in the life of the church around the world.